YOUNG HEROES OF THE SOVIET UNION

YOUNG HEROES OF THE SOVIET UNION

A MEMOIR AND A RECKONING

ALEX HALBERSTADT

RANDOM HOUSE
NEW YORK

Published in the United States by Random House, an imprint and division of
Penguin Random House LLC, New York.

RANDOM HOUSE and the HOUSE colophon are registered trademarks of Penguin
Random House LLC.

Grateful acknowledgment is made to Margarita Novgorodova for permission to
reprint "Northern Elegies" by Anna Akhmatova. Reprinted by permission of
Margarita Novgorodova.

Photo credits are located on page 291.

Library of Congress Cataloging-in-Publication Data
Names: Halberstadt, Alex, author.
Title: Young heroes of the Soviet Union: a memoir and a reckoning /
    by Alex Halberstadt.
Description: First edition. | New York : Random House, [2020]
Identifiers: LCCN 2019019658 | ISBN 9781400067060 (hardcover) |
    ISBN 9780593133071 (ebook)
Subjects: LCSH: Halberstadt, Alex—Travel—Russia (Federation) | Jews,
    Soviet—United States—Biography. | Halberstadt, Alex—Childhood and
    youth. | Jews—Soviet Union—Biography.
Classification: LCC DS134.93.H35 A3 2020 | DDC 305.892/4047092 [B]—dc23
LC record available at https://lccn.loc.gov/2019019658

Printed in the United States of America on acid-free paper

randomhousebooks.com

9 8 7 6 5 4 3 2 1

First Edition

For my grandparents

You who do not remember
passage from the other world
I tell you I could speak again: whatever
returns from oblivion returns
to find a voice.
   —Louise Glück, "The Wild Iris"

CONTENTS

FAMILY TREES

FATHER'S SIDE

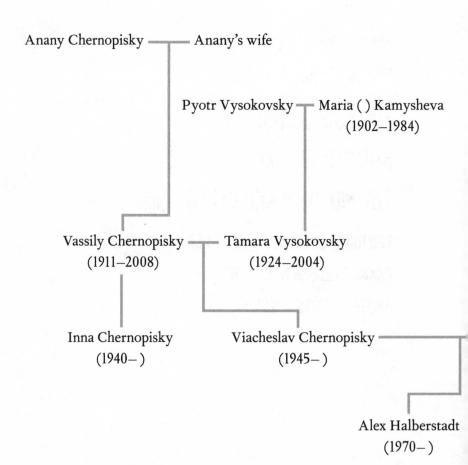

Anany Chernopisky ——— Anany's wife

Pyotr Vysokovsky —— Maria ( ) Kamysheva
(1902–1984)

Vassily Chernopisky ——— Tamara Vysokovsky
(1911–2008)   (1924–2004)

Inna Chernopisky   Viacheslav Chernopisky
(1940–)   (1945–)

Alex Halberstadt
(1970–)

MOTHER'S SIDE

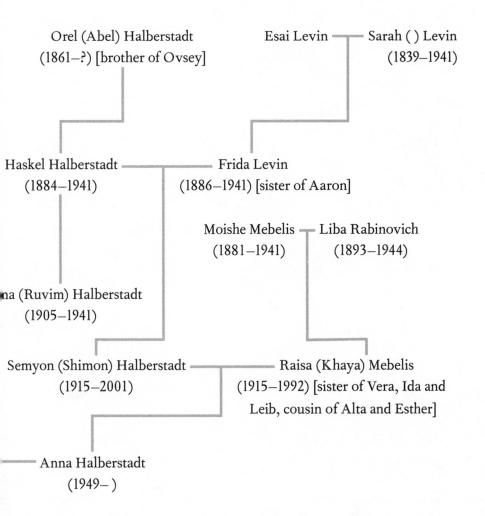

Orel (Abel) Halberstadt
(1861–?) [brother of Ovsey]

Esai Levin —— Sarah ( ) Levin
(1839–1941)

Haskel Halberstadt
(1884–1941)

Frida Levin
(1886–1941) [sister of Aaron]

Moishe Mebelis —— Liba Rabinovich
(1881–1941)   (1893–1944)

na (Ruvim) Halberstadt
(1905–1941)

Semyon (Shimon) Halberstadt
(1915–2001)

Raisa (Khaya) Mebelis
(1915–1992) [sister of Vera, Ida and
Leib, cousin of Alta and Esther]

Anna Halberstadt
(1949–)

THE FORGOTTEN

WHEN WE ARE CONFOUNDED OR LOST, STORIES HAVE THE POWER TO LEND meaning to our disorder, and not long ago I found just such a story in the pages of a science magazine. Or maybe it found me. It described how a team of researchers at Emory University in Atlanta had blown air scented with a chemical that smells like cherry blossoms into a cage of baby mice, then administered an electric shock to the animals' feet. Eventually, the mice learned to associate the scent of cherry blossoms with pain and trembled with fear whenever they smelled it. The surprising part, though, came after they had babies of their own. When exposed to the scent, the second generation also trembled, though they had never been shocked. Their bodies had changed, too. They were born with more smell-sensing neurons in their noses, while the structures in their brains that receive signals from these neurons had grown larger.

Puzzled by these results, the researchers worried that they were witnessing an anomaly. And so they made sure that the next generation of mice—the grandchildren—had no contact with their parents whatsoever; in fact, they were conceived using in vitro fertilization in a laboratory on the other side of campus. But these mice also trembled at the cherry-blossom scent and demonstrated identical brain changes. The experiment appeared to show that one generation's trauma was passed on *physiologically* to children and grandchildren—even in the absence of contact. What the researchers couldn't explain was how or why this was happening.

After these findings were published in 2013, studies of human subjects confirmed that the Emory researchers were on to something: Markers attached to certain genes are influenced by one's environment. A study conducted at Mount Sinai Hospital in New York found that children of Holocaust survivors showed changes to the genes that determined how they responded to stress—changes identical to those found in their parents. Another study showed that pregnant mothers who were near the World Trade Center during the attacks of September 11, 2001, gave birth to children with similar alterations to their genes. The children in these studies showed a propensity for post-traumatic stress disorder that had no explanation rooted in their own lives, a condition that one researcher described as a tendency to "feel unsafe in a safe environment." Most theories attempting to explain these findings rely on the relatively new field of epigenetics—the study of changes in gene expression rather than the genetic code itself—though aspects of the theories remain poorly understood and controversial.

I first read about these studies at a particularly unsettled time in my life, when I was trying to piece together my own family's history. The studies seemed to speak to something I was coming to believe, something I wanted to believe because I sensed it so acutely—that the past lives on not only in our memories but in every cell of our bodies. It was a deterministic notion to be sure, but it helped explain certain recurrent and mystifying experiences shared by the past three generations of my family: ruptured relationships, presentiments of disaster, clinical depression and anxiety, chronic sleep disturbances, a proclivity for keeping secrets and an ever-present sense of danger.

For some reason, I kept returning to the study of the mice at Emory. Eventually, I realized that what drew me to it were not only the provocative findings but its potency as a metaphor. Could it be that we, too, were trembling at stimuli we could neither identify nor remember, stimuli that had their origins in the decades prior to our births? It was unnerving to imagine that the past could be living through us without our consent or knowledge. But if it were true, it also meant that with time and effort these long-gone stimuli could be named and, at long last, acknowledged.

THERE WERE ALWAYS dogs barking in my dreams, my mother said. In the bad ones, anyway. They began the year I turned nine, while my mother, her parents, and I were making our nomadic way from Moscow to New York. They happened in budget hotel rooms in Austria and Italy and Manhattan and later in a succession of apartments in the wastes of Queens.

Most of the dreams weren't particularly memorable, but there was a recurring one that stood out. It takes place in Stepanovskoye, a village near Moscow where, in summers, my family rented the front part of a blue clapboard house with green shutters. In the dream it is dusk, and I stand at the gate in the picket fence in front of the house, wanting badly to go inside. My parents are in the house, and I can smell the wood smoke from my great-grandmother's stove. But the landlady's bulldog has gotten off the chain and is barking on the other side of the fence, constricting my throat with fear. I can't decide what to do, but it is getting dark and I need to get home, so eventually I throw open the gate and lunge for the door, and the bulldog lunges after me, snarling just over my shoulder. That's when I'd wake, my pulse juddering, my pillow damp with sweat. Right away the events of the dream seemed to break apart, to turn to dust even as I reached out for them. Sometimes, if my mother was asleep, I snuck into the kitchen, took a knife out of a drawer and kept it under my pillow until morning, lying in bed uneasily and watching the cold light through the curtains. The dream has refused to go away, even all these years later.

Several months after it began, my family and I arrived at John F. Kennedy International Airport in New York City. Right away, and for many years afterward, New York felt more like home than any place I'd lived. For me, the rest of North America existed as a notional territory. From the first day on, I loved nearly everything about our new city, where the tread of history pointed to the future instead of the past. In Moscow, the metro ran below the streets, and the stations doubled as bomb shelters; in parts of New York, the subway ran on girders high above the sidewalks, up near the billboards, neon and postmodern pediments. I marveled at each of the city's providential gifts: the ground-floor two-room apartment in the Ravenswood housing projects in Long Island City where the four of us lived; the booklets of crisp, colorful food stamps that arrived in the mail; the Swanson's Hungry-Man frozen dinners that my maternal grandfather, Semyon, and I shared nearly every night, admiring their gleaming foil and perfect Euclidean shapes.

In those years, I wanted nothing to do with our Soviet past—which included my father. During our first five years in New York, I spoke to him on the phone about a dozen times, and only because my mother thrust the receiver into my hands and furrowed her forehead. In school, I told everyone that he'd died, first from cancer and then in the Afghan-Soviet War. What was the harm? Before boarding the westbound Tupolev Tu-154 jet in Moscow, we'd renounced our Soviet citizenship and passports, and with them the possibility of returning. My father had chosen to stay behind, and I knew I wouldn't see him again. The Soviet Union had endured for nearly seventy years, and as far as we could tell in 1985, it would last for another seventy.

The name I brought with me from the Soviet Union, my father's name—Aleksandr Viacheslavovich Chernopisky—was a catastrophe in both the old language and the new one. In more courtly times, our surname might have been translated as "he of the dusky loins." Middle-school classmates truncated it to "Pissky" or "Pissed On" or simply "Piss" and sometimes, in those closing days of the Cold War, they called me "Big Red," after the brand of chewing gum and my expanding waistline.

And so at fifteen I found myself in a government office with a metal desk, metal chairs and a framed portrait of Ronald Reagan. My mother sat beside me. About the woman across the desk, I can recall only that she was pretty and black and wore a blazer and a shade of lipstick sometimes called Wild Raspberry. She was a supervisor with the Immigration and Naturalization Service, and she announced, her posture erect under the president's baking-soda smile, that I could have my mother's name instead, right then and there, by government fiat.

My mother looked at me and I nodded. The supervisor wrote something on a form and slid it across the desk, my mother signed it in ballpoint pen, and it was done. The foreign patronymic and the surname that the men in my family shrugged and joked about—and those Slavic syllables—were gone. I was the first Chernopisky who wouldn't have to go on being one.

My name was one of many things I'd brought with me that I tried to give away. I was beginning to understand that the immigrant project of internalizing a new culture had a necessary flip side, which was eradicating the old one. To exist in two cultures at once was disorienting and oddly uncomfortable, like listening to a radio tuned between two stations. And as a teenager, I was happy to forget Russia, and Russian, because I believed their absence would clear space inside my brain for our new language and manners.

The forgetting was helped along by my mother's disdain for the country of my birth. What had it ever done for her, she liked to say, except unburden her of her youth? She'd grown up in Soviet Lithuania, a place she disliked nearly as much as Russia, salvaged for her only by childhood nostalgia. For her, Moscow had been as foreign as New York and signified little except state-sponsored discrimination against Jews, consumer deficits, appalling architecture, months-long stretches of uninterrupted sleet and snow, and an overabundance of synthetic fibers. On the subject of my father, whom she divorced after seven increasingly unhappy years, she was even less charitable. Her parents didn't think much of him, either.

Semyon and Raisa, who came to New York in their sixties after a comfortable middle age in Vilnius, remained bewildered by their new surroundings, but neither went in for retrospection. When I asked about their youth—knowing some details about the war and the extended families each had outlived—my grandparents rarely said much. They believed in the ability of the past to corrode the present and thought of me as a product of peacetime, which is to say pure and soft as a cloud. If I persisted with my questions, they grew tight-lipped and glum. "Those are terrible memories," Raisa said at those awkward moments with a conviction that sounded religious. "It's more prudent to be an optimist."

My father was the one I tried hardest to forget, because when I remembered him, I also remembered his voluntary absence from our lives. For about a year and a half after our arrival in New York, he called occasionally and once sent a package that contained a letter addressed to me along with several books, including a Russian-language biography of Peter the Great, which I devoured. Afterward, his calls dwindled to one or two a year. Calling *him*, my mother decided, was simply too expensive.

Most of the time, my father and I communicated only in my imagination. My favorite memory was of him teaching me to swim the summer I turned seven. It happened at one of the weedy ponds in Stepanovskoye. My father waded into the water up to his waist and laid me across the pond's surface, placing one hand under my chest and the other under my belly. "Kick," he instructed and spun me around while I kicked water in his face. The first time he took his hands out from under me, I swallowed a mouthful of water and plummeted to the pond's muddy bottom; it took a few tries before I could stay afloat without him, windmilling my arms and legs as fast as I could. "Constant motion!" he hollered over my thrashing.

Most of the time, I tried not to think about him at all, until I began to forget the sound of his voice, which for some reason scared me. I must have been twelve or thirteen. And so at night, after I got into bed and turned off the light, I tried to hear him repeating, "constant motion." After a while I thought I could hear it faintly, like the sound of the surf in a seashell, and every time I found it comforting.

NOT LONG AFTER I went away to college, my mother called to say that my father had suffered a heart attack and spent nearly two months recovering in an intensive-care ward. Apprehending my father's mortality made me determined to know him, and so, with a calling card, I dialed the international codes followed by his seven-digit number. I did this every two or three months. He was pleasant enough when I called, and could be funny and wry. Sometimes he grew cagey when I asked about his new family or brought up the past, but mostly he sounded drained of vitality, exhausted by the task of speaking. At times he sounded like someone half-alive. Mostly he liked to talk about old movies, often the same ones as during the last call; after fifteen or twenty minutes, he would begin to sound distracted and eventually said he had to go.

I didn't understand why my father wanted no part of fatherhood. From my mother, I heard that he'd stopped speaking to his own father, Vassily, several months after I was born. Everyone in my family mentioned my grandfather only in passing; they treated his existence as an open secret. Vassily saw me only once, when I was three months old. My mother said it happened on an autumn afternoon in Moscow and that he'd bathed me and combed my hair. Of course I have no memory of this meeting. From these snippets, I pieced together that he had been an officer in the organization that would come to be known as the KGB and, for more than a decade, served as a personal bodyguard of Joseph Stalin. I was a teenager when I learned this, and for me this made Vassily the moral equal of a Gestapo officer, so the fact that I didn't know him hardly registered as a loss. He was born before the revolution, my mother remembered, and she and I assumed that he'd died some time before the Soviet Union's fall.

By my early thirties, my reinvention seemed complete. I'd become a writer who'd published dozens of articles in the new language and was working on a book. I shared an apartment in Brooklyn with my college boyfriend, the grandson of a Lutheran minister whose parents met in a high school class in Grand Forks, North Dakota. I'd worked diligently at forgetting. When our friends asked about my childhood, I couldn't explain with any conviction what it meant to have grown up in Russia, or why I had a relatively young father with whom I barely spoke, and a grandfather I hadn't met, and a native language that I spoke worse with every passing year.

Of course I didn't manage to forget much of anything, not really. During these years, the recurring childhood dreams became more insistent and disturbing, unwelcome visitors staking a claim to the unattended corners of my mind. On those mornings, long before I read about the mice at Emory, I wondered whether dread could be passed down like a gene. As it happened, the dread spread to my waking life, too: I became obsessively fearful first of strangers' footsteps in the hallway, then of noise coming through the bedroom walls from neighbors' apartments, then of the neighbors themselves. What made this fear unfamiliar is that I couldn't connect it to a threat in my environment, and so couldn't negotiate with it or rationalize it away. At times it felt like a visitation from outside myself, like a medieval possession.

Then, one morning in the summer of 2004, during one of our not-quite-quarterly telephone conversations, my father mentioned a cousin two or three times removed who lived somewhere in Ukraine. He said he barely knew him, but this man had called unexpectedly several weeks earlier and demanded to know why my father didn't visit Vassily. At ninety-three, Vassily was still alert, the cousin reported in a chiding tone, and "he misses you." I was surprised to hear that my grandfather was alive, that he still lived in the apartment where my father had grown up in Vinnytsia (known in Soviet times by its Russian name, Vinnitsa), a drab industrial city near Ukraine's center. The last time my father and Vassily exchanged letters had been twenty-six years earlier; they hadn't seen each other in thirty-five. I blurted out that I wanted to meet Vassily. My father sounded almost as surprised as I was. "In that case," he said, "you'll have to find him."

After I hung up, I sifted through what I knew about Vassily. It wasn't much. One night, when I was nine, my maternal grandmother, Raisa, uncharacteristically drunk after a glass and a half of Asti Spumante, said that he'd worked in the secret police and done "unmentionable things." Raisa was a cautious woman and permitted herself this indiscretion only after we'd left the Soviet Union. It was the winter of 1980, and we were living a twenty-five-minute train ride from Rome in a windy beachside town called Lido di Ostia, where stunted palms dotted the traffic islands and the beaches were littered with trash and mussel shells. It was a Red Brigades headquarters and a stopover on the route that the four of us, along with thousands of other Soviet refugees, were taking to New York. No one at the table said anything in response to Raisa's outburst. This was typical. Whenever Vassily's name came up, the air in the room seemed to grow colder. Depending on who was speaking, he was described as a Communist zealot, an emotional cipher, an imbecile, a negligent father and husband, an impeccably mannered gentleman, a dandy, a martinet. My father spoke about him the least. The little he did say was tinged with a resentment that bordered on hatred.

The only physical proof I had of my paternal grandfather's existence was a black-and-white photograph pasted into an album that my mother brought with us from Moscow. In the photo, Vassily sits on a grassy slope beside his second wife, my grandmother Tamara. A trim, well-proportioned man with a flair for clothes, he wears high-waisted slacks, a short-sleeved shirt and a straw fedora; he glances into the lens with an ambiguous, contained smile. The two of them look fine together, but the photo offers few clues about who the man in it was and what he might have been thinking. On the back, a spidery pen inscription reads, "Vassily and Tamara, Vinnitsa, 9th of September, 1953."

I wasn't sure what I wanted from him. He was a stranger in his nineties whose mental acuity I wasn't certain of, an army officer and secret policeman, a man my father once called a heartless thug. Of course I wanted to meet him, but that wasn't all of it. Vassily's existence was a thread that might lead me to a past that I couldn't fathom or explain but that I somehow knew was living through me. Could this past explain my grandparents' blank silences, my parents' unhappiness, and my own nightmares and dread? Could it be that the past wasn't gone at all, but existed alongside our present-day lives, in ghostly superimposition? And so several days after the long-distance telephone conversation with my father, despite entirely reasonable doubts, I had resolved to find my grandfather. Mostly, I was afraid that he'd die and take what he knew with him. I wasn't sure what I'd do when I found him, but I began to plan the trip, afraid of losing my nerve.

The following morning I picked up the receiver, dialed directory assistance, and asked to be connected to an operator in Ukraine. After a dozen long, low-pitched beeps, a woman's voice on the other end asked for a street address in rapid-fire Russian. I didn't have one; my father told me he no longer remembered it. Vinnytsia was a city of half a million, the operator said. What was I expecting? She hung up. I redialed, was asked again for a street address, hung up, dialed again. The third operator agreed to look up the name. She came back on the line almost immediately. "There's only one Chernopisky in

Vinnytsia," she said, and dictated a number. I stared at the scrap of paper where I'd written it. This felt too easy.

I dialed. After two beeps, an old man's voice answered. Was this Vassily Chernopisky? It was. We could barely hear each other over the noisy line. "Who's there?" he kept shouting. I shouted back that I was the son of his son, Slava, that he'd seen me when I was an infant in the autumn of 1970, and that I wanted to come to Ukraine and meet him. I could hear him breathing into the receiver. He sounded confused. "I don't have a grandson," he said finally.

I listened to the crackling static for what felt like minutes, thinking he'd hung up, when a woman's voice came on the line. "This is Sonya, his wife," the voice said. "We have a photograph of you. If you come, he will remember."

THE BODYGUARD 1.

THE PLANE PITCHED TO THE LEFT AND BEGAN TO DESCEND. A DIORAMA
flashed into view through a break in the cloud cover: low cabins
standing in puddles of pea-green grass, a pond and a sluiceway and
some obsolete factory buildings dreaming in pastureland. Then fog
rolled in from somewhere below. Sheremetyevo airport, a linoleum
labyrinth lit dimly by fluorescents, was watched over by soldiers
barely out of their teens who leaned languidly against the walls, assault rifles slung over their shoulders. I waited beside a church group

from Michigan, half a dozen families in pristine white sneakers who joked heartily with one another, as though they were waiting out a lull at the Department of Motor Vehicles back home. Just then, their American sense of inviolability reassured me.

My case of nerves, I knew, was shared by many Soviet immigrants returning to the motherland: the worry that the gates won't open again when it's time to leave. The customs inspectors' opaque, somehow familiar faces—faces professionally immune to interpretation— told me that liberties I hadn't questioned the previous morning were now granted and revoked at the whim of these men, and men in other, different uniforms. In my Levi's and windbreaker, I blended in with the church group, but I was a returning refugee, a category of traveler the customs men regarded with suspicion and possibly envy. I shifted my weight from one foot to the other and strained to pick up scraps of conversation. When my turn came, I stepped up to the window and slid my passport under the glass. The inspector, fiftyish with a comb-over, didn't look up. When his eyes moved across the column of text that read, "Place of Birth: Russia," the corners of his mouth widened into a foreshadowing of a grin. He stamped the passport, slid it back and, looking up at last, said, "Welcome home, Mr. Halberstadt."

LATER THAT AFTERNOON, my father and I sat in his kitchen, smoking. I'd quit cigarettes in college, but I pulled on one of his Winstons, watching the smoke drift to the ceiling, where it was forming a storm cloud. My father had been smoking since he was sixteen. He was remarried and had a college-age daughter and had never recovered completely from the heart attack he'd suffered nearly fifteen years earlier. "Why don't you quit smoking?" I prodded. He said he would quit "when things get easier" and that he was "crazy about cigarettes." We both knew things wouldn't get easier and that he wasn't going to get any less crazy, so I lit up in guilty solidarity.

My father liked a brand of vodka called Peter the Great, and on that first day in Moscow I drank enough to begin liking it, too. My father and I hadn't seen each other in seven years. I wondered if I'd recognize him, thinking of the way some men in their late fifties begin to look elderly almost overnight. But my father looked as I remembered him, still handsome and confoundingly fit, only his temples were grayer and the lines around the eyes more pronounced.

We spent nearly the entire day talking in the kitchen, but to me our voices sounded tentative and oddly formal. Since I'd left Russia, we'd spoken occasionally over a sputtering long-distance phone line and met a handful of times, adding up to maybe three or four weeks spent together over two and a half decades. Unlike that of most fathers and sons, our relationship hadn't been worn into a recognizable shape by familiarity. We were closely related strangers.

To my frustration, I once again became quiet and strangely passive around my father—a condition exacerbated by my shortage of Russian words to describe adult emotions. Well, not a shortage of words, exactly. What I lacked was the ability to put them together in ways that enabled adult modes of conversation: irony, doubt, tenderness, reserve. And so in my father's presence I spoke less than I did otherwise and was cowed by my silence, which in turn made me feel not only mute but dumb.

He asked, as he always did, whether I'd seen any movies lately. My father liked old films enough to make them his livelihood: he dubbed classic Hollywood and European films into Russian and sold the not entirely legal VHS tapes and DVDs at a storefront in one of the new-ish strip malls that ringed Moscow. Sometimes he was paid—by scrap-metal magnates and natural-gas-company lawyers—to assemble private video collections in loose-leaf binders with titles like "The New Wave" and "Early Hitchcock." He had been an academic of sorts once but was a business owner now in the fledgling post-perestroika middle class. We shared the fondness for old movies, particularly American ones, and after a few glasses of vodka he began to recite lines of film dialogue in hilariously accented English: "Whoa, take her easy there, Pilgrim." He told me about *The Band*

Wagon, an MGM musical from 1953. It had a dance scene he liked, filmed on a set that looked like Central Park. Halfway through, my father said, you can tell that Cyd Charisse and Fred Astaire have fallen in love, and just then his eyes looked excitable and impossibly young, the way they did when I was a child. I always liked how easily he laughed. When he did, our awkwardness and odd formality gave way to something like joy—both unfamiliar and childishly primal—and I could tell he felt it too. But after a moment or two, a self-consciousness intruded and the elation was gone.

When I asked about Vassily, my father became evasive and glum, and I said nothing more until I remembered that I came to Moscow to find out about the two of them. "There isn't much to tell," he said, looking away. "It's all pretty boring." In spite of my discomfort with Russian, I knew that I had him pinned, there behind the chipboard table in his kitchen. He responded to my questions with gestures of bodily discomfort. His eyes beseeched me to change the subject, but this was important, I told him, I needed to know. He winced and lit another cigarette, chain-smoking irritably in silence. When he spoke finally, it felt like the giving of a heavy door.

My father's first memory of his father was watching him count money. They lived in a communal prerevolutionary apartment near the Hotel Metropol, a few steps from Red Square, alongside families of other state security officers. Vassily coaxed the bills into neat stacks and laid them gingerly into a shoe box that he kept on a high closet shelf, along with his pistol. He never quite figured out how to spend his extravagant major's salary and lavished much of the money on clothes, for which he had a keen eye, ordering dozens of monogrammed shirts and gabardine suits from the Kremlin tailors. My grandmother Tamara designed women's clothes for an atelier that furnished the city's dress shops. When the two of them went out, they looked like one of the smart modern couples from the pages of *Harper's Bazaar,* a magazine Tamara pried away from a colleague of Vassily's who lived upstairs and whose job it was to monitor foreign mail. It was 1949 and my father was three or four years old.

It occurred to me that my father's was a decidedly uncommon set of memories for someone growing up in Moscow in the late 1940s. Ninety percent of Moscow's apartments had no heat, and nearly half had no plumbing or running water; in winter, people going out for water carried axes along with their buckets, to hack through the ice that grew around the public water pumps; workers stacked firewood brought from the countryside on street corners in piles that sometimes grew taller than a building; siblings went to school on alternate days because they shared a single pair of shoes.

But the Kremlin elite never prided itself on being egalitarian. The war was over. Vassily and Tamara went dancing, vacationed on the Black Sea. At home, my father remembered, she covered every surface with red and white carnations in cut-crystal vases, floral bouffants that gave the room the look of a funeral parlor. They dined on caviar and smoked sturgeon sent over as part of Vassily's rations. On New Year's Eve—the secular Soviet Christmas—Tamara put out porcelain bowls filled with pomegranates and oranges and decorated the tree with tinsel and crystal bells, arranging presents and sometimes a pineapple under the bottom branches. My father tore the wrapping open after supper on the thirty-first, and after he was put to bed, the neighbors gathered around the radio console in the hallway and waited for midnight, toasting the New Year with a sparkling wine labeled Soviet Champagne. Moscow was rising from the wartime mire. Nearly identical wedding cake–like towers, known as the Seven Sisters, were going up around the city. They were built mainly by German POWs; the most elaborate among them was the Moscow State University high-rise on Lenin Hills.

The family lived in a single room: Vassily, Tamara, my father, and his older half sister, Inna, Vassily's daughter from his first marriage. As in many such rooms in Moscow's communal apartments, a screen partitioned Vassily and Tamara's bed from their children's; the bathroom and kitchen were shared with other families. There wasn't much privacy, but the apartment was larger and better furnished than most. The four of them spent many hours together on

that rectangle of parquet, but my father could recall only a handful of conversations with Vassily. Whether posted abroad or working less than an hour away, at Stalin's "nearer dacha" in Kuntsevo, he was gone for weeks and sometimes months at a time. My father didn't remember how or when he found out about Vassily's job; he recalled somehow always knowing, though Vassily rarely said anything about it.

But over supper one evening, Vassily described a remarkable altercation. Earlier that day, he had been standing guard in the hallway at the entrance to the Presidium of the Supreme Soviet when Marshal Zhukov—the man widely credited with turning the tide of the war in the Soviet Union's favor and keeping Hitler from breaching Moscow—came walking toward him with his head down. Today, a statue of Zhukov astride a stallion stands in front of the State Historical Museum, near the entrance to Red Square. But Zhukov was not a member of the Presidium and was not allowed inside, and Vassily stepped in his way. For a moment, he outranked the nation's top military commander. "I put my hand right in his chest and said, 'Comrade Zhukov, you may not enter!'" Vassily said at the table, grinning, to my father's obvious delight. "His chest, it was all covered in medals."

For the most part, though, my father glimpsed Vassily in drowsy early-morning sightings between waking and sleep, when he seemed to float around the apartment. When he was stationed in Moscow and kept more or less conventional hours, Vassily came home in late afternoon, put his sidearm in the shoe box, changed out of his uniform into a suit and another pair of shoes, hung a Leica from his shoulder (it was a war trophy, and he was a skilled photographer) and went walking, usually staying out well after dark. Other than to discuss my father's weekly grades—and only when they were poor—he rarely spoke to his son, leaving the child care to Tamara.

Vassily did teach my father to fight. He was home one afternoon when my father ran into the room sobbing after an older boy, the son of another NKVD officer, had knocked him down on the neighborhood playground. "Next time you see him," Vassily instructed, "pick up a stick and hit him as hard as you can on the bone between the knee and the ankle." The following day my father carried out his father's instructions. The older boy yowled in pain and hobbled off the playground. He stayed away for three weeks.

In March 1953, Stalin's body lay in state at the Hall of Columns. Crowds of mourners descended on Moscow; hundreds were trampled to death in the streets. Several weeks later, Vassily had a driver take Tamara, my father and his half sister, along with the family's belongings, to the Kievskaya railway station, where they boarded an overnight train. The move was sudden; they had less than a day to pack. The train traveled southwest, to Vinnitsa, a Ukrainian city that spanned a muddy river called the Southern Bukh, not far from the village where Vassily was born. If the city was known for anything at all, it was for being the onetime home of Nikolai Pirogov, a popularizer of ether and an inventor of field surgery (a service to science for which he remains entombed, mummy-like, in a glass coffin inside his former estate). For Vassily and Tamara, the move was akin to relocating from New York City to Terre Haute, Indiana. Eight years after the war, prison crews were still tearing down buildings damaged by German shelling. Wehrwolf, Hitler's easternmost bunker, still stood in pine woods just north of the city. The sidewalks were pocked by shrapnel. Ration cards remained in effect. Vassily rented a one-bedroom apartment not far from the city center at 19 Voroshilov Street, named after Stalin's defense chief, whom he had known well.

Vinnitsa had little to offer in the way of after-school recreation, so when classes let out, my father, an eight-year-old loner, walked past the bombed-out buildings and newly planted birches to the

movie theater. The Khrushchev thaw was beginning, and for the first time the theaters were screening Hollywood films. My father watched *Sun Valley Serenade,* with the bandleader Glenn Miller, nine times. He told me once that he still remembered almost every note of the soundtrack. Once, years later in Moscow, when Miller's "Moonlight Serenade" started playing on a friend's shortwave radio, my father burst into tears.

His grades were dismal. He detested algebra, but not as much as the morning assemblies, with their recitation of oaths to the party and field trips to place flowers at the pedestal of Lenin's statue. To my father, these felt like odious forms of thought control. In his class-rooms' back rows, he recognized fellow miscreants and cynics, some of them united by an obsession with American movies, jazz, and rock and roll. One boy had access to his father's record-cutting ma-chine. It used shellac disks that had disappeared from stores during the war, likely melted down for munitions. The discarded X-rays that my father and his friends fished out of the hospital's garbage bins made serviceable replacements. When he was twelve, my father brought home a record of Bill Haley's "Rock Around the Clock" engraved on an X-ray of a lung. That afternoon he and two friends played it over and over on Vassily's record player, dancing in their muddy felt boots on the lacquered dark-wood dinner table. When Vassily walked in, the boys scattered. His classmates, my father said, were terrified of him. Vassily beat my father with a belt until he lay sobbing on the kitchen linoleum, pleading for him to stop.

It wasn't the first beating, just the worst one yet. Afterward, the four of them—Vassily, Tamara, my father, and his half sister, Inna—ate in silence. By the time my father was thirteen, the indoctrination he was undergoing in school had turned him into a zealous anti-Communist. He knew that Vassily's job in a local factory's "human resources department" was a euphemism for the KGB minder who worked at every large Soviet establishment, and this knowledge made him hate his father more. The factory was named Pribor—Device—and no one in my family ever remembered what it pro-duced.

Tamara was a native Muscovite who never learned to enjoy life in the small, provincial city. She chafed against it by adopting an air of amused haughtiness and ignoring her neighbors' invitations. When my father was around thirteen, Tamara began an affair with a taxi driver, and one morning she introduced him to her son. My father thought of his glamorous, vain mother as a co-conspirator and an equal; it didn't occur to him that there was anything odd about meet-ing her new lover on a street corner not far from home. Gradually, mother and son united against Vassily. When Tamara and my father walked to Gorky Park, or to the fabric store to pick out a worsted pattern for a blazer or a roll of cotton for a shirt she'd make for him, they didn't tell Vassily. At home, they whispered secrets to each other while he slept.

Then, a few months after my father turned fifteen, Tamara told him that she was divorcing Vassily and moving back to Moscow— alone. He would stay in Vinnitsa until he graduated from school two years later. He felt betrayed, but what could he do? After Tamara left, my father and Vassily saw each other even less often than before, mostly over meals. Neither one could prepare even the simplest dish, and they ate dinner together at a nearby cafeteria. After dinner, Vassily went out on his nightly walks, and my father went to the movies; in the summer of 1962, *The Magnificent Seven* played in Vinnitsa for three months, and my father said he saw nearly every showing. Afterward, in his bedroom, he listened to Willis Conover's Voice of America broadcasts on the shortwave. In his mind, he had already left.

Even before my father saw his tenth-grade final exam grades posted on a bulletin board in the school hallway, he knew they weren't high enough for an army deferment. Vassily was pleased; the army had given him discipline and purpose, and now it would do the same for his bookish, lazy son. My father resigned himself to another three years in a different sort of prison. He knew that in the army a skinny city teenager would be a target for the sons of collective farmers and coal miners, and he spent his last weeks in Vinnitsa practicing soccer. Eventually, his soccer skills would redeem him.

At the army base in Belorussia, near Minsk, his new tormentor was a Ukrainian lieutenant determined to strip him of his intellectual airs. For eight months, he forced my father to run laps around an ordnance storage depot while hugging a twelve-kilogram kettle. One morning, after a sleepless twelve-hour shift of peeling potatoes behind the mess hall, he returned to the barracks to find the lieutenant rifling through his foot locker. The other soldiers stood at attention while the officer fanned out photos of Duke Ellington and Stan

Kenton that my father had clipped from *Down Beat* and other American magazines Tamara had mailed him. Then the lieutenant tore
them to pieces, telling the men that "cosmopolitan influences" were
a poison to the mental state and battle readiness of a Soviet soldier.

My father reported these events in dismal weekly letters to Tamara, and eventually she came up with a plan. As it happened, a
colonel's wife on the army base was pining for a refrigerator and a set
of tortoiseshell buttons. And so one Sunday, Tamara's fiancé, Mikhail
Mikhailovich—a slight, balding hustler with a permanent grin who
managed a fruit-and-vegetable warehouse on Moscow's outskirts—
pulled up outside my father's barracks in a van with a lightly used
refrigerator strapped to the roof. Days later, my father received a
transfer to an ICBM silo less than an hour from Moscow. His job
there was to trap the rats that gnawed the missiles' looms of precious
wire, some made from platinum. His tools were a box of spring traps
and a crowbar. He was left unsupervised for weeks and spent his afternoons lounging in a hammock, sipping weak instant coffee and
reading *A Farewell to Arms*.

He returned to Vinnitsa in his fatigues, his head still shaved,
three years later. Vassily looked happy to see him; he had good news.

After months of letter writing and cajoling, he'd gotten my father admitted to the Military Institute of Foreign Languages, which catered to the sons of KGB officers and career diplomats. A diploma from the institute would mean a good salary and opportunities to travel abroad. My father told Vassily that he'd wasted his time. He said that he was going to Moscow and tossed a few changes of clothes into a suitcase. He shook his father's hand when he left.

The following morning, Tamara waited for him at Moscow's Kievskaya station. She'd come up with another plan. Mikhail Mikhailovich got my father a job driving a produce truck at his warehouse, which meant my father was now legally a proletarian, a distinction that gave him an inside track to being admitted to Moscow State University's philosophy department. He spent the nights leading up to the admission interview poring over his mother's antiquarian books by prerevolutionary historians like Soloviev and Kostomarov. At the interview, the head of the department's admissions committee remarked that he had never met such a well-read truck driver.

My father enrolled at the university on Lenin Hills in 1968. "I met your mother a year later," he said. "You know the rest." We sat in his kitchen; it was nearly dark. His face looked drawn in the lamplight. I asked him when he last saw Vassily. "A few years before you and your mother left," he said. In Vinnitsa, he and Vassily spent two tense days at the old apartment, arguing and sulking. Vassily complained that he hadn't been invited to his own son's wedding, and had met his grandson only once; my father replied that he hadn't received a letter from Vassily in over a year. He was convinced that Vassily was avoiding him because his wife—my mother—was a Jew, a circumstance that might harm his KGB career. There was shouting before my father left for the train station. "I've always known who my mother is," he told Vassily before walking out, "but I'm not so sure about my father." It was the most hurtful thing he could think of.

My father smoked one cigarette after another while I took notes in a spiral-bound notebook. Months earlier he'd agreed to come with me to the city now called Vinnytsia, but as the date approached, he began to equivocate. The dates, he said, may not be good after all; there was a fishing trip, and his wife, Irina, was having stomach pains. My father tended to reduce broken promises to inevitabilities. I'd spent months imagining the two of us wandering around the city of his childhood, and when he told me he wasn't going, a few weeks before my flight to Moscow, for reasons "too numerous, really, to discuss," I hung up and spent days mired in anger.

Sitting in his kitchen, I felt the anger well up again as I watched him from across the table. Emboldened by my interrogator's role and trying to make my Russian sound authoritative, I demanded to know the real reason he wasn't going.

My father pulled on a Winston and cocked his head, as though debating something with himself, then let the smoke drift from his nostrils. He seemed to flatten into the wall behind him. "One night, I came home with a week's worth of failing grades," he began, glancing up at a spot where the wall and ceiling met behind me. "I was twelve. My father took off his belt and began beating me on the living room floor. For some reason, on that night he wouldn't stop, so I got free and ran down the stairs into an alley behind the building. He ran after me and dragged me out by my collar. It was a warm night and everyone was sitting outside, on the benches. He threw me on the sidewalk and finished beating me in front of our neighbors." He took another drag and tilted back in the chair. "I know I'm wrong, but I can't see him again." He snuffed the Winston in an ashtray and stood up. "It gets cold there in the winters," he said before walking out. "Bring him a sweater."

I stared out the window through the kitchen's nimbus of smoke. The rooks in the plane trees were gone. A seven-story cinder-block apartment building the color of old snow stood across a patchy field of grass. It was identical to the building I was in and the row of buildings behind it, disappearing into the distance like dominoes. In the late 1960s and the 1970s, they went up by the hundreds along the city's periphery. The building I was looking at happened to be the one where the three of us lived before my mother and I left for America and my father remarried and moved here, across the field, with his second wife. For years after leaving, I visualized this unremarkable building, trying to reconstruct its features from memory. Now, abundantly real, it gave off nothing but a prosaic homeliness.

In the summers when I lived there, my friend Volodya and I set fires on that field, and in the winters, when the snow piled taller than a man, we tunneled under its frozen crust. But there was something there now that I didn't remember, something new. A handful of women in caftans and baggy coats, most of them elderly, waited in a line clutching empty plastic jugs and kitchen kettles. There had been more of them earlier in the day. The women took turns filling their containers from a rusty pipe topped with a spigot that jutted from the ground, because the water was reputed to be medicinal and possibly holy, springing from a spot discovered by a dowser of some renown. A metropolitan in his vestments came to bless the site, my father said. Residents of a European city of eleven million, the women waited to take their turn, lit by the violet glimmerings above the tenements.

I stubbed out my cigarette and went to say goodbye to my father. He was in the study, dozing on a daybed, a TV remote in his hand. A stack of VCRs and a row of monitors, one lit, occupied the shelves. I recognized the Western and sat down beside him. In the blue glow, my father's face looked placid for the first time; a framed photograph on a desk showed him in a boat somewhere on the Volga, smiling, holding up a large glittering fish. On the monitor, Jimmy Stewart washed dishes in an apron. "Men out here solve their own problems," somebody said. Later, Stewart staggered in front of a saloon, grimacing, clutching the bloodied arm where Lee Marvin had shot him. In a villain's black vest and hat, Marvin raised his gun again and laughed a braying laugh. "Okay, dude," he said loud enough for everyone in the street to hear, "this time, right between the eyes."

. . .

ON THE FOUR-LANE near the Konkovo metro stop, I flagged down a guacamole-colored Lada. Most private cars double as taxis in Moscow; it's the city's most common form of part-time employment. I exchanged a few words with the driver, a thirtyish computer programmer named Maxim. "Where're you from?" he asked. "West of here," I told him. The car radio was turned up loud. A woman's voice sang about deep oceans and sighing winds over a drum machine that sounded like uncooked rice sprinkled on foil. For half an hour, the Lada's high beams swept rows of kiosks and the outlines of ghostly, identical apartment towers along Profsoyuznaya Street. They were interrupted only once, by a billboard depicting a psychedelic alpine meadow superimposed with the English word "love."

Maxim let me out near the Kievskaya railway station, beside the twelve-foot-high Cyclone fence of the Radisson SAS Slavyanskaya Hotel. I handed him a pair of hundred-ruble bills and walked past two security checkpoints into the frosted-glass lobby. I was paying for the trip by writing about it for a magazine, and the magazine's travel agent in New York booked me a room here. I wandered through the lobby, past black-suited security men with earpieces who followed me with their eyes. At the bar, men wearing more expensive suits nursed cigars and tumblers of single-malt scotch or spoke loudly into mobile phones. Several young women in cocktail dresses hovered near them. Anodyne electronic music provided a barely audible soundtrack; like everywhere in Moscow, its throb was meant to signify Western luxury. A light rain began to fall beyond the sliding glass doors, out in the night where chauffeurs and bodyguards smoked beside idling black sedans, the kind with curtains in the backseat windows.

I was jet-lagged and unsure of the time, and I stepped into a boutique where a model-handsome salesperson of about twenty wearing pressed trousers and a cravat the color of rare venison arranged cuff links in a glass case. In the window, there was a crocodile briefcase with gold latches; the tag read 640,000 rubles (about $22,000). "We sell quite a few of those," he said. "Mostly people buy them to give as gifts." Someone's chauffeur walked into the store, and after a quick exchange the salesperson handed him a handful of garment bags embossed with the word "Brioni." "Just bring back the ones he doesn't want," he told the chauffeur.

Besides Russians, there were Americans and Canadians at the Radisson, a surprising number of whom were completing the final stages of adoption. In 2004, along with caviar, oil, and natural gas, infants numbered among the country's few exports. In a restaurant called Balanchine, a sconce-lit grotto decorated with oil paintings and bronze-colored drapes, a woman in an Atlanta Falcons sweatshirt carried a bright-eyed infant girl past a buffet table, studying the smoked salmon and deviled eggs. "Anything you want, darlin'," she cooed in a buttery Georgia drawl. "Tomorrow, Momma's going to take you home."

Though the man at the front desk advised against it, I went out for a walk just after eleven. The Kievskaya station, with its pretty domes, was busy and brightly lit, and I made my way past the facade to where trucks and vans were parked alongside a small plaza. There, a man sat on the asphalt and picked food out of a can with his fingers; when I walked past him, I saw that it was a can of dog food. Nearby, a policeman was having a conversation—entirely amiable and sotto voce—with a young woman wearing clear-plastic stilettos and a sequined halter top. The sequins trembled in the dark.

I walked past them to a shantytown of kiosks, most shuttered for the night. Two sailors loitered in front of a stand selling a fermented bread drink called kvass. I bought a glass and drank it beside the sailors, who were drunk and in a fine mood. A radio played "It's Raining Men." The redhead threw his arm around my shoulders and showed me his new mobile phone. The sailors agreed that the phone was *krutoi*, hard-core. I said I thought so too. They laughed, with or at me, I wasn't certain, but I laughed too. For some reason, I took out my phone and handed it to the redhead. After he handed it back, I dialed my home number. I heard my boyfriend's voice on the answering machine.

"I'm here," I said. "I miss you. Everything is fine."

.   .   .

MY GRANDMOTHER TAMARA was a month shy of eighty. She lounged on the velvet sofa in a frayed velvet robe, a pair of bifocals perched on the tip of her nose. I hadn't seen her in seven years, and to my dismay the imperious, impeccably dressed woman I remembered looked disheveled and old, her speech vague, her eyes watery and unfocused. I tried on a smile. "Please try to remember," I pleaded.

She held a photo close to her face and squinted. All afternoon we'd been looking at photos from the 1940s and 1950s, most taken with Vassily's Leica. Most were portraits of Tamara posing in feathered hats and fur collars like someone out of a Fitzgerald novel: exotic, slim and utterly at odds with the bleakness of the wartime city.

By the 1970s, she'd grown plump and began dyeing her hair a lustrous blond, but she retained the bearing of a beautiful woman, someone accustomed to flattery, attention and getting what she wanted. She was impressive in a way some men call "handsome," her gravity reinforced by her actual, considerable status. She worked near the Danilovsky Market at the House of Fashion, one of Moscow's most desirable ateliers, where she designed bespoke dresses, suits and

gowns for several dozen of the city's most prominent women. They paid her mostly in gifts from abroad; in Moscow, these mattered more than cash. During televised party speeches and holiday telecasts, she delighted in spotting her clients wearing her creations. She pointed at the screen with a blood-colored nail and announced, "Nadezhda Ivanovna, in the blue organdy, is mine." Tamara maintained an appearance in line with her reputation. Even when heading out for a loaf of bread, she never left home in anything plainer than a navy silk wrap dusted with polka dots, patent-leather pumps, soaring sapphire eye shadow and a mink turban. On her left hand she wore an amethyst the size of a hazelnut that hypnotized me as a toddler.

The winter before my visit, Tamara's third husband, a cantankerous Jewish engineer named Isaac Zinovitch, died of stomach cancer, leaving behind a handful of suits and a drawerful of empty jars of shark-fin cartilage that his son mailed him from Canada. After the funeral, Mikhail Mikhailovich—Tamara's second, and favorite, husband—paid a visit to console her and ended up moving in. He, too, died five months later, and ever since Tamara had been occupying the three-room apartment alone. She misplaced her keys daily. She forgot the names of friends and complained to my father of burglars who entered her bedroom in the night or of a long-dead aunt who called on the telephone. These delusions came imperceptibly, leaving her good spirits unruffled.

As I sat beside her, Tamara flipped over the photos carefully, hoping for an inscription on the back to remind her of the faces in the picture. I asked why she hadn't kept photos of Vassily. She peered at me sharply over the top of her glasses and pulled her tatty robe tighter around her. "He needed no one but himself," she said with a spark of her old vehemence. "That's why I stopped loving him."

They met in 1943, in a loud, smoky dance hall where a band played Benny Goodman tunes and jazzed-up Soviet marches. Tamara was unusually self-reliant for a nineteen-year-old: she had a well-paying job designing women's wear for the city's dress shops and came to the dances in pleated skirts and wool crepe hats that she made herself. That she was strikingly attractive was not in itself an advantage at the dance hall. It was packed with enlisted men and junior officers on leave from the front; they smoked and drank too much and brawled in the alley behind the building. "It was wartime, and no one knew whether they would be alive a month later," Tamara said. "So if you danced with the same boy twice, he expected you to go to bed with him."

She told me that in those years she was "feral." Maria Nikolaevna, her compact, severe mother, doled out her affection stingily. She told Tamara that her own brother was taken by Gypsies when she was four. Maria Nikolaevna had been beautiful, too, with chestnut hair that fell to the waist and slate-colored eyes, beautiful enough to marry a son of a Moscow University history professor, an educated man from an aristocratic family, in the years following the revolution. By the time he vanished, in 1924, a few months before Tamara was born, he'd suffered a series of breakdowns and, haunted by paranoid delusions, refused to leave their apartment. Shortly before his death, he turned up in a psychiatric hospital (the same hospital where my mother would work decades later). This is all Tamara managed to learn about her father besides his fine-sounding Polish surname: Vysokovsky.

As a young woman, Tamara liked to say that she had no use for the past. She lived in a twenty-five-square-meter room with Maria Nikolaevna and her second husband, a taciturn, disapproving man who dressed cadavers at a morgue. Their daughter, a cheerful brown-eyed girl named Lyusia, shared Tamara's bed. At fifteen, Tamara began working seventy-hour weeks as a seamstress and pattern maker. The long hours suited her, and the job provided a supply of good fabric and kept her away from home, where she usually ended up arguing with her stepfather.

She first noticed Vassily because he was square-jawed and trim, with a major's boards on his shoulders and, at thirty-two, older than the other men at the dance hall. He seemed, Tamara said, masculine yet self-effacing, one of the few men she'd met who was entirely without bluster. He had a soft, unhurried way of speaking, but what impressed her most were his manners; he didn't kiss her until their third date. They married three months later. After she moved in, Vassily sent for his daughter from a previous marriage, a timid, brooding girl named Inna who never warmed to her stepmother. My father was born two years later, during the first winter following the war.

Tamara looked forward to going out walking with Vassily on Sunday mornings. Both were particular and vain about clothes. He wore his parade uniform and she her couture, and when they strolled arm in arm along the boulevards in the city center, they reveled in the surprised glances of Moscow's plainer, grayer residents. Though he was often gone, Vassily sent plenty of money and arrived home with a suitcase of presents for her and the children. He was fastidious, rarely drank and never complained about taking a turn sweeping or washing dishes. Vassily didn't speak about his job and Tamara knew not to ask. When he was away, after the children were asleep, she spent the last hours of the night reading books she bought or borrowed, by Pushkin, Gogol, Turgenev, Strindberg, Shakespeare, Balzac. Though she never enrolled in a university course, on those nights she discovered a fondness for books that never left her.

Her devotion to Vassily began to waver only after the family relocated to Vinnitsa. There, Tamara said, she began to see him clearly. For the first time she noticed his near-total absence of curiosity about the world and his habit of sitting in a chair and staring into space, sometimes for hours, as though watching something unfold in the middle distance. In all the years she knew him, she saw Vassily read only one book, *Pot-Bouille* by Émile Zola, a satirical novel about bourgeois strivers set in a Second Empire Paris tenement. He kept it at his bedside like an icon or a lucky coin. Before falling asleep he'd skim a page or two and set it back on the nightstand. Tamara never found out whether he finished it.

When they were alone, Vassily seemed distracted and listless; their conversations petered out. He took little interest in the children,

and Tamara knew never to discuss politics, which prompted Vassily to lapse into icy silences. When my teenage father began to volunteer his anti-Communist views at the supper table, Tamara glared at him until he was quiet.

About a year before they left Moscow, Tamara found out that her design for a women's gabardine trench had won an international competition and would be shown on a runway in Milan. Of course she wasn't allowed to attend, but the prize brought her plenty of attention at work and even a raise. It also convinced her that designing clothes could be not just a job but a career. Yet after all that, she found herself in Vinnitsa, sewing dresses from second-rate fabric for women who couldn't distinguish rayon from silk and who'd never seen Western clothes, not even in a magazine. She hated Vinnitsa, and the bond that kept her there was the marriage to her increasingly remote husband.

The first affair began almost by accident. Vassily was gone for a few days, and she felt resentful and bored. "My pride was the culprit," Tamara told me. It was her pride, too, that kept her from doing a better job of concealing the affair. When she passed neighbors on the staircase, she could hear them whispering. Even after Vassily heard the rumors, he said nothing, and his moods remained constant. He refused to confront her even after she began seeing her lover openly, and his indifference infuriated her. His emptiness, Tamara said, occupied the apartment like an odor.

She was spending more time visiting her mother in Moscow, and on one spring night aboard the northbound train she met a short, bald manager of a fruit-and-vegetable warehouse. He was too talkative and homely but had an appealing grin and an easy laugh. Like her, he was married. Mikhail Mikhailovich proposed to her just before the train pulled into Moscow's Kievskaya station; afterward, he sent a dozen carnations every day to her mother's apartment until she agreed to marry him. It was 1960. When Tamara returned to Vinnitsa she asked Vassily for a divorce, packed two suitcases, kissed her son goodbye, and took a taxi back to the train station. She said when she told Vassily, he didn't argue or ask her to reconsider; he merely walked into the kitchen and began boiling water for tea.

"I never think about him anymore," she said, clutching the armrest of the sofa, fatigued by the effort of shaking the stories loose from the sieve of her memory. "He had an empty place where his heart should be." It was cold outside, and a draft bothered the curtains, so I shut the window, banging at the rusty latch until it slid into place. Back on the sofa, I pointed out a greenish color photo of me at six or seven, my hair still curly, squeezing a child's plastic accordion. My grandmother held it in front of her and lowered her chin slightly to peer at it over her reading glasses. A look of confusion passed over her face like a sudden gust passing across a field.

"Look, Grandma, it's me," I said.

"No," she chided me, as though I'd made an obvious mistake. "That's my grandson. He moved to New York. I like you, but he was my favorite."

.   .   .

ON THE DAY before I left for Vinnytsia, my father and I took the metro to the city center. Every time I visited, he took me on a walk around the center, to point out the same landmarks and tell the same stories. Still, I enjoyed hearing him talk, something he otherwise did reluctantly. The metro was crowded. The passengers kept their eyes closed or scanned the floor, as quiet as patients in a doctor's waiting room.

Outside it was a cloudless, warm late-autumn day, and the city looked as radiant and hopeful as a bride. We made our familiar rounds, passing the Bolshoi Theater with its apple trees wearing their last leaves, the glass-covered Hotel Metropol, and the tall windows of the GUM shopping center facing the russet marble of Lenin's Mausoleum. Behind the Hotel National, we passed the First Medical Institute and stopped in front of the building of classrooms where my parents had met. My father glanced up warily at its windows, stubbed out a cigarette, and pulled his hat down over his ears.

"I want to show you something," he said slyly, and led me down a series of smaller streets. He stopped on the Stone Bridge and pointed over my shoulder. I turned and found myself looking at the reconstructed Cathedral of Christ the Savior. It wasn't there the last time I'd visited Moscow, seven years earlier. I stood for a while staring at the church's improbable white-and-gold enormity; it loomed above the river like a visitor from some humorless alien civilization. My father wanted to take a look inside.

I'd seen the original cathedral in old photos and on postcards. No other structure expresses so much about the place—Russia's singular aesthetics, the relationship between the rulers and the ruled, and its extreme, sometimes absurdly violent history. The mammoth church on Volkhonka Street epitomizes the city's tragic past and its penchant for outsize, eschatological gestures, the combination that gives Moscow its unusual scale, its heaviness and its peculiar, grandiose beauty. So much meaning is packed into the cathedral that for most Muscovites it functions as allegory.

The salvation in the cathedral's name was, partly, that of Russia from Napoleon's army. According to a manifest Tsar Alexander I signed in December 1812, it would "signify Our gratitude to Divine Providence for saving Russia from the doom that overshadowed Her." As a monument to Russia's victory over a Western power, Alexander envisioned the largest, costliest and most impressive Orthodox church in Christendom, modeled on the Hagia Sophia, with room for ten thousand worshippers. No foreign visitor could miss its meaning: Moscow, resurgent from the steppe, was proclaiming itself the Third Rome. The cathedral was proof that Russia exceeded all other nations not only in size but in the magnitude of its people's devotion.

Crews had pulled down the Alexeevsky Monastery's fifteenth-century bell towers and chapels, near the Kremlin, to clear space for it. Construction, financed mainly by public donation drives, lasted for forty-three years. After Alexander died, his brother Nicholas I took over the project, and his son Alexander II completed it. The court architect Konstantin Thon enlisted Kramskoi, Vereshchagin,

Surikov and other renowned Russian painters to adorn its interior; they worked among expanses of Altaic and Podolia marble and inlaid semiprecious stones. Tchaikovsky premiered the *1812 Overture* there while it stood in scaffolding. When it was finally unveiled, in 1880, the effect was that of an intimate medieval Russian church scaled upward to incomprehensible dimensions, a gold-domed Neo-Byzantine cube out of proportion with the city around it, at once disrupting and unifying the skyline.

By the beginning of the Soviet age in the 1920s, the cathedral had become an impediment, an albatross from a decadent age. The Moscow party chief Lazar Kaganovich proclaimed that the new capital would physically embody the ideals of Socialism and become "a laboratory to which people from all over the Union will flock to study its experience." Under his watch, landmarks like the sixteenth-century wall encircling Kitai Gorod and the Kazan Cathedral in Red Square were demolished, streets were widened in anticipation of the automobile age, and nearly every alley and square was renamed after a luminary of the new state.

The most ambitious feature of Kaganovich's plan was the splendid new metro system, its deep tunnels doubling as bomb shelters and its stations, decorated with colonnades, stained glass and statuary, intended to serve as "people's palaces." Thousands of students— members of the Young Communist League, the Komsomol—were conscripted into heavy labor on the metro's construction, during which hundreds were gravely injured or killed.

In 1936, a British delegation led by the Liberal MP Sir E. D. Simon visited Moscow and took in the city's wholesale transformation into a futuristic Socialist metropolis. When the Brits asked government officials why so much capital and labor were being spent on a vast, sumptuous underground transportation system at a time of severe housing and food shortages, they were told that "the metro is a symbol, an expression of the power of the people to create gigantic and beautiful things, a foretaste of the wealth to be at the command of all." The first part was certainly accurate, because Russia's architecture, like many aspects of its civic life, has always functioned primarily as a symbolic language. Though Stalin's rule became identified with brutalist monoliths conceived on a monumental scale, the Cathedral of Christ the Savior was a reminder that Stalin didn't originate Russian gigantism, but merely lent it new forms of expression.

In 1931, the year Kaganovich unveiled his plan for a Socialist Moscow, Stalin demolished the cathedral with truckloads of dynamite. The world's grandest Orthodox church, nurtured into being by three tsars and a multitude of ordinary Russians, which took nearly seventy years to complete, existed for a mere fifty. For days a crew of men, including squads of secret policemen, worked through the nights removing tons of gold and malachite, marble plaques inscribed with dates of Russian military campaigns, gilt vestments, priceless icons. Gold leaf was scored from its domes, and the bells were taken down. It took two weeks of explosions to level the massive structure section by section, and nearly another year to haul away the debris. Much of the marble used in the opulent station halls in Kaganovich's metro, as it was known for a time, came from the demolished cathedral.

Of course, the razing was symbolic, too. In order to create in Russia "a proletarian religion without God," Stalin destroyed the people's holiest temple. In its place he would give them something even grander, a futuristic palace to house party congresses and proclaim the triumph of world Socialism and the Five-Year Plan, a structure large enough to blot out not only God the Father but the entire Trinity. And so that no one would miss its meaning, it would stand on the site of the demolished church.

An international design competition for the Palace of the Soviets brought hundreds of proposals, most optimistically constructivist or modernist in style, including submissions from Walter Gropius and Le Corbusier. Stalin chose the Moscow architect Boris Iofan's proposal for an awkwardly gloomy neoclassical tower—the world's tallest building would resemble a hockey trophy. Stalin's Palace of the Soviets, thirty meters taller than the recently erected Empire State Building, was topped with a statue of Lenin three times taller than the Statue of Liberty. Lenin's arm swept out over the city and toward the future; his extended index finger was six meters long. The main hall would hold twenty thousand while another, smaller one, seven thousand more. Crews excavated the foundation in 1937, the deadliest year of the Terror, the year Frank Lloyd Wright, speaking to an audience of architects in Moscow, warned the Russians about "grandomania." A thirty-foot model of the design was exhibited at the 1939 New York World's Fair.

River water flooded the foundation almost immediately, and children jumped the fences to swim and fish for carp. Trucks brought tombstones from the city's cemeteries to reinforce the sides; construction was halted in 1941. Workmen dismantled the building's steel skeleton for use in the war effort, while the city's residents, in constant need of firewood, pulled apart the fence enclosing the site. The nearby metro station kept "Palace of the Soviets" as its name until the year of Stalin's death; factories continued to illustrate matchboxes with Iofan's design.

A family friend in New York remembers the site. When he was a teenager in the years immediately following the war, it was covered with trash and stinging nettles. He ate his midday meal while dangling his legs over the edge of the watery foundation. Pious old women whispered that after the cathedral's demolition the ground under it was cursed. The fact that both Kaganovich and Iofan were Jews figured in anti-Semitic conspiracy theories that never died out entirely in Moscow. Finally, on Khrushchev's orders, the chasm on the embankment became a heated open-air swimming pool named, blandly, Moskva—it, too, the world's largest. Russia's two grandest structures—one demolished, the other unrealized—were replaced with a poured-concrete basin. My mother remembers swimming there several months before my birth.

My father and I wandered through the rebuilt cathedral, which was crowded with visitors. Like the previous version, it was paid for in part by ordinary Russians, more than a million of whom donated money to its reconstruction. It was intended to be an exact replica, but at the last hour the Georgian-born sculptor Zurab Tsereteli, a close friend of Moscow's famously corrupt mayor, added awkward, inexplicably modern embellishments. Tsereteli's widely despised monument to Peter the Great stood elsewhere along the river; Moscow police had arrested two separate groups that tried to rig the statue with explosives.

We walked past statues of Nicholas and Alexander and took a flight of stairs down to a smaller chapel, where a service was under way. A priest chanted in front of a gilt iconostasis. Amid the candles and incense smoke a trio of singers and a few dozen parishioners in overcoats crowded around the altar. The singing was almost unbearably beautiful. Watching them, I thought for some reason about a midnight Mass at a Lutheran church in Bethesda, Maryland. My boyfriend and I had gone there one Christmas to hear his mother sing a solo from Fauré's *Requiem*. Parishioners in the pews chatted pleasantly before the service. Later, women in cardigans and pearls and neatly combed boys in navy blazers knelt along the railing around the altar and waited for Communion. The scene felt cautiously optimistic. Here in Moscow, the mood was darker. There were no pews and the air was tense with devotion. Unlike Fauré's airy melodies, the singing resonated with earthly life. A woman beside me, a satchel of groceries at her feet, rocked back and forth on her heels, eyes closed, repeating a prayer under her breath.

My father began to whisper something in my ear when someone behind us shouted. It was a man in a patched suit jacket and felt boots; he was on his knees, touching his forehead to the floor in the old Russian way. When he rose, his cheeks were streaked with tears. *"Zhidi rastoptali Rossiyu!"* he shouted again. "The kikes trampled Russia!" My face grew cold. My father turned from me and walked quickly away. I followed him up the stairs and stumbled into the afternoon light. He flagged down a privateer cab and we sat side by side in the backseat while the old city receded, giving way to apartment blocks and sidewalk kiosks. He lit a Winston and blew the smoke out the window. Twenty minutes passed before he looked at me again.

IT WAS PAST midnight when the Bucharest-bound train ground to a stop. Vinnytsia was still fourteen hours away. In place of a station house, there was a sign lit by a bulb in a metal shade that read, "Sukhinichi." Seen through the window, the place looked like any of the pinpricks on the map that owe their existence to the railroad, a strip of packed dirt alongside a length of track. At first I barely noticed the procession of silhouettes—indistinct shapes, first one or two, then dozens—that crowded around the train car. After my eyes adjusted to the dark I made out outlines of people bent under the largest stuffed animals I'd ever seen. When the passengers filed off the train, life-size panthers, tigers and bears surrounded us, their hard plastic eyes glittering in the moonlight.

The conductor, a woman with severely parted bangs and apricot lip gloss, explained that these people worked at a nearby toy factory that, like many others, was nearly bankrupt and paid employees in merchandise. They hawked the enormous stuffed animals on the platform to train passengers who stretched their legs and smoked during the ten-minute layover, because they were the only visitors who passed through Sukhinichi regularly. After I declined to buy a canoe-size panther for about seventeen dollars, the woman underneath it asked whether I was hungry. "I've got a cooked chicken leg," she offered. A boy of about eight, dragging a duffel on the ground, yelled, "Beer, cigarettes!" "When you come through on your way back, it will be daytime and the prices will be higher," a man in a knit cap said bitterly. The whistle blew and the conductor climbed aboard. I weaved past a mermaid and a leering humanoid mushroom to the train's metal steps. The train lurched. In the compartment I pressed my face to the glass and watched the surreal zoo recede into the night.

"How do you like our country?" Petya asked with a grin. I was sharing a four-berth sleeper compartment with my stepfather's son from his brief first marriage. A few days earlier he volunteered to join me on the trip to Vinnytsia, and I was relieved and grateful not to be traveling alone. Petya was a year older than I. He grew up in Moscow, where he worked as a freelance magazine photographer. We'd met only a few times, and I asked one question after another. He told me about his army stint in the Urals and his recent trip to Chechnya, on assignment for a Moscow magazine, to photograph the dead. I think he found my halting Russian and my circumspect tourist's manner amusing. Built like a trapeze artist, with buzzed yellow hair and humorous hazel eyes, Petya shepherded me up and down the train, at ease and cheerful in its ecosystem but touchingly concerned about my well-being. He grew dour only when our conversation turned to his father, my stepfather, a painter who left the Soviet Union under government pressure in 1978. Petya was eight when his father left, and he asked about him with a cowed, tentative expression. I wondered whether he resented me for my proximity to his father, proximity that by rights should have been his, but he brushed my awkwardness aside. "You're stuck with him now," he said, and grinned his reassuring grin.

The night before we left for Vinnytsia, Petya called to say that he was bringing his wife, or more precisely his ex-wife, Anya. He didn't explain why. She sat on the berth beside him, a thin, pretty blonde in her mid-thirties with a scattered manner and a piercing, slightly unhinged laugh. Anya said she designed "abstract" women's clothes. She and Petya had split up several times but reunited in the end, mostly because of her son from a previous marriage, an eight-year-old whom Petya adopted. We sipped tea and vodka and stared out the window while the suburbs gave way to cabins, outhouses, vegetable patches, crank wells and low undulating wooden fences missing an occasional slat. Anya told dirty jokes and howled with laughter at the punch lines.

On the way to the dining car we walked through a section called *platskart*—the train's equivalent of steerage. There weren't doors or even curtains to separate the passengers, and entire families dozed on wooden berths, faces turned to the wall for privacy. Soldiers sprawled in their boots. Women played cards, snacking on radishes and sliced cucumbers from cellophane bags. The windows were bolted shut, and the air was thick with the smell of cured sausage and sweat. We stumbled down six rattling cars and huddled around a cold metal table. Anya ordered a bottle of Moldovan brandy and a plate of lemon slices sprinkled with sugar. Before the brandy arrived a pair of passengers squeezed in beside us. There were plenty of empty tables in the dining car, but it would have been boorish to object aboard a train, a form of travel that brings out a benevolent courtesy in Russians.

Our companions—two curly-haired, dark-eyed men in their late twenties—slurred at us with Uzbek accents. They looked as if they had been drunk for a long time. The more talkative one, Zhora, said they were coming from Samarkand; he didn't mention where they were heading. He gaped admiringly and not in the least self-consciously at Anya. They seemed too friendly, too open, but I told myself that I'd lost my feel for Russian manners. The door at the end of the car opened, revealing the conductor's uniform, and Zhora and his friend dashed into the lavatory and locked themselves inside. After she passed, they stuck their heads out, looking dogged and comical. Zhora admitted that they had neither tickets nor passports and that they'd been kicked off another train several days earlier.

The sweet brandy was making my head buzz when Petya leaned toward me and whispered in my ear, instructing me to look at the men's hands; their fingers were tattooed with elaborate blue rings between the second and the third joints. "Convicts," he whispered calmly, enunciating the word *zeki*. Just then Zhora asked whether any of us were carrying cash; a gold incisor flashed under his mustache. We glanced at each other, sobering up, realizing that there was no one else in the dining car. Just then the conductor made another pass, sending Zhora and his friend to the lavatory. When the metal door clicked shut behind them, Petya signaled for us to go. We skittered through the cars and locked the compartment door behind us. Petya took a wine cork from his suitcase and slid it under the latch so that the door couldn't be jimmied open.

We sat laughing for a long while, taking a last round from the vodka bottle. Later, groggily, we folded down the upper sleeping berths and covered them with stiff white sheets. Petya and Anya were asleep within minutes, but when I closed my eyes the film of the preceding day played on the backs of my eyelids. After half an hour of staring at the night-light and listening to the wheels' stutter, I put on headphones. The music made me alternately scared and homesick until I found a record by Sonic Youth. "Love has come to stay in all the way / It's gonna stay forever and every day," Thurston Moore and Kim Gordon's voices chanted in my head; outside, ghostly forest stretched in all directions. "You got a cotton crown / I'm gonna keep it underground." I fell asleep with guitar feedback squalling in my ears.

It was dark outside when the whine of brakes woke me. My watch said four thirty. We were at the border. There was a sound of boots on the metal steps. "Where's the American?" a man's voice demanded. The train's manifest listed the names and nationalities of the passengers, and I was the only foreigner aboard. A moment later someone was pounding on the compartment door. Petya pocketed the wine cork and flicked on the lights. Two border guards with the Ukrainian flag on their coat sleeves walked in and stood over us; the bigger one did the talking. We handed him our passports and he feigned examining them. I couldn't see his eyes under the visor. "Where's your customs declaration?" he barked, turning to me. The conductor didn't give us any customs forms, I replied. We were startled and still a little drunk, and Anya and Petya were protesting loudly.

"Your documents are not in order," the guard intoned as though reading from a card. "You're behaving disgracefully and holding up this train, and if you do not produce customs declarations in ninety seconds, I will detain you here."

I glanced out the window. Located in the night somewhere along the endless Russian-Ukrainian border, "here" was a corrugated shed that looked as if it weren't heated. We lay undressed on our berths and looked up at the guards. I was slightly nauseated with fear but also worried that I might start laughing at the obvious setup. The floor began to tilt toward some catastrophic outcome when Petya reached into the back pocket of his jeans and handed the guard a crumpled twenty-dollar bill. (Russians often carry dollars for precisely these kinds of transactions.) The man brightened, then actually smiled. "Welcome to the sovereign Ukrainian Republic," he said. "Enjoy a safe and pleasant stay!" He snapped us a cordial salute, stepped out into the hallway with the other guard and, after another, jauntier salute, slid the compartment door closed.

WE WAITED BESIDE our luggage in the corridor outside the compartment and looked out the windows, watching the countryside transform into the wreckage of a medium-size city. The train passed the shells of buildings of indeterminate age, warehouses and waterworks, their bricks scattered along the tracks; young, soot-darkened trees sprouted randomly among dandelions and crabgrass. The Vinnytsia train station, a concrete bunker under a corrugated-metal roof, waited amid the detritus. Petya hustled us into a privateer's taxi that took us, at a bicycle's pace, down the main street to our hotel.

In my *Rough Guide* to the region, Vinnytsia merited a single paragraph. The city, the book claimed, was "remarkable for being utterly unremarkable." In the taxi I thought about childhood stories my father had told me about this place; they didn't jibe with the shabbiness and apparent poverty around us. An outdoor market occupied both sidewalks along River Street. Sitting on a crate, an old woman stooped over a pair of plucked hens that lay at her feet on the asphalt. At improvised stands women sold pirated DVDs, homemade sweets and yard after yard of fashions: black lace-ups with pointed toes, acrylic sweaters with names of famous designers inscribed in sequins across the front (one misspelled), Gucci handbags, Swiss wrist-watches from China. There were indoor shops in Vinnytsia, too, the driver assured us, but almost everyone shopped here, where prices were lower.

After checking into our hotel, we sat down for breakfast in an empty cafeteria and waited for a boy of sixteen in an apron to bring enormous menus, conceived with the Soviet absence of irony and penchant for abstract nouns—a banana-and-ham appetizer was named Tenderness. Petya, Anya and I agreed to meet here at the end of the trip. I told them I didn't know when that would be, but they didn't look concerned. It wasn't yet noon. I left my suitcase in my room, threw water on my face and went to look for my grandfather.

No one here had heard of Voroshilov Street. I began to think that I must have written down the address incorrectly when a woman in her fifties smiled and nodded. The street was renamed a few years back, she explained. The 50th Anniversary of the Victory over Fascism Street was a grand name for a narrow two-lane road with scrawny birches planted every twenty feet in the sidewalk. A cold wind had started to blow and a red Japanese sun was setting behind a factory when I spotted number 19, a five-story brick walk-up dating from the 1930s. Timid graffiti covered the door. A sign in the window of a shuttered beauty salon on the corner promised unisex electrolysis and "Afrobraids."

Laden with presents from the outdoor market—daisies cinched with a rubber band and a cake in a plastic bag that read, "HUGO BOSS"—I lingered by the door and inventoried the possibilities. I considered silence, dementia, rejection. I considered my lack of a meaningful contingency plan. I considered the absurdity of traveling five thousand miles after a single phone call with no memories of this man and no messages to deliver to him.

I'd imagined meeting Vassily for months, but for some reason just then all I felt was dull anxiety and a desire to get this over with. Suddenly I wanted more than anything to be home. To be pedaling up the Brooklyn Bridge until, at the top of the climb, I could see the morning's glimmer in the windows above South Street, and beyond them Governors Island and the ferries fanning out from Whitehall Terminal. The desire was so vivid that I nearly turned around and walked back to the hotel. Instead I checked my watch and climbed an unlit stairwell.

A woman in a flower-print apron opened the door. "I'm Sonya," she said, smiling. "I saw you on the sidewalk and recognized you from the photo." Sonya was tiny, around eighty, with a kind, inquisitive face. She folded me in a strong hug, then ushered me inside and led me along a linoleum-floored hallway to a small living room that smelled of cleanser and old age. It was full of outmoded furniture, overgrown plants and floral lace curtains. A maroon rug hung over the sofa. On top of an old television a blond doll sat splay-legged beside a rabbit-ear antenna held together with electrical tape.

It took me a moment to realize that the spindly, ancient man on the sofa was my grandfather. He perched there in the dark like a flightless seabird and regarded me with pale, watery eyes. Before I got a good look at him, he embraced me and kissed me on both cheeks, over and over, the way old Russian men do, repeating my name. When he released me I searched his face for the one in the photograph. I took it out of my backpack and showed it to him. He put on glasses that dangled by a piece of yarn on his chest and looked at it with something like disbelief. "Was that me?" he muttered. His voice was clear, his cheeks clean-shaven. The faded navy blazer he wore had recently been pressed. His nose bent at the end like the beak of a bird of prey, like my own. It was him, I thought, genuinely surprised. I'd found him.

We passed that first night around the lacquered living room table (it turned out to be the table my father and his friends danced on fifty years earlier) sipping lukewarm tea and picking at the cake. Sonya did most of the talking. She told me about Vassily's daughter, Inna, my father's half sister, who lived several hundred kilometers to the west, and showed me photos of the grandchildren: a skinny boy and girl with oatmeal-colored hair clinging to a middle-aged mother whose face I couldn't connect to the two or three childhood photos in which she stood pensively, always unsmiling, beside my father. The grave rectangular face of Sonya's son, a military judge in Moscow, looked down from a framed photo on the wall.

As the night wore on, Sonya said more, and I was surprised, and then ashamed, that many of their difficulties came down to lacking trivial sums of money. There was a dangerously unstable balcony they couldn't afford to reinforce, a sofa with a sharp spring poking out of the seat that cost too much to fix. Like most of the elderly here, Sonya and Vassily talked about pensions: hers was thirty-five hryvna a month, about seven dollars, his slightly higher. When he broke his hip they couldn't afford the surgery a doctor recommended, and now, after a year and a half spent immobile in bed, Vassily got around on crutches. The operation would have cost around three hundred dollars.

Vassily didn't get many visitors, and he sat grinning under over-grown brows. When he smiled in the lamplight I saw that three of his front teeth were capped in gold. His mood soured only toward the evening's end, when he asked about my father. I told him what I knew and watched his face register surprise and then, gradually, embarrassment. "I thought he'd gone to America, with you," Vassily muttered at last. For some reason I felt embarrassed, too. I wanted to say something to comfort him. "He asked me to say hello to you," I stammered. The lie sounded idiotic even as it left my mouth, but Vassily was transfigured by a look of such unabashed joy that my face flushed with shame.

ON THE FOLLOWING morning, on the 50th Anniversary of the Victory over Fascism Street, we moved the chairs near the window, where sunlight slanted in and lit the daisies and the scuffed parquet, making the room look almost cheerful. Vassily had spent the morning talking about his childhood in Aleksandrovka, a village located a short drive from Vinnitsa. These were the grinding years of civil war, collectivization and famine, but to me Vassily's memories sounded incomprehensibly bucolic. Then the stories segued to his return to Vinnitsa after Stalin's death in 1953, as though the intervening years in Moscow had been taken up with gardening and paperwork and weren't worth mentioning. Every time I asked about Moscow, he deflected the question. He looked up from time to time, shooting me furtive, guilty glances, because he knew that I knew he was doing it. Sonya looked uneasy, too. I expected her to tell me to leave the old man alone, to quit discomfiting him with my questions, when she slammed her hand on the table so hard that all of us flinched. "Tell him the truth, Vassily!" she nearly shouted, and then vanished into the kitchen.

Vassily was silent for a moment, then turned to me with what looked like relief. I stared wordlessly until he cleared his throat and resumed speaking in a slightly lower register that sounded more like his natural voice. "The first time I saw Stalin was on November 8, 1932," he said. "I remember walking across Red Square, past St. Basil's Cathedral. Voroshilov was hosting a banquet on the fifteenth anniversary of the revolution, and someone had sent for me. Imagine! A beet farmer's son. I had just turned twenty-one." Vassily's apologetic look was gone and he appeared transfixed by his words, as though years had passed since he had spoken about these things aloud.

He said he'd been invited because he was secretary of the Komsomol chapter at the OGPU academy in Moscow. He was admitted after enlisting at eighteen and serving two years with a Red Army cavalry unit near Vinnitsa. OGPU was the name of the organization that had been known as the Cheka and would come to be called by other acronyms, including NKVD, MGB and KGB. Vassily was one of a handful of men from the cavalry unit selected for the academy. In the army, he'd been good at everything. His commanders liked him for his seriousness and lack of guile, for not complaining and not speaking until spoken to. Until he traveled to Moscow, with everything he owned packed into a cardboard suitcase, Vassily had never been aboard a train.

The guards at Spasskaya Tower smirked while he produced his identity papers. *"Kuda idyosh paren?"* one of them greeted him: "Where are you going, kid?" They walked him along the Kremlin's flagstones to the narrow Horse Guards building, the residence of the defense chief, Kliment Voroshilov, and his wife, Ekaterina. Someone else, Vassily remembered, led him to a crowded banquet room with a long table and seated him beside a pretty opera singer—possibly, he surmised, from the Bolshoi. He barely registered her presence.

He was the youngest person in the room. He sat woodenly and studied the faces of the guests, some of whom he recognized from the pages of newspapers. The country's leadership was gathered around the table: the squat, punctilious premier, Molotov; strapping Voroshilov in an ornate uniform; the old revolutionary cavalryman Budyonny, who twisted the ends of his walrus mustache with tobacco-stained fingers; and moonfaced Yagoda, soon to be OGPU chief and his boss. They sat so close he could touch them. Vassily spoke to the pretty singer and quickly downed two glasses of vodka. He grew warmer and more unlaced until a hand took firm hold of his elbow. A frowning officer in a medal-spangled parade uniform, his academy's headmaster, pulled him into a corner and reminded him that in the presence of the nation's leaders an OGPU agent's task was to observe and listen, not to wallow in drink and chatter like an ingenue.

During this exchange, Vassily missed Stalin's entrance. He was admittedly easy to overlook among the decorated commissars, standing a mere five feet, six inches and wearing a corporal's plain tunic and baggy trousers. Vassily was surprised by the smallpox scars on his cheeks, which were airbrushed from official photos.

At state banquets, Stalin liked to substitute water for the vodka in his glass, enjoying the game of watching his guests drop their inhibitions while he remained sober. In the coming years, Vassily saw this happen many times. But on that night, Stalin drank glass after glass of vodka, neglecting to eat, and grew unusually talkative and loud, leering red-faced at a slim young woman several seats away. Published accounts of that night suggest she was Galina Yegorova, an actress and the wife of General Yegorov. In her tailored flapper dress she looked a breed apart from the matronly Kremlin wives around her. She acknowledged Stalin's glances but looked coquettishly away.

The accounts suggest that to get Yegorova's attention, Stalin balled up pieces of bread and tossed them at her, aiming at her décolletage; Vassily remembered only that Stalin flirted with a pretty young woman. Those seated around them pretended not to notice, all except the dark-haired woman sitting across from Stalin—his wife, Nadezhda Allilueva. She glared at him, incensed, and when Stalin stood to toast "the destruction of the enemies of the state"—the peasants resisting the man-made famine he'd unleashed upon the countryside—she defiantly did not raise her glass. "Don't you drink?" he shouted at his wife, bringing a hush over the table. When she didn't answer, Stalin tossed orange peels and cigarettes at her until she ran, sobbing, from the room. Polina Molotova, the premier's wife and Allilueva's closest friend, followed. The guests at the table remained quiet, except for a few whispers that only Stalin's intimates permitted themselves. "My mouth probably hung open," Vassily said, his eyes growing damp. "I was so young. I didn't know to look away."

That night turned out to be a pivotal one in the nation's history, though it remains fragmented and obscured by the enforced secrecy of totalitarianism. Much of this history continues to be filled in from newly declassified documents and research, but some of its set pieces will never be reconstructed completely. What's known is that many of the events that would come to be called the Great Terror trace their origins to that early November night, recounted in a multitude of rumors, second- and thirdhand accounts, facts, pseudo-facts and other pieces of information. It isn't always clear which are which, and some contradict others, but in their aggregation they suggest something about what happened.

Here are some of them. On the morning of November 9 the Stalins' housekeeper discovered Allilueva in her bedroom at the Poteshny Palace, lying on the floor in a pool of blood, her pearl-handled German revolver beside her. The official report, signed by a Professor Kushner, stated that the cause of death was a self-inflicted gunshot to the chest. But an autopsy conducted by the physician who first arrived at the scene, Boris Zbarsky—the country's leading anatomist and Lenin's embalmer—concluded that she'd died of a gunshot to the left temple from a handgun that was fired from at least four meters away. Allilueva was right-handed; when the housekeeper found her, she was holding a blood-soaked pillow in front of her like a shield. An obituary in *Pravda* omitted the cause of death altogether. At her funeral, friends noticed that her hair was swept over her left temple, though she'd always worn it parted in the middle. A small crowd had gathered at the Stalins' apartment before Zbarsky was called, and several hours passed before it was decided that the general secretary should be woken. Upon learning of his wife's death, Stalin is said to have wept, to have cried out that he couldn't go on living. He didn't attend the funeral. "She left me like an enemy," Stalin reportedly said while a horse-drawn carriage led Allilueva's casket past a throng of mourners from Red Square to the cemetery at Novodevichy Convent.

Perhaps Allilueva's violent death bent Stalin's mind further toward isolation, distrust and malice. Perhaps it did nothing of the kind; perhaps the terror that followed was inevitable. What's been established with greater certainty is that after her death the revolutionary camaraderie that bound the Soviet Union's ruling families was replaced with suspicion, fear and paranoia that eventually engulfed the country. "How did our life," the banquet's hostess, Ekaterina Voroshilova, wrote in a diary, "become so complex that it was incomprehensible to the point of agony."

I asked Vassily whether he remembered how the night ended. He cocked his head, thinking. "I walked home," he said. "I didn't know why any of it was happening to me, but I remember being happy." Back home in Aleksandrovka, OGPU detachments drove kulaks—prosperous farmers like Vassily's father—from their homes and orphaned scores of his former schoolmates. The liquidation was carried out by agents of the secret police, because ordinary soldiers couldn't be trusted to shoot farmers. But on that night Vassily walked to his dormitory room, lost in happy thoughts, certain that the future he imagined for himself was drawing near.

.   .   .

AS I AMBLED back to the hotel, my mind felt like a snake that had swallowed a large rodent and now needed stillness and time to digest it. The sky was starless and the streets quiet, but in the park couples still strolled and teenagers lingered on benches, and I walked among them for a while, becoming pleasantly lost. A breeze rustled the lindens and the air smelled of damp leaves. I sat on a bench, looking around me, and began to think.

Prior to the trip, while trying to find information about this city, I stumbled unexpectedly across one of the Holocaust's most famous photographs. It was captioned "The Last Jew in Vinnitsa," and was first circulated by UPI during the trial of Adolf Eichmann. In my mind, this haunting image transformed the ordinary provincial city of my father's stories. In the middle of the last century, catastrophe on a mass scale affected nearly everyone here, arriving from both the east and the west as the city passed back and forth between warring powers. In Vinnitsa, the epicenter of the catastrophe turned out to be not some abandoned field at the city's edge, but the pretty, verdant park where I now found myself.

In 1943—when the place was called People's Park—the Nazi occupiers exhumed nearly 10,000 bodies in its vicinity. All but 149 were men, mostly Ukrainians. During Stalin's mass executions in 1937 and 1938, they were forced into long lines and shot in the back of the head by NKVD agents. (Did Vassily take part in cleansing his native city of enemies?) Entrenched in a propaganda battle with the Soviet Union, the Germans publicized "the Communist Terror" and flew in a panel of international experts to pore over the ninety-one mass graves. Locals managed to identify fewer than 500 of the bodies. The remains were interred in a public ceremony; Metropolitan Vissarion of Odessa presided at the mass burial; a monument was erected.

What the Reich declined to publicize was a series of "actions" carried out nearby in the fall of 1941 by the SS officers of Einsatzgruppe D. On the morning of September 15, German command ordered every Jew residing in the vicinity of Uman, a city east of Vinnitsa, to report to the local airport. There, at gunpoint, they were made to strip and line up along a ditch. SS men then walked along the line behind the assembled, shooting them in the head with Lugers. They brained infants with the pistol butts and tossed them onto the pile of bodies before shooting the mothers. The next group of Jews were given shovels and ordered to cover the still-moving bodies with chloride of lime. Then they, too, were shot. Twenty-four thousand Jews died in Uman, and on September 22, when the SS carried out a similar action in Vinnitsa, another twenty-eight thousand bodies were buried in shallow ditches.

Soon after September 22, yet another massacre took place in People's Park. This one claimed approximately six thousand victims and was carried out by Ukrainian militiamen commanded by the SS. In 1945, a captured Wehrmacht officer, Oberleutnant Erwin Bingel, described the event to his Soviet interrogator.

"In the morning, at 10:15," Bingel testified, "wild shooting and terrible human cries reached our ears. At first I failed to grasp what was taking place, but when I approached the window . . . Ukrainian militia on horseback, armed with pistols, rifles and long straight cavalry swords, were riding wildly inside and around the town park. As far as we could make out, they were driving people before their horses—men, women and children. A shower of bullets was then fired at this human mass. Those not hit outright were struck down with the swords. Like some ghostly apparition, this horde of Ukrainians, let loose and commanded by SS officers, trampled savagely over human bodies, ruthlessly killing innocent children, mothers and old people whose only crime was that they had escaped the great mass murder, so as eventually to be shot or beaten to death like wild animals.

"Over the next few hours," Bingel continued, "we were to see the following. In the municipal park in Vinnitsa there was a pit. In front of this pit human corpses, that had been brought hither from the entire neighborhood, were dumped on the ground. The bodies were

those of some of the murdered Jews. The corpses were then placed in
the above-mentioned pit, layer upon layer, and covered with chloride of lime. In this way 213 bodies were disposed of, after which the
opening of the pit was bricked up."

The well-known photo was probably taken on that day by an un-
identified German soldier. It shows a gaunt Jewish man in a black
coat kneeling by the edge of a pit; a tangle of bodies is visible below.
A handsome German officer in wire-rimmed spectacles stands above
him, pointing an automatic pistol at the back of the man's head. The
most remarkable thing about the image is the assembled soldiers and
officers gathered just behind them, calmly posing for the photographer in postures of stoicism and pride. Writing about the image, one
commentator remarked that, judging by the men's expressions, they
could have been watching a barber cutting hair.

After the war, the dead buried in the park continued to be used as
little more than political ballast. Communist Party authorities in
Vinnitsa rededicated the original Nazi monument to the victims of

Nazi killings. Later, when the park was renamed for the Soviet novelist Maxim Gorky, they ordered the monument bulldozed. The Ukrainian government erected another one in the year following my visit. I saw it only as a JPEG on a computer screen: a homely grouping of three modern crosses with an inscription that reads, once again, "To the victims of Stalinist terror."

The park looked well kept, even cheerful, as darkness settled over the trees. Here, history inundated every square centimeter—it seemed more real and urgent than the present—and yet the ground under my feet didn't quake. No one wailed. Here in a city that was allegedly remarkable only for being unremarkable, it was a warm autumn night and somewhere farther in the park a radio was playing "Have You Ever Seen the Rain?" Someone on the benches laughed and the wind blew so loudly through the lindens that for a moment I couldn't hear the music.

AFTER I SPENT several fourteen-hour days beside Vassily on the ragged sofa, the lacunae in his stories began to close. Whatever else he might have been, I was learning, he was neither a dullard nor simple. My grandfather answered questions about his past with a studied ear for narrative, emphasizing certain details and omitting others, eager to portray himself as a harmless invalid, and on occasion he introduced inconsistencies that he refused to clarify. "That's how it happened," he remarked opaquely, or when I pressed, he draped the fiction of a weak memory over scenes that he described in otherwise lapidary detail. Several times he fixed me with a peculiar wounded look as if to say, "You came here as my grandson, not my interrogator."

He was vaguest about the years just prior to the war, and it wasn't difficult to guess why. In those years the Soviet government's war against its people reached an apex; in its savagery and ultimate irrationality, it has few historical parallels. Between 1935 and 1941, nineteen million Soviet citizens were arrested, and seven million executed, many by quota. The purges were bookended by millions of other deaths brought about by civil war, mass starvation, collectivization and the catastrophic war with Germany. The mass arrests and executions decimated the ranks of the country's leading intellectuals, writers and artists but also its inventors, engineers and military tacticians, to say nothing of the political elite. Most of the victims, of course, were neither prominent nor well-known.

In those years, arriving to work five minutes late was sometimes a pretext for arrest; Stalin's government sought to turn every citizen into an informer, claiming that enemies were all around, hidden in plain sight. At this it was uncannily successful. Monthly quotas from Moscow to find and arrest "terrorists," "anti-Soviet agitators" and other "enemies of the people" were received by local NKVD offices, demanding as many as sixty arrests each day. Every morning, lines formed outside their doors as people waited patiently to file denunciations. They lined up to denounce neighbors, colleagues, family. Some estimates suggest that one in seven Soviet citizens became an informer.

In its rejection of personal experience and common sense, the Soviet mentality of those years resembled mass psychosis. Decades after Stalin's death, hundreds of thousands continued to believe in the accusations that were given as the reason for the disappearance of their family members—they died believing that their parents, siblings and spouses had been conspirators and spies.

The daily work of the purges fell to men like Vassily. He answered questions about his time in the OGPU and NKVD in the middle and late 1930s by relating vague episodes about following foreigners to restaurants and eavesdropping on their conversations, about surveillance and stakeouts, about filing reports. He did admit that beginning in 1935, he worked out of an office at Lubianka, a place central to the Soviet imagination. A death's-head come to life as a building, it was a secret-police headquarters, prison and torture chamber, and there are few chronicles of the Stalin years where it does not figure prominently. Prisoners detained there spoke about secret drug labs, about recordings of women weeping piped into the ventilation ducts to break prisoners' morale, about subterranean levels hundreds of meters belowground, about crematoriums. In what had once been a courtyard there stood a prison for high-profile political prisoners— a series of cells with windows so occluded that they allowed a single ray of light—called the Isolator.

Vassily glanced away often when I asked about Lubianka and his job there. Instead he talked about convictions: being a true believer in Communism's difficult mission and the need to periodically cut the rot from the apple's core. "Of course, we believed it all," he said, resorting to the boilerplate response of those who carry out atrocities. At times he sounded as though he'd been duped, at other times irritable and defensive. He was, he allowed, an investigator of low rank, one among many. What were his duties? Beyond "interrogation" and "paperwork," he refused to elaborate. While he spoke, I struggled to connect Vassily's mild, diffident expression, the invalid's mask, with what I knew he must have seen and done: torture in pursuit of false confessions that, in many cases, led to death sentences and summary executions. Vassily shrouded himself in the softening ravages of age, the creases and lines that erased from his face the look of mastery and even cruelty I thought I saw in photos of his younger self that Sonya had shown me. I knew that to accept his bland, innocuous accounts at face value would have been naive. "To do that job, you have to have a particular vocation," the poet Osip Mandelstam said of his interrogators at Lubianka. "No ordinary man could stand it."

After I returned to New York, I thought about Vassily's evasions when I came across a strange, short, out-of-print book by Walter

Krivitsky, a high-ranking Soviet intelligence officer who, at the height of the purges, managed to defect to the United States. "It is one of the peculiarities of the Soviet judicial process," he wrote in 1939, of Lubianka, "that despite the tremendous number of executions, there are no regular executioners. Sometimes the men who go down to the cellar to carry out death decrees . . . are officers and sentries of the building. Sometimes they are the investigators and prosecutors themselves. For an analogy to this, one must try to imagine a New York District Attorney obtaining a first-degree murder conviction and then rushing up to Sing Sing to throw the switch in the death chamber."

Later, I wondered why the star student of the secret-police academy—who was invited to the Kremlin to dine beside Stalin and the Politburo—failed to move up the organization's ranks. Vassily's name appeared nowhere on lists of the NKVD's top-ranking officers, nor of that organization's recipients of important medals and orders, nor of its deputies to party conventions and congresses. Eventually I realized that he must have purposefully avoided these distinctions in the interest of survival. "Those were black years," Vassily said, trying to add substance to these vapid words with a slight narrowing of the eyes. "One had to keep one's own counsel." And then, less audibly: "You always had to know how to play the situation, because the situation changed daily."

In March 1937, Stalin's newly appointed secret police chief, Nikolai Yezhov, a diminutive bureaucrat with a wolf's face and the title of people's commissar for internal affairs, addressed a meeting of senior NKVD staff in a Lubianka annex. He accused his predecessor, Genrikh Yagoda—the man who had hired Vassily—of being a tsarist sympathizer, an embezzler and a German spy. After Yezhov finished speaking, some of the high-ranking officers present at the meeting rushed up to the podium to denounce colleagues and superiors in a futile bid to be saved. Yagoda's department chiefs had already been arrested; much of the leadership followed. Yagoda, after being further accused of plotting to poison Stalin and most of his deputies, was executed. Two years later, after overseeing the deadliest phase of the purges—a period that would come to be known as Yezhovshchina—the man nicknamed the Poison Dwarf was himself charged with espionage and shot, replaced by Stalin's fellow Georgian Lavrenty Beria. Stalin called Beria, who would hold this job far longer than his predecessors, "our Himmler" and "Snake Eyes." It was Beria who would become the most powerful of Stalin's deputies and the most feared, and it was Beria who would play the pivotal role in my grandfather's career.

"A whole generation must be sacrificed," Stalin decreed, and in the 1930s no part of the Soviet power structure was purged as thoroughly as the secret-police apparatus. The defector Krivitsky wrote, "Men of prudence sought obscurity, demotion to a clerical position if possible—anything to avoid importance and get out of the limelight. . . . The reasons for a man's arrest had no relation to the charges lodged against him. Nobody expected them to have. Nobody demanded it. Truth became completely irrelevant. When I say that the Soviet government became a gigantic madhouse, I mean it literally. . . . It is not funny when your lifelong friends and comrades are

disappearing in the night and dying all around you. Please remember that I was an inmate of that gigantic madhouse." In 1941, two years after having written these words, Colonel Krivitsky was found at the Bellevue Hotel in Washington, D.C., just blocks from the Capitol; he was in bed, dead of a gunshot. Three suicide notes found in his room were judged to be poor fakes, and to this day his death remains unsolved.

In Vinnytsia, I began to understand that the very fact of Vassily sitting beside me attested to what could only be his uncommon combination of intelligence, cunning and luck, only I wasn't sure of the ratio. Maybe because of the spooked look on my face, Vassily leaned toward me, into the lamplight, and poured me a shot of local strawberry wine. "Good for the heart," he croaked, and flashed a golden smile.

"I WAS AT the front when I received the telegram," Vassily said, revived. Petya had stopped by earlier to take some photos, and after a supper of white-bread-and-cheese sandwiches, Vassily and I drank tea from china cups decorated with wreaths of roses. Sonya decamped to the kitchen, leaving us alone. Vassily was telling me about 1941. Dug in near Smolensk, he was a member of an NKVD blocking unit that marched behind the front lines. It was an innovation of the Soviet secret police designed to deter potential deserters, offering the ill-equipped and often outnumbered Red Army troops the choice of Hitler's panzers in front of them or the bayonets of their countrymen behind them. The telegram recalled Vassily urgently to Moscow. Upon arriving, he discovered that he had been attached to Stalin's personal security detail and on the following morning was to report to Lieutenant General Nikolai Vlasik at the Kremlin.

The bodyguards were eventually incorporated into the KGB and came to be known as the Ninth Chief Directorate, but during the war years they operated as a semi-autonomous force reporting directly to Stalin. Their chief, Vlasik, a former secret-police operative from Belorussia, acted as the supreme leader's factotum, even tutoring and chaperoning his children after school. In her memoir, Stalin's daughter, Svetlana Allilueva, remembers Vlasik as semi-literate and crude but unquestioningly loyal. He derived his power from a hermetic proximity to his patron. Along with Stalin's secretary, Aleksandr Poskrebyshev, he constituted the innermost barrier between the state and its leader. Vlasik was probably the man whom Stalin, a paranoiac, distrusted least.

"From the first day," Vassily admitted, "I was in awe of Stalin. He comported himself modestly, he listened, he valued honesty and directness." Vassily's brief was to walk ten meters ahead or behind the supreme leader and sometimes to ride in the passenger seat of the generalissimo's Packard. He was to speak only when it was required. He told me about nights he spent at Stalin's country residence, the dacha at Kuntsevo, where Stalin bedded down on the sofa. Vassily would patrol the lanes and the quiet house while Stalin slept. In later years, he stood with his back to a wall and observed nightly bacchanals where Politburo members, whose presence was mandatory, danced and obliterated themselves with drink for the edification of their sober leader. At dawn, Vassily walked these barely coherent officials to their limousines. Of those early-morning departures, one Politburo member wrote, "You never knew whether you were going home or to prison."

At Kremlin banquets, too, Vassily stood in the wings and watched. When overzealous guests rose and tried to approach Stalin to toast his health, Vassily intercepted and guided them back to their seats. "Stalin pretended not to notice," he remembered, grinning, "but I could tell he enjoyed the show of force." There was a note of trepidation in his voice whenever he mentioned Stalin's physical proximity, as though the Georgian were standing in the room beside us. I asked whether Stalin ever spoke to him directly. "Maybe half a dozen times," Vassily replied. "I remember the first time, at the dacha. I'd been an officer for maybe ten years, but when I heard his voice and noticed him looking at me, I broke out in a sweat and began trembling. All Stalin wanted to know was whether I was receiving my salary." He laughed.

A bodyguard's job, Vassily admitted, was "less political"—in other words, safer—than his former post at Lubianka. Still, he couldn't help but notice the disappearances. On certain mornings co-workers didn't show up at work and were never mentioned again. Neighbors moved out in the night. Former instructors at the secret-police academy, veteran investigators and prosecutors who'd taught him ideology and methods, were scrubbed from public records, their very existence erased. Many were arrested, some took their own lives, others simply vanished.

In 1943, at the plenary conference in Tehran, where he traveled as a member of Stalin's security detail, Vassily befriended an American, one of the Secret Service men traveling with President Roosevelt. "Consorting with a foreign agent?" a fellow bodyguard teased him one night when the two were sharing a cigarette. "Suspicious behavior for a Socialist." Vassily heard a trace of menace in the comment. Afterward, whenever he ran into the American, he pretended not to notice him: "Every time he waved and called my name, I ran and hid."

In 1941, the year he was recalled to Moscow to guard Stalin, Vassily's young wife died suddenly in the night; abdominal hemorrhage is listed as the cause on her death certificate. They were married for less than three years. Vassily sent their one-year-old daughter to live with his parents in Aleksandrovka, on what had become a collective farm. He stayed on in Moscow alone. How did he spend his spare hours? I wondered. "I had no friends," he said. "I'm not sure what I had to offer anyone." The work had changed him from the eager academy recruit who arrived in Moscow a decade earlier. "Many of the men I'd known in Moscow were gone. I knew that the phone was tapped and the apartment bugged. Someone watched everyone then.

"By the time I met your grandmother, I'd become a different person," he said. It was only the second time he'd mentioned Tamara. Earlier, when I asked how they met, he grimaced. "She showed up at my apartment, hiked up her skirt, and never left." He spat out these words with palpable spite and was about to say more when Sonya put her hand on his arm. Later, his bitterness dissipated. He looked impassive when he told me about arriving home after a two-month posting abroad to find the apartment empty. "I went looking for Tamara and walked all over Moscow. It was already dark when I saw her in the window of a café. She was sitting at a table across from a well-dressed younger man, speaking to him intimately. I knew I should've felt angry and betrayed, but just then I felt nothing, so I turned around and walked home. I never told her about it."

When my father surfaced during our conversations, sometimes he, too, set off Vassily's ire. "What kind of son abandons a father?" he asked while describing their last visit. He claimed my father shouted at him, even suggested they weren't related—a barbed reminder of Tamara's infidelities. He asked Sonya to confirm his version of the meeting and she nodded, sadly and without anger. According to Vassily, it was my father who cut off communication first. "He simply stopped writing," he said, inverting my father's accusation. "Not a letter or a call in twenty years. Or has it been twenty-five?"

When Vassily was in a more reflective mood, I asked him about being a father. "I provided for them," he replied woodenly. "I always left Tamara money. There was never a day when they went without a meal or new clothes or shoes. Not many children could say that then." Then, as though sensing the whiff of defensiveness in his words, he relaxed. "We didn't speak much," he added after a pause. "When I was home, there wasn't a lot to say."

On our last day together, Vassily told me about the girl. I could tell he'd been saving it, waiting, not sure he wanted to let it go. The story took place in Moscow in 1943. It was the worst year of the war, and the city was a place I can scarcely imagine: lead-colored barrage balloons, protection from German pilots, hovered above the Kremlin, and a decoy village of hammered-together plywood occupied Red Square. The streets were half-deserted; the city was mired in a perpetual brownout. Bread, electricity and gas were rationed, but factories operated through the night. A woman or a man of working age who missed a day on the job received a mandatory prison sentence of five to eight years, and even prisoners were taken to their offices and assembly lines six days a week to work twelve-hour shifts before being returned to their cells. Sirens howled during nightly air raids; residents slept on tiled floors in subterranean metro stations; radios were confiscated. Military law was in effect. In 1943 in Moscow, twelve-year-old children were summarily executed for stealing bread.

On an overcast afternoon, Vassily was riding in the back of a black limousine, one of the armored Packards that Stalin lavished on his deputies. Civilian cars were a rare sight, and pedestrians along the embankment stopped to watch it pass. The limousine slowed near the entrance to Borodino Bridge. A girl was walking quickly on the sidewalk; she looked as if she were hurrying home. Vassily recalled that she appeared to be sixteen or seventeen and was slender and tall, with a round face and auburn bangs. The car pulled to the curb and coasted for a time beside her. A driver in a colonel's uniform leaned out the window and called to her. The Packard rolled to a stop. The girl approached shyly and bent down to peer into the automobile's dark interior.

The man inside the car who studied her with the most interest was bald and pale; he wore a nondescript uniform and a pince-nez over acute, intelligent eyes. Not yet a full-fledged member of the Politburo, First Deputy Lavrenty Beria—commissar general of state security and warden of the prison system known by the acronym GULAG—was nonetheless the most feared person in the country.

The men unnerved the girl, but as she backed away, a three-hundred-pound Georgian who had gotten out of the limousine—a deputy of Beria's named Kobulov—enfolded her. He lifted her off her feet and tossed her headfirst into the car as easily as if she were a bundle of firewood. This took no more than several seconds. No one on the sidewalk stopped.

Vassily sat in the backseat. The youngest of the men in the Packard, he'd been borrowed from Stalin's detail. The secret police chief enjoyed befriending Stalin's bodyguards, Vassily said, an expression of his contempt for their boss, Stalin's slow-witted majordomo Vlasik. Vassily was taking his first ride with Beria. He knew he was being tested. He sat in the backseat and watched the girl's frightened, rapidly moving eyes.

The limousine traveled to a mansion on Malaya Nikitskaya Street that had belonged to the tsarist general Kuropatkin. Inside, servants had laid out a Georgian feast—roast mutton, *satsivi,* bottles of red wine. Beria's men sat around the table laughing, getting drunker. Vassily stood in the corridor and watched: there was one of the commissar's senior bodyguards, Sarkisov or Nadaraia (he didn't remember which), the enormous Kobulov, a few others he didn't know, and at the head of the table Beria himself, picking at the eggplant, entirely sober. They'd nearly forgotten about the girl when Kobulov waddled in and hoisted her onto the table, sending a plate crashing to the floor. Somewhere in the bowels of the house a Chopin waltz warbled on a gramophone. The girl stood frozen until Kobulov gave her a shove and she began to sway slightly to the music. Vassily recalled that she still had a child's face that reminded him of his younger sister's.

He watched the awkward striptease, the Georgians jeering and laughing, and he dug his fingernails into his palms because he wanted to shout, to upend the table, to unholster his gun and shoot into the air. But he stood in the corridor and watched one of them carry the girl upstairs. Beria stood, draped his napkin over the back of his chair and walked after them. Vassily knew the girl wouldn't return home or be seen again. "I just stood there," he said. "Watching."

Vassily related the end of the story looking straight ahead, without even a glance in my direction, his jaw turning hard at the mention of her. Just then he looked less guarded than I'd seen him, the performative airs forgotten. The mild, sunken-cheeked face of the ninety-three-year-old shut-in took on its former severity.

He caught a glimpse of Beria shortly after Stalin died, at Kuntsevo, on March 5, 1953. After the bodyguards were told of Stalin's death that morning, Svetlana Allilueva recalled in her memoir, two of them shot themselves. The entire household staff, down to the scullery maids and cooks, was dismissed. Days later, Vassily said, Beria summoned him to his office and announced that he was transferring him to work in the administration of a penal camp in eastern Siberia. Vassily recognized the transfer for the deportation it was, knowing that Beria was working rapidly to eliminate everyone who'd been close to Stalin. Over the following weeks, in what must have been an act of unthinkable audacity, Vassily lobbied Beria—now arguably the most powerful individual in the Soviet Union—to send him instead to Vinnitsa, where he could care for his aging parents. Apparently Beria granted his request, because in April 1953, Vassily reported to the Vinnitsa office of the MGB (as the state security directorate was briefly known), assigned to monitor the activities of Ukrainian nationalists while ostensibly working in the human resources department of a factory. He'd brought Tamara and his children with him.

Vassily knew that he'd gotten off easy. Vlasik, his former chief, had been outmaneuvered by Beria and found himself in prison, convicted on trumped-up embezzlement charges. Some months later, when Nikita Khrushchev emerged as Stalin's successor, Beria himself lost his grip on power. After running the Soviet Union's state security apparatus for nearly fifteen years, he became a prisoner in his Lubianka dungeon. There, on December 23, 1953, a general named Batitsky stuffed a rag in Beria's mouth and shot him in the forehead at point-blank range. Batitsky was made a marshal for doing this.

I sat on the sofa, scribbling in a notebook, but something about Vassily's account nagged at me. How had a mere bodyguard managed a one-on-one meeting with Stalin's presumptive successor? How did he then manage to persuade him to amend his own order? "You worked for Beria the entire time, didn't you?" I asked. Vassily nodded, seeming pleased with my acumen.

He said that during his time at the Kremlin he was caught in a battle of influence between Vlasik and Beria, a battle that Beria nearly always won. In 1944, on Beria's orders, Vassily was sent to Crimea to take part in the deportation of the Tartars, an ethnic group that Stalin considered "unreliable." Vassily described watching families beaten and turned out of their homes, watching a mass rape, then described how he himself herded women and children into unheated cattle cars and wrapped wire around the door handles. More than a quarter of the 190,000 deported Tartars aboard those trains died. For a moment, in the dim lamplight, Vassily's eyes welled up. Anger distorted his voice. "I was a major," he nearly shouted. "I had an office in Lubianka and supervised fifty-five men. He used me like a common thug. Beria was the smartest of them, and I loathed him."

It was the first time he acknowledged being not an investigator of small rank, as he'd claimed, but an officer who commanded fifty-five agents. More important, he admitted to being Beria's man, not Vlasik's. My brain was humming, trying to fill in the gaps in his stories. Did Vassily inform on his Kremlin superiors? Did he provide evidence that led to Vlasik's arrest? The thought of my grandfather working for Beria made my breath catch in my throat. I'd read that soon after becoming head of the secret police, Beria locked a former superior and his wife in a Lubianka cell and made them watch as guards beat their teenage son to death. Then, before leaving, Beria tossed a poisonous snake in their cell.

How many abductions, how many murders, did Vassily witness? How many did he take part in? Did he merely demand confessions, a cigarette in hand and a guard posted at the door, or did he administer the beatings and torture? Did he carry out the executions? I needed more information, needed to square the inconsistencies and make a mental time line, but already Vassily realized he'd said too much. I asked him to explain, to provide details, but he smiled weakly. The mute, apologetic invalid returned.

It was nearly ten o'clock. The only sounds were the ticking of a clock and, outside, the ratchet-like whir of a trolley. The headlights of passing cars fluttered across the ceiling, first yellow, then red, then a washed-out pink. Vassily and I sat across a table and took each other's measure. I sensed the weight of everything he had concealed or left unsaid, everything he would take with him. Its presence was palpable between us.

I'd traveled five thousand miles to meet this man, almost certainly Stalin's last living bodyguard, this man who happened to be my grandfather, unwittingly thinking of myself as an amateur mapmaker of his life. I imagined decoding his roles as perpetrator and victim, trying to piece together and weigh his motives, charting his involvement in decades-old events. I realized how naive I'd been. His culpability was an immense, unknowable continent filled with indecipherable ambiguities. Vassily had merely permitted me into the vestibule of his past.

I was realizing, too, that Vassily's role in these events affected all of us who were connected to him. My father had to nourish himself on the leavings of humanity Vassily brought home and on his frightening past. He cut off communication with this man partly to shield my mother and me from his past. *This,* I understood finally, was history: not the ordered narrative of books but an affliction that spread from parent to child, sister to brother, husband to wife. It took Tamara from Vassily, Vassily from my father, and my father from my mother and me. Fifty years after his death, Stalin—the scarecrow of black-and-white newsreels—had reached into my life, too.

Sonya stood listening in the kitchen. All night I could tell she wanted to say something, and when I walked to the stove to pour myself a cup of tea, she beckoned me into a corner, out of Vassily's earshot. "When I was twelve, my mother was arrested," she said, her hand on my arm. "She owned a farm and was denounced by a neighbor. My father ran away. My brother was nine. The orphanages didn't admit children of enemies, so for three years we lived in the street, begging. A pious Orthodox family took us in. Then one day, they heard my brother singing a Soviet song he'd learned in school, and they made us leave. Two years later my brother was killed at the front." She looked out the window at the empty sidewalk. "Sometimes I hate this country," she said with a fervor that made tears well up in her eyes.

Out in the living room, Vassily was eating a piece of cake, oblivious to our conversation. They had been married for thirty-five years. How did she manage, caring in her old age for Stalin's infirm bodyguard? "We lived in terrible times," Sonya said, guessing my question. "All that is left now is to be kind to each other."

It was nearly midnight, and I told Vassily that I would stop by again tomorrow to say goodbye, before catching the train back to Moscow. Sonya handed me a stack of photographs I asked to copy. "Keep them," she said, "or they will end up in the trash." Before leaving, I sat beside Vassily for a while, studying his face, trying to remember everything that had been said earlier. When I told him good night, he grasped my hands and didn't release them until we were alone and his face was so close to mine that I could smell his breath.

"I was frightened every single day," he whispered, and let go.

IT WAS JUST after sunrise, and Petya and Anya were asleep on their berths. The train rocked steadily as I fanned out the photos that Sonya had given me across a blanket. There were a dozen portraits of Vassily. In the earliest he poses at attention with the flag of his OGPU division, several medals already pinned to his chest; on the wall behind him there's a famous painting of Stalin in a white tunic addressing a crowd. On the back of the photo is an inscription from his commander, dated 1935 and stamped with the seal of the NKVD.

A hand-colored photo from the following year shows my grandfather looking a little like a young Cary Grant, grinning in a tweed newsboy cap, sheepskin-collared coat, pin-striped shirt, gabardine blazer and striped tie with a needlework pattern. The coat flaps open to reveal a medal pinned to the blazer by a gold chain. This gaudy portrait is inscribed to his parents and sister back home: "From your son Vasya, in Moscow."

The oddest image, remarkable for its unmissable vanity, was taken at the communal apartment in Moscow. Vassily sits at a table covered in a white tablecloth, beside a vase of flowers. He leans on his elbows and rests his chin on interlaced fingers, looking like a raptly listening poet. The pose is strangely flamboyant, almost feminine. I wondered for a moment who took this photo before realizing that Vassily must have staged and taken it himself, mounting his Leica on a tripod.

For a while I studied an official portrait from 1950: Vassily wears an officer's insignia on his uniform's shoulders and collar; an overlapping curtain of medals hangs on the left side of his chest; on the right, there are three orders—two Red Stars and an Order of the Patriotic War, awarded for "heroic deeds." Unlike the conceited poseur in the earlier, more lighthearted photos, here Vassily looks savage and unmistakably sad.

What had happened to Vassily in the years leading up to this photo, taken three years before Stalin's death and his family's sudden departure from Moscow? By 1950 he was a twice-married father of

two and a decorated war veteran, an officer who commanded fifty-
five men, a secret policeman who took part in arrests, interrogations,
disappearances and, in Crimea, what amounted to a genocide. I could
only guess at what else he had seen and done, but certainly he understood better than most the peculiar fragility of his and his family's
existence. What did it mean to be descended from a man like this?

In the envelope Sonya had given me, there were several photos of
Tamara, too, each studiously posed. In one she stands beside a row
of sunflowers in a floral-print robe, like a golden figure from Klimt.
In another she slices a cake in a ravishing polka-dot dress. She never
smiles. Elsewhere she stands beside my father in a park. It's one of
Vassily's few poor compositions, with a fountain hovering above Tamara like a headdress. My father is three or four, in short pants and a
cap. He clutches his mother's hand and peers shyly from behind her
sleeve at his father.

In the last photo, Vassily and my father look at each other, smiling. Vassily wears a dark suit and tie; his hair is swept back. My father

must be six or seven. His hair is cropped, to minimize barber visits and outbreaks of head lice, and he glances up into Vassily's face with an expression that manages, all at once, to express excitement, apprehension and longing. The most telling detail is my father's hands. Soviet schoolchildren were instructed to keep their hands folded on their desks, and this gesture—in its formality, obedience and desire to please—jarred me. I'd never known my father to need anyone, and it occurred to me, looking at his upturned face in this photo, that as a young man he must have worked hard to never need anyone again. I took the photo out of the envelope and laid it on the fold-down table beside me, where it remained until the train reached Moscow.

My father was waiting for me at Kievskaya station. On the drive to his apartment I could tell he wanted to ask about Vassily, but he allowed me to do the talking, not wanting to betray too much interest. There was something newly respectful in his manner, as though I'd accomplished a feat that he didn't dare attempt. "He asked about you," I offered, but couldn't muster more encouraging news. While we sat drinking tea in his kitchen, I handed him two of his class photos from grade school. His thin face, set in an expression of protest, peered from a row of taller boys. Then I showed him the rest of Sonya's photos. "He looks handsome in this one," my father said, pointing to a snapshot of Vassily sitting pensively at a desk, and it occurred to me that it was the first time I'd heard him say anything admiring about his father. He asked whether he could have it, and I slid the photo across the table toward him.

WHAT DISTINGUISHES MOSCOW from other European cities is the extent to which the needs of its residents didn't figure in its design. More than any other place I've been to, it's a city of monuments. Many of the splendid churches and monasteries, the neoclassical palaces and mansions, were raised to glorify military victories and the wealthiest among the nobility and merchants. The Soviet-era structures— ten-lane boulevards spanned by dim underground walkways, dande-

lion clusters of apartment blocks that swallowed entire forests and lakes—were conceived on a scale reminiscent of some particularly severe strain of science fiction. The architecture here is short on humanism but abundant in variety, strangeness and lovely unexpected juxtapositions, which lend the city its perpetual ability to surprise.

And so on my last day in Moscow I planned a long, meandering walk across the city that Vassily, my father and I had in common. I suppose I wanted to decipher something in the architecture. Why had this place extracted so much grinding labor from its residents and visited upon them so much upheaval and loss, which continued into the present day? What explained its unmistakable heaviness? On a map I drew a route that might teach me something about the city of my birth. It began at the Bolshoi Theater; proceeded south through Red Square and over the Bolshoi Moskvoretsky Bridge, past the Church of Resurrection in Kadashi, a former KGB archive, its belfry like the rigging of a sailboat, past the Tretyakov Gallery and the custard-yellow Church of St. Nicholas in Tolmachi; then turned east near the grandiose Scientific Pedagogical Library, with its massive columns and wrought-iron gates; continued past the storm-gray house and museum of the playwright Ostrovsky on Malaya Ordynka Street and the splendid old mosque on Bolshaya Tatarskaya . . .

The escalator at the Teatralnaya metro station ferried me up into the bright overcast afternoon. Out on the street, metal detectors stood at every intersection and soldiers cordoned off the Bolshoi Theater. Unexpectedly, I found myself in the midst of a crowd of mostly el-derly Muscovites, moving in the direction of the Kremlin. I was swept up in the march, or perhaps it was a demonstration, pulling me in the wrong direction, when I remembered with a start that it was November 7, the anniversary of the Bolshevik Revolution, the high-est holiday of my childhood. I had imagined that it had been scrapped along with all the pulled-down statues of Lenin. But as I walked among hundreds of people clutching tiny red flags in their mittens, I caught a glimpse of a bundled-up man in a fur hat standing in the back of a flatbed truck, belting the Soviet anthem into a microphone.

A line of picketers on the sidewalks held hand-lettered signs. One depicted a Jewish Bolshevik with a grotesquely elongated nose; another admiringly quoted "U.S. Senator David Duke." Under a granite monument to Karl Marx, a strikingly tall woman stood on another truck bed, her chest covered with gold- and silver-colored medals. In a booming voice, she intoned a speech about an empire that once blanketed half the globe, about squandered wealth and military might, about encroaching decadence and Westernization. "These criminals sold our nation!" a woman in a rabbit-fur hat shouted beside me, shaking her fist in the direction of the Kremlin's tomato-soup-colored battlements.

An LCD billboard above Marx cycled ads for Dolce & Gabbana shoes and Bulgari jewelry. Then it flashed a full-length image of the Ukrainian presidential candidate Viktor Yanukovich, an ex-convict backed by Russia, his pixelated face set in a smile. The crowd cheered halfheartedly. I learned later that the government vowed that every year's Revolution Day will be the last, but the celebrations continued, part of Putin's calculated double-talk about the Soviet past. The Communist Party paid some among the elderly to show up today, but most would have come anyway. They belonged to Vassily's generation. At the rallies they could wear hard-won medals and orders and believe that the social experiment they'd sacrificed for was something other than a colossal mistake.

Somewhere along the parade route, entropy took over. Like billiard balls, some marchers moved in vectors of their own devising; others gathered around loudspeakers to sing along with Soviet songs. I retraced my steps along Mokhovaya Street, heading west against the current. On the sidewalks, people had stopped to watch. Inside a Bentley dealership's plate-glass storefront, two young salesmen in ash-colored suits watched the passersby. The clouds rolled away suddenly and sunshine flooded the street. Almost involuntarily, everyone smiled; the singing grew louder. I finally set out in the direction of my walk, and the crowd ahead of me dissipated. I found myself at the entrance to a square. On a rise, there was an empty pedestal once occupied by a statue of the first Soviet secret police chief, Feliks Dzerzhinsky, and behind it I saw the massive old Lubianka prison, still the headquarters of the secret police, now called the FSB. Sunlight painted a swath of gold across its windows.

FOR THE FIRST time since I'd been in Moscow, a warm breeze was blowing and the sky was clear. I sat in the passenger seat of my father's jeep, headed to the airport. The part I disliked most about our visits was that last ride to the airport, and I think he did, too. For ninety minutes we sat side by side in Moscow's roisterous traffic, making stabs at conversation, acknowledging neither the misery nor the relief of my departure.

My father stared ahead, navigating the beltway. On our right, we passed the skyscraper at the center of my parents' alma mater, Moscow State University. Rising more than two hundred meters, it remains the apotheosis of Stalinist architecture: three concrete slabs topped with a gold spire, embellished with sheaves of wheat, barometers and figures of muscular striding proletarians. Stalin commissioned seven of these wedding-cake towers, the "Seven Sisters"; they say that no matter where you stand in Moscow, you can see at least one of their spires. Today Muscovites refer to them simply as *visotki*, high-rises.

When the university building was completed, in 1953, it was the tallest in Europe. Erected on Sparrow Hills, a site that Ivan the Terrible considered too windy to build on, it offered one of the city's finest views; Chekhov declared that to understand Russia, one had to see it from this promontory. The project was assigned to Boris Iofan—the architect who designed the grandiose, ill-fated Palace of the Soviets—but he decided to situate the building at the edge of what was then called Lenin Hills. In the event of a mudslide, it might have tumbled down the precipice into the Moscow River. Reportedly Iofan refused to consider changing the location and was replaced with Lev Rudnev, a younger, more pliable monumentalist. Rudnev received the Stalin Prize for his work on the university in 1949, four years before it was completed.

The tower was raised by a crew of prisoners from the Gulag; among them were thousands of German POWs. On Beria's orders they transported the building's steel skeleton from the Ukrainian city of Dnepropetrovsk aboard sixty trains. Hundreds died during its construction. Muscovites sometimes remark that the skyscraper was "built on bones." According to an urban legend, a prisoner working on the spire fashioned a pair of wings from plywood scraps and leapt to freedom.

My mother lived there as a student. I thought of her stories about cramped dorm rooms where listening devices were hidden in the closets, about ventilation so bad that the smell of cabbage boiled on the floor below by exchange students from Ho Chi Minh's Democratic Republic of Vietnam permeated her room, about the thirty-three kilometers of dark corridors, about unexplained sounds in the night, about suicides. Many believed the building was haunted.

My father turned to grin at me. "You were conceived in that building," he said, pleased at the memory. I turned to get a last look at the tower's bright needle, but he floored the gas and it vanished behind us in a blur.

AFTER I RETURNED to New York, Vassily grew to occupy more and more of my time. He even found his way into my dreams: always alone, sitting across from me in the apartment in Vinnytsia. I spent weeks in libraries, trying to corroborate his stories with published histories. I was assured by those who knew these things that Vassily's FSB file was not something I could reasonably expect to see in my lifetime.

I watched and rewatched a Russian documentary, titled *I Was Stalin's Bodyguard*, about a man who claimed to have had a career nearly identical to my grandfather's: Aleksei Rybin had been a major in the NKVD and a bodyguard who served under General Vlasik. The stories he tells—about Stalin's grooming habits and appetite for elk meat—struck me as both banal and evasive. But at one point, after naming a litany of coworkers who had been arrested or committed suicide, Rybin remarks: "All any of them had to do was say that I was connected to them, and I would've disappeared, too. My wife would have never found my grave." The film, made fifteen years before I met Vassily, described Rybin as "the last living witness to history."

As my obsession with Vassily's stories grew, so did my doubts. The episodes he'd supposedly participated in—the fateful banquet at the Kremlin, Beria's sidewalk abduction—were well-known episodes of the Stalinist period. But published accounts corroborated only so much. Some of Vassily's claims were documented in family photos and in my father's and Tamara's stories, but others seemed out of reach, tangled in a tight knot of plausibility, probability and motive. When I called Vassily after my visit, he turned silent about the past, refusing to clarify or explain.

So I wrote letters and emails. An elderly Soviet scholar, whom I met by chance at his summerhouse in New Hampshire, made introductions. I began corresponding with two specialists who'd studied documents declassified in the post-Soviet period and had amassed more reliable information about Stalin's circle than probably anyone else in the West.

After listening to my story, Stephen Kotkin, a Princeton professor working on a magisterial three-volume biography of Stalin, began talking in an excited torrent. I held the phone to my ear with my shoulder while taking notes. Beria was a frequent supper guest at Stalin's dacha at Kuntsevo, Kotkin told me; he was cunning and brilliant and regarded the hapless Nikolai Vlasik—my grandfather's boss—with a mix of envy and contempt. Beria enjoyed showing up Vlasik by befriending and cultivating close ties with the bodyguards, whom he drew into his circle partly to obtain information about and exert influence on Stalin and his entourage. So it was entirely plausible, he concluded, that Vassily maintained a close relationship with the secret police chief while employed by his nemesis. Could Vassily have maintained an office at Lubianka while working as a bodyguard? I asked.

"Why not?" Kotkin replied. "What you have to understand is that Kremlinology operated by keeping nearly everyone—even people within the innermost circles of power—in the dark. No one knew everything that was going on around them. Hypersecrecy was the rule."

Simon Sebag Montefiore, the British author of several superb books about Stalin, emailed to say that Vassily's presence at the 1932 banquet was questionable—it was a relatively small event attended mostly by top officials—but possible. The etiquette among the former revolutionaries, after all, was still largely informal. He wondered whether perhaps Vassily had heard of these events from associates and unwittingly merged them with his memories. Yet both he and Kotkin agreed that, from the vantage of the present day, Vassily's version of his past was impossible to either confirm or refute. "Overall," Montefiore wrote to me from a stop on his book tour in Australia, *"it is all plausible."* Then he wished me good luck.

SEVERAL DAYS BEFORE I left Vinnytsia, during an unseasonably warm afternoon, Vassily told me about his father, and it's *this* story that for me has come to epitomize the lives of the men in my family. Appended to our ridiculous surname was my great-grandfather's even more comic Christian name—he was called Anany, after Onan, the Old Testament masturbator. Among the photos Sonya gave me there is a snapshot of two elderly men sitting in front of a farmhouse with a thatched roof. The man on the left, the one with my six- or seven-year-old father peering from behind his shoulder, is Anany. With his work shirt buttoned to the top, cropped hair and large gnarled hands, he looks every bit like a lifelong farmer. Anany was a devout Communist and a devout Christian. Though he became a director of a collective farm, he remained an elder at his church and kept on the mantel a leather-bound Bible with gauffered edges and 208 illustrations by Gustave Doré. My father remembered that despite losing much of his hearing and sight in old age, Anany remained cheerful and kind to his last day.

According to Vassily, in 1915 Anany was conscripted into the tsar's army and left his wife and two young children to march on Poland; later that year, he was wounded and taken prisoner by the kaiser's troops. Because he'd passed himself off as a Pole, instead of being shot he was transported under guard to a Berlin hospital, where surgeons removed shrapnel from his thigh. He remained in Germany for six years, working sporadically as an orderly and a chimney sweep. Eventually he managed to stow away aboard a freighter to Denmark. From there he made his way to Sweden and Finland, and in 1923 he crossed the border into the country that, in his absence, had become the Soviet Union. Anany made much of the rest of the journey home on foot, walking until he reached his village of Aleksandrovka, only to discover that a funeral had been held in his absence and everyone there believed him to be dead. It was already dark when he walked into the house he'd left as an army conscript eight years earlier. His wife was putting away the supper dishes.

His son Vassily, who was twelve, didn't recognize the gaunt stranger in the doorway.

"Hello," Anany said to the boy. "I am your father."

2.

NUMBER 19

IN THE YEARS AFTER I ARRIVED IN NEW YORK, MY IDEA OF WHO MY FATHER was grew fainter by the day, colored by my mother's and her parents' stories and their prejudices and fears. I was realizing I didn't know much about my father and his family, and after a while I wasn't sure I wanted to. Possibly the strangest thing about leaving the country of your birth is renegotiating the relationship with your past. Once the past is reduced to a handful of photos and family stories, it becomes optional. Or so I believed.

The man I did come to know intimately in those early adolescent years was my maternal grandfather, Semyon Efimovich Galbershtad (he preferred the weird Russified spelling). He was a large-featured, solidly built man with a hemispheric belly; glaucous, buggy eyes; and an outsize, two-storied nose that jutted from his face like a wood-ear fungus. He'd been a teacher of neurophysiology, zoology, Darwinism and half a dozen other subjects at Vilnius University; an author of twelve books on scientific topics, including a textbook, *The Nervous Regulation of Muscular Tissues,* that for a time a professor had assigned at the Sorbonne; a pioneer of the spectrogram; a cavalry lieutenant in the armed forces of interwar independent Lithuania; a Red Army mortar operator in World War II; a middle school German teacher; a book and magazine hoarder; a Verdi enthusiast who could whistle the entire first act of *La traviata;* an improbable bullfighting aficionado; and an amateur, albeit ardent, morphologist of women whom he appraised largely, though not entirely, from afar—when speaking about a university secretary or a bookstore cashier, he described her, disregarding all evidence to the contrary, as a "gorgeous redhead," a "blond beauty" or an "exquisite brunette." He rarely drank. Every time he heard or read something funny, his shoulders wobbled gently and the oversize topography of his face contorted like a sea anemone until he was blinking away tears, all without making a sound.

In those years, I spent most of my nights in Semyon's company. My mother worked late shifts at a mental-health clinic on Coney Island, and my grandmother Raisa, addled by Parkinson's, spent her evenings in front of the TV, so after I came home from school it was Semyon and I who walked up Broadway, sometimes all the way to the subway station on Steinway Street, to partake of his idea of a constitutional. His favorite conversation topic was wild fauna: the platypus's genetic odyssey, the number of vertebrae in a giraffe's neck, the iridescent coloring of the *Colibri cyanotus,* the second posterior brain of the *Apatosaur* and other large herbivores of the late-Jurassic.

The destination of these walks was a corner store where he bought a bag of Brach's sour-apple candy. At first I nagged him for it, but after I came into an adolescent self-consciousness, I refused. Brach's is going to make me fat, I told him one day in the store. I must have been eleven or twelve. Semyon glanced down at the middle of my puffy winter coat and considered my recent enlargement; I was beginning to resemble a miniature version of him. "You're right," he agreed. "Look at you, you're practically obese!" I slammed my boot into his shin, drawing disapproving looks from the counter women, snatched the paper bag of still-unpaid-for green candy from his hand, and ran out.

I didn't stay angry. I couldn't. Semyon was a natural scientist; he liked to say that he trafficked in facts, not niceties. Manners were for intellectual weaklings in the humanities. At home I liked to interrogate him about the war, and he told reluctant stories about the Polish front and the Battle of Berlin.

"I calculated the distance between our foxholes and the Germans', and then I fired the mortar."

"And then?"

"And then we marched to their foxholes and everyone in them would be dead."

"What did they look like?"

"They were young boys and usually their intestines were out, and they were green, because of the bile, and they smelled strongly."

One night we were coming home from one of our walks when, near the entrance to the apartment building where we lived—a housing project on the corner of Twenty-fourth Street and Thirty-fourth Avenue in Long Island City—we spotted Jason, who lived on the sixth floor. He was about my age, a reedy, well-mannered middle schooler. Everyone in the building liked his parents. Al was a housing cop from Trinidad; Brenda, who was round, light-skinned and friendly, stayed at home with Jason and his two brothers. Semyon said something I didn't make out to our upstairs neighbor, and then I saw his large, meaty hand rise and stroke the top of Jason's Afro.

My grandfather smiled broadly. His English was too loud and inept. "Your hair . . . ," Semyon rooted around in his meager vocabulary, "like . . . Brillo pad." Jason's eyes opened in surprise. He slapped Semyon's hand away, hard. "Get off me, man," he said, and squeezed past us. This upset Semyon for weeks. "Jason is a good boy," he said. "What did I say to make him angry?"

If New York bewildered him, he felt most in control hunched over the chessboard. We played chess every night, and beside the board Semyon kept an open notebook where he took notes and diagrammed his favorite openings, especially the daring gambits: the Alekhine, the Nimzowitsch, the Scandinavian. I'd made a Swanson's Hungry-Man dinner for each of us, making sure to turn up the square of foil over the cobbler, and Semyon took a bite out of a perfect lozenge of Salisbury steak. He considered the chess pieces. "There are billions of possible games!" he remarked. "All of them take place on these tidy sixty-four squares, and whether you win depends on logic and patience." He'd opened with the Sicilian and was making inroads onto my side of the board, on his way to another victory. "Not like in life," he added, and tapped the button on the chess clock.

THOUGH I'D SPENT many nights with my maternal grandparents, I'd learned little about their lives prior to my birth. They didn't disseminate this information happily. I knew that only about 5 percent of Lithuania's Jews had survived the war, making Semyon and Raisa—and by extension my mother and me—statistical marvels. Of course their lives had disposed them toward secrecy. I knew that my own wariness, excessive vigilance, and reluctance to plan for a future that may never arrive amounted to an adoption of their mental habits and worldview, a patrimony for dealing with the unexpected.

After I returned from Ukraine, the gaps in what I knew about their lives began to unnerve me. Meeting Vassily created a rupture in my understanding of my family; a rupture, really, in my understanding of human behavior. I began to grasp something about the ways in which the political and the personal interacted. Relationships I had assumed turned on affinities, grudges and misunderstandings had in fact turned on these vast collective events and the daily realities they imposed on individuals. I was coming to see that all four of my grandparents had lived in a country and a time when the buffer between history and biography became nearly imperceptible.

By that point I'd waded too far into the past. My days in New York were increasingly spent there—in my family's past—and I needed more information. I'd found Vassily; now, to understand all of it better, and I needed to learn about Semyon and Raisa, too. By the time I visited Vinnytsia, both of them were gone, but much about their lives survived in my mother. And so several years after I met Vassily, my mother and I flew to her birthplace, Vilnius, the Lithuanian city where I'd spent several summers as a child. As it turned out, the past there was vanishing, too, though not quickly enough for some.

THE FIRST ANCESTOR I know something about was a great-great-grandfather named Abel; in the language of the occupying Russian Empire, he was called Orel. In the second half of the nineteenth century, many places and people in Vilnius were known by more than one name. Abel/Orel lived not in the Jewish quarter but in the newer part of the city, on Novogorodskaya Street (now called Naugarduko). Even more unusually, he lived in a four-story stone house that he owned, thanks to a minor fortune he made reselling scrap metal. In a clothbound ledger that contained the births of the tsar's subjects in his territories during the year 1861, I found Abel's: November 12, or 9 Kislev according to the Jewish calendar. There was also a note about his circumcision, performed six days later. The entry recorded the names of his parents—Aron and Risa—and of his grandfathers, both named Abram, who came from the nearby town of Stakliškės, but about them I've found nothing. In another ledger there was the Russified name of Abel's brother, Ovsey, born fifteen years later. About Ovsey, too, I learned little except for the dates of his birth and circumcision, recorded in loopy old-Russian script, the ink curlicues identical as though set from type.

I pored over these ledgers in a concrete bunker that houses Vilnius's municipal archives. The furnishings and employees inside appeared to have taken on the brownish gray of the concrete walls, as though the rain drumming on the roof had leached them of pigment. An archivist, an early-fifties bottle blonde in a flower-print shawl, typed absentmindedly at her desk while I turned the brittle pages. Other ledgers and databases contained further Halberstadts— Arons, Girshes, Tsernas, Chaykas, even a Frade, dead of suicide at age eighteen in August 1930—but whether these were relatives or strangers I couldn't determine.

The thread of my grandfather's family was the one I managed to trace furthest. According to his stories, they came to Lithuania from the Bishopric of Halberstadt in the Lower Saxon Circle of the Holy Roman Empire, now in Saxony-Anhalt, probably after a periodic expulsion of the Jews by the Church or one of the many massacres. Halberstadt was known for its Torah scholars and religious academies, but exactly when or why these people left my grandfather didn't know. It's likely that along with many others they came east in the fifteenth or early sixteenth century to take advantage of the favorable conditions that existed for Jews in Lithuania. The last country in Europe to adopt Christianity, it was gifted for a time with uncommonly egalitarian and farsighted rulers.

As a boy, my grandfather knew older neighbors who kept sacred snakes in their homes— Lithuania had once been a nation of animists. The country's name first appears in the year 1009, in an ecclesiastical document called the Annals of Quedlinburg; it records that Bruno of Querfurt, a Saxon missionary, "was struck on the head by Pagans . . . at the Rus and Lithuanian border." (Today the Lithuanians date the founding of their country to this allusion.) Some accounts claim that Saint Bruno attempted to convert the local chieftain and was killed by his brother, while others suggest that the local pagans beheaded him for spending a night in a sacred grove.

Lithuanian rulers held fast to their animist faith until opportunity— to rule Catholic Poland through marriage to its eleven-year-old queen, and to put an end to attacks from the Teutonic Knights, who fashioned themselves eastern crusaders—persuaded them to convert. King Jogaila's people burned their dead together with their horses, dogs and falcons and threw the claws of wild animals onto the pyres, so the departed would have an easier climb up the hill in the next world. In February 1387, Jogaila and his party rode into the grove he and his ancestors had worshipped. They cut down the oaks, toppled the idols, killed the sacred snakes, and extinguished the sacrificial fires. In their place they erected crosses.

A few years later, Jogaila's cousin Vytautas granted a charter to the Jews of Troki, Brest and Grodno that eventually extended to all those living in Lithuanian lands. The document was striking in its opposition to the intolerance and religious fervor that characterized much of the rest of Europe. To get a sense of how unusual it was, one only had to look west: In 1290, Edward I expelled the Jews of England. Sixteen years later, Philip the Fair followed suit in France. In Spain, Columbus's patrons, Ferdinand and Isabella, ordered more than sixty thousand Jews to leave the country in 1492; Spaniards murdered thousands as they attempted to leave their homes.

In contrast, the Lithuanian charter outlawed blood libel and punished Christians who vandalized Jewish graves. It decreed that when a Jew stood accused of a crime, the crime had to be corroborated by both a Christian and a Jew. It levied a fine on any Christian who failed to respond to a call for help in the night from a Jewish neighbor. Today, the charter reads like a small-town zoning ordinance, codifying the Jews' right to "live in the areas where they live in Grodno, that is: starting from the bridge of the Castle of Grodno to the market, on both sides of the street, to the street which goes from Castle Street to Podol; on the areas facing the church houses and the house of Ivanovsky; from the other side of the street to the cemetery, and across the cemetery to the lot of the Church even up to the very river, the Gorodnitza." The grand duke's descendants upheld the charter, for the most part, and by the sixteenth century Jews poured into the country from the west and east, eventually making Lithuania's Jewish community the largest in the diaspora—larger than any since Babylonian times. Lithuania became nearly as important to the Jews as it was to the Lithuanians.

Still, the large-mindedness of the Warsaw kings who ruled Lithuania rarely trickled down to the mayors or local guilds: merchants and tradesmen saw the Jews as competitors and continually petitioned officials to restrict their rights. By the seventeenth and eighteenth centuries, Jews were permitted to settle in a single overcrowded sliver of Vilnius that gentiles named the Black Quarter. Its courtyards became beehives of shops, craftsmen's kiosks, religious study houses and synagogues. The tenement doors and latching shutters were made of iron to ward off potential intruders.

The early Litvaks (as the Lithuanian Jews called themselves) whom I encountered in histories turned out to be unlike the famous secular Jews in Semyon's stories: Horowitz, Wittgenstein, Freud and the Nobel laureates in chemistry and physics whose company he aspired to. Photographs and tintypes taken in the shtetls depict bearded men in dark heavy coats and humped caps and women in kerchiefs and black ankle-length dresses. They brought to mind Mendel Singer, the protagonist of Joseph Roth's *Job,* who observes his gentile neighbors in the Pale of Settlement with a sour and sometimes caustic disinterest. In their insularity from and apparent indifference to the gentile society in which they lived, these eastern European small-town Jews reminded me of the Lubavitcher Hasidim I came to know in Brooklyn.

The source of this indifference to the gentile world was set down in scripture. The Litvaks saw themselves as existing in an epoch of indeterminate duration—a span between the handing down of the laws in biblical antiquity and the future arrival of the Messiah. About the present they were ambivalent and sometimes unenthusiastic. Compared with the word of God interpreted through thousands of years of unassailable rabbinic commentary—and a tradition dating to the settlement of Canaan by Abraham's clan some eighteen hundred years before the Common Era—what significance could a transitory gentile culture have? The Litvaks' chief duty was to study the Torah, the Talmud and the many subsequent volumes of scholarly reckoning. Besides the commandments Moses brought down from Sinai, rabbinical authorities extracted 613 laws from the Bible's first five books—248 thou-shalts and 365 thou-shalt-nots. Every day, a Jew devoted hours to prayer and reciting blessings before many activities, particularly if they happened to be pleasurable. Except for Yiddish-language popular entertainments (often authored by women and viewed by the rabbinate with suspicion), the literary output of the Jews comprised commentaries upon commentaries on scripture written in Hebrew and Aramaic, known as *pilpul*. Their writers distinguished themselves through originality and rhetorical brilliance, extemporizing on the internal laws of a stateless people.

For my grandparents' ancestors, the question of assimilation barely existed. To be a Litvak was to maintain an inborn awareness of being alien and a heightened sense of the potential dangers of one's environment. For many, *kiddush hashem*—dying for God—was not a religious ideal or a fantasy. They grew up hearing about the massacres, expulsions and forced baptisms their ancestors endured and other Jews continued to suffer elsewhere in Europe. For centuries Litvaks were forced into professions that most gentiles avoided. Some were craftsmen and merchants who traded largely among their own people; others collected tolls and taxes, distilled and sold liquor, operated taverns. They lived in a tense equilibrium with their gentile neighbors and kept them at a vigilant remove.

Even the political upheavals of the day barely registered—it was typical of a Litvak to remark that he cared little about which side prevailed in the latest war. Still, conditions in Lithuania were more hospitable than elsewhere, and Jews by the thousands pulled up roots and made the journey to the banks of the river Neris. Vilnius's first synagogue opened in 1573. By the nineteenth century, Jews made up nearly half of the city's population. It was said that Napoleon called it "the Jerusalem of the North" when he saw the Renaissance-style interior of the Great Synagogue and strolled the Black Quarter.

In the archives' ledgers I also found a record of my great-grandfather—Abel's son Haskel Halberstadt, who opened a dental office at 12 Kalvariyskaya (now known as Kalvarijų) Street, just north of the Neris, in 1897. That year, nearly sixty-five thousand Jews called Vilnius home. Having been driven out of rural districts by a Russian edict, Jewish newcomers—mostly dejected-looking small-town refugees—wandered the city's streets and alleys. It was said that every evening four-fifths of the city's Jews didn't know where their next meal would come from and nearly half lived on charity.

Owing to his father's profitable business, Haskel didn't count himself among them. He graduated from the city's university and trained as an oral surgeon in Kiev. To minister to the residents of a metropolis as diverse as Shanghai or Berlin, Haskel learned to speak at least passable Russian, Lithuanian, Polish, Ukrainian, Yiddish and Belorussian, and to read Hebrew. Around the time my grandfather was born—when several of the kaiser's officers from the recruitment station across the street became his patients—he also learned German.

A dentist who treated as many gentiles as Jews, he was a delicate-featured, dark-eyed, rather small man with an agreeable face and a calm, formal manner. He married young and had a son—a sweet-natured, solitary, painfully shy boy named Ruvim, whom everyone called Roma. Haskel was thirty when his wife, Sarah, began to complain of abdominal pains. My mother recalled Semyon telling her that she died of peritonitis, though her entry in the ledger lists the cause of death as stomach cancer.

In any case she died suddenly, leaving Haskel with a busy dental practice and a nine-year-old son. He couldn't manage being a widower for long. Thanks to a matchmaker, in less than a year he wed a woman from Švenčionys (called Svintsyán in Yiddish), a small town to the north. The willful, independent Frida Levin was two years younger than Haskel—and far luckier than he to find a spouse. At twenty-eight, she was well into spinsterhood, a condition she owed to a cheerful disregard for religion and a worldliness unusual in a woman from a country town of six thousand.

The career prospects of most Litvak women were largely circumscribed by their gender. Fathers taught sons simple prayers as soon as they could speak and took them to a heder, a religious school, when they turned five. Some boys married as young as ten (in the belief that the messianic age would not begin until every Jewish soul had

been joined to its destined mate); often, the groom lived with the bride's parents until he completed Talmudic studies and thereby attained manhood. Girls received little formal education, usually from their fathers, and sometimes none at all. Few Litvak women chose their professions, and even fewer had access to universities. Their work was to bear sons and prepare them for a life of Torah study and righteousness.

Frida had no intention of becoming one of these women. She scandalized the Jews of Svintsyán by attending a secular gymnasium and later enrolled at a medical school in Hamburg, graduating with a dental degree. Another obstacle to finding a potential groom was her ungainly size. She towered over her husband and outweighed him by at least twenty pounds. Yet she had a cheerful, uncomplaining disposition and radiated an easy kindness even while spinning up the foot-operated cast-iron drill, and became a well-liked addition to Haskel's dental practice. When Haskel was about to extract a tooth, he called Frida into the office. She grasped the patient's head and held it firmly against her bountiful bosom while her husband braced a knee against the metal chair. While he pulled, Frida whispered consoling promises in the patient's ear.

Prior to the marriage, she informed Haskel that she wanted another child and wasn't inclined to wait. She gave birth to my grandfather ten months after her wedding, on October 9, 1915. His father named him Shimon, but Frida insisted on calling her son by his Russian name, Semyon. Just a few weeks earlier, on Yom Kippur, the kaiser's troops had occupied Vilnius. (Somewhere to the west, Vassily's father, Anany, the Ukrainian beet farmer with the Old Testament name, was wounded and taken prisoner by the same army.)

The German occupation intensified the city's poverty and overcrowding and hobbled the Jewish quarter. Another twenty-two thousand Jews, expelled from Kaunas, Grodno and elsewhere by the tsar's edict, arrived in Vilnius along with ten thousand Christian refugees. Many of these newly homeless Jews wandered the streets and slept on the floors of synagogues and kosher slaughterhouses. The government issued bread cards, and more than a hundred communal kitchens provided bread and soup not only to the city's poor but also to members of the newly impoverished middle class. Travel bans led to widespread unemployment. German officials declared that holders of bread cards who didn't find work within ten days would be conscripted into labor battalions. As a result, Litvaks were deported by the thousands to work in coal mines in the Ruhr and Upper Silesia or on the docks of Tilsit. Soldiers marched other laborers into the countryside to build roads and clear forest. They slept on planks in unheated wooden barracks, and in the winter of 1915 hundreds froze to death in their sleep. The city roiled with typhoid and dysentery. Mothers left children in the streets, knowing they would be better fed in orphanages.

In the space of seven years, the sovereignty of Vilnius changed hands eight times. By 1918, after the major powers—the Germans and Russians—had been driven out, it became even more lawless and hungry. St. Anne's brick-colored spires and the city's old horse chestnuts rose over a slum of food smugglers and prostitutes, of child beggars and nightly random stabbings, where a plate of horse meat and radishes was not an uncommon supper. The death rate among the city's Litvaks rose five times, to nearly one in ten. Many of the wealthiest residents had fled. In 1918, when Frida took to bed with the Spanish flu, a stranger showed up at the apartment and produced a single egg from his coat. Haskel paid for it readily. "Give it to Senechka," Frida said, using their younger son's pet name. Semyon was two and for weeks hadn't eaten anything except bread soaked in milk. Haskel had to concede that the city of his birth, the city he loved, had become uninhabitable.

He shuttered the office on Calvary Street and loaded his family and two cast-iron drills onto a horse-drawn wagon. They relocated about a hundred kilometers to the north, to a nondescript outpost on the Vyžuona River called Utena. A census from that time describes it as a settlement of seven hundred houses, thirty-four shops, three mills, a sawmill, a leather works and a few small factories. About half of the residents were Jews who called the shtetl by its Yiddish name, Utian. Hunger and disease there were less extreme, the prices lower, and the chaos and misery of Vilnius quieted to a distant thrum.

Haskel bought a six-bedroom house near the center of town and opened a dental office nearby. My grandfather spoke about those years with a nostalgic lilt; often he saw the large, drafty house in his dreams. His memories of it suggested Chekhovian provincial comfort just short of affluence. There were cut flowers in every room, a piano, a Lithuanian housekeeper and a cook. In the mornings Semyon sat around the dining room with his brother and father while Frida bustled in the kitchen. Haskel sipped strong coffee and spread gooseberry jam on his toast, all the while muttering to himself and skimming the Yiddish daily. "An omelet for Romochka and a soft-boiled egg for Senechka," the matronly cook intoned in singsong Lithuanian. From the kitchen she brought a soft-boiled brown egg, still steaming, in a porcelain egg cup and cracked the top with a spoon before setting it down on Semyon's plate along with a sterling-silver saltshaker.

I've tried to reconcile my grandfather's bucolic recollections of this time and place with historical accounts. Political historians thin their narratives of it to a sequence of interlocking violent upheavals, while cultural historians reduce theirs to the peregrinations of a dispossessed minority. Here's a sample: Vilnius passed back and forth between Bolsheviks and Polish legionnaires. The Poles accused the Jews of siding with the enemy and desecrated the old Shnipishok cemetery, where the Russians had made their last stand, expecting to disinter caches of currency and rifles from the graves of long-dead rabbis. Soldiers then shot some eighty Jews and threw others, hands tied behind their backs, into the frigid waters of the Vilia (the Polish name of the Neris).

If these events intruded into my grandfather's consciousness, it was as the subject of quiet talk among adults. What *he* remembered best about those years was going to the movies. In Utena, a stroll away from his parents' house, a movie theater opened for business: its seats were upholstered in burgundy velvet and a bald music teacher hammered at an upright piano during screenings of silent films. Semyon spent afternoons there engrossed in watching Mary Pickford, Buster Keaton, Ivan Mozzhukhin and, most memorably, Marlene Dietrich in *Der blaue Engel,* a film he claimed as his favorite for the remainder of his life. On holidays, when relatives came to visit, Frida staged plays for the children in the cavernous living room. She sang, someone sawed on a violin or played the upright piano, and later Haskel manned the hand-cranked gramophone that blared Chopin or Strauss into the night. The adults drank too much slivovitz and danced.

Haskel recited kaddish at the local synagogue, muttered hurried blessings over wine and potted flank, and spoke to his sons in Yiddish. Frida addressed them in the tsar's Russian. She considered the religiosity of small-town Litvaks an embarrassment and didn't think much of their language. By any measure, her family was extraordinarily strange, something Semyon began to discover whenever maternal uncles, aunts and cousins visited them in Utena.

Frida was one of thirteen children. Her father, Esai Levin, was a lawyer who achieved the unheard-of distinction of being appointed a magistrate. Even in their dotage, his grandchildren swore that he was the sole Jewish judge in the entire Russian Empire. To his children he bequeathed a blithe disregard for the painstaking commandments of the Jewish faith, and a belief in secular education, science and modernity. He advocated the necessity of travel and managed to instill it in his children. Frida's German schooling was typical of her siblings' nomadic lives. Her younger brother Aaron, another Hamburg-trained dentist, lived with Haskel and Frida in Vilnius, where he stayed on after they left for Utena. Leah went to St. Petersburg, enrolling in one of the empire's few university programs for women. David became head of the international Communist organization in Shanghai and later opened a bicycle factory in China. Max, the youngest and most handsome, became a prosperous lawyer in Munich. In his early thirties, he sat down on his bed, put the barrel of a revolver in his mouth and shot himself. Two sisters said he was despairing over a woman who spurned him, but Aaron claimed poor Max had contracted syphilis.

By the time Frida came to Utena, her father, Esai, was dead and her mother, Sarah, had moved in with her and Haskel. Nearing eighty, Sarah enjoyed entertaining the children with stories about Sunday mornings at Esai's large, comfortable house in Svintsyán. The long dining room table often had two dozen people seated around it, with Esai at the head, while Sarah circled the room with a tray of warm bialys. She proudly pointed out that their guests numbered as many gentiles as Jews.

She told her grandsons a story that would become a founding myth for the family. On an autumn night sometime in the 1890s, a man climbed into an open window in the kitchen. Esai, an insomniac who sat reading at the kitchen table, didn't recognize the intruder. The bedraggled man pulled a pistol from his waistband and pointed it at Esai. He reminded the magistrate that he'd presided at his trial (Semyon could never decide whether the charge was manslaughter or murder) and sentenced him to decades in prison. Now the escaped prisoner had come to get his revenge.

Everyone else in the house was asleep. Esai asked the intruder to hold off shooting him for a few minutes and offered him a cup of tea and some food. He laid out challah, butter, sour-cherry preserves and leftover cold beef. The fugitive laid his gun on the table and ate and drank greedily. In the meantime, he poured out his story to Esai, who listened as though nothing were wrong. Several hours later, before anyone in the house woke, the two men strolled like friends to the police barracks, where the intruder turned himself in. Sarah swore that every detail of the story was true.

I never learned what Esai Levin looked like. The sole surviving photo of Semyon's family was taken years after his death. In it, my grandfather must be around fourteen; he stands in a double-breasted suit behind his parents, Haskel and Frida. His grandmother Sarah sits beside her daughter. His half brother, Roma, stands behind her. Uncle Aaron, holding his daughter on his lap, sits on the left. The young boy in the center, the only one permitted to pose without a necktie, is Aaron's son. Whenever I look at the photo, my attention drifts to the lace curtain and the picture of the seated figure tacked to the wall. For some reason the mundane details—the picture, the

tacks, the coat hanger, the pansies embroidered in the lace—are what allow me to imbue the image with the slowness and verisimilitude of ordinary life. To fix these people in a moment when the terrible future looming over them was still one possibility among many.

At the periphery of these private lives, the country continued to change. In 1920, the year my grandfather turned five, General Żeligowski's Polish troops captured Vilnius and a broad swath of Lithuania. Afterward, the birthplaces of my grandfather and his parents, a few hours away, lay inside an enemy nation. The new border, a ten-kilometer-wide no-man's-land cordoned with land mines, would remain impassable for almost twenty years. Semyon wouldn't see Vilnius again until the next world war had run its course.

WHEN MY GRANDFATHER was old enough, Frida sent him to the famous Vilkomir Reali gymnasium. Though there was a perfectly respectable yeshiva in Utena, the school in Ukmergė (Vilkomir in Yiddish) was one of only two schools in the country that instructed students in Yiddish instead of Hebrew. It was an incubator for the left-leaning, secular ideas of the Yiddishists, who believed that the

rightful homeland of the Jews was Lithuania—not Palestine, as the Zionists insisted—and that the language of Jewish literature and pedagogy should be European-derived Yiddish instead of biblical Hebrew. The eminent linguist and journalist Yudel Mark was the principal. The school was the only one Frida would consider, undaunted by the fact that it was located sixty-five kilometers away. There she rented her son an attic room in a teacher's house a

short walk from the school, and afterward saw him only on vacations and the more important holidays. In addition to Yiddish, Semyon studied sciences, poetry, music and foreign languages. He came to classes in an ironed uniform, a starched shirt and a cap with the school's brass insignia above the shellac visor.

Semyon returned home on holidays loaded down with books. He read at night by the light of a lamp, falling asleep at dawn and usually sleeping through breakfast. Many of the books were in German, a language he picked up easily because of its similarity to Yiddish, and he read and reread Goethe's *Werther* and *Faust* and spent hours memorizing poems by Schiller, Heine and Hölderlin. During Sabbath suppers, he liked to recite Frida's favorite—Schiller's "Song of the Bell"—to her unvarnished delight. Semyon claimed to have memorized all 430 lines of the famous poem. At those holiday meals, Haskel mumbled blessings over the challah and wine. Then Semyon—still high-voiced, gazing adoringly into his mother's face—stood up to deliver the German stanzas:

> Denn mit der Freude Feierklange
> Begrüßt sie das geliebte Kind
> Auf seines Lebens erstem Gange,
> Den es in Schlafes Arm beginnt.

> *Because with the festive sound of joy*
> *She greets the well-loved child*
> *On his life's first walk,*
> *Which he begins in the arms of sleep.*

AFTER MY GRANDFATHER graduated from the gymnasium, Haskel moved the family again, this time to Kaunas, Lithuania's new capital. The facts I've gathered about their life there flatten to a few key events, mostly because Semyon avoided talking about his years in Kaunas, which reminded him of the terrible shocks that arrived at the beginning of the 1940s. The war divided his narrative of early adulthood into an overture that grew increasingly pastoral in hindsight, and a period of calamities that he described as warping his understanding of what it meant to be human.

Haskel's dental practice had been stagnating in the country, and Kaunas was not only the largest city in the newly partitioned Lithuania, but also the cultural capital of the Jews. After the Polish occupation of the older, more cosmopolitan Vilnius, Kaunas came into its own. The main thoroughfare, Laisvės Alėja—a tree-bound boulevard that terminated in a ponderous neoclassical cathedral—sprouted hotels, cabarets and restaurants that aimed for the splendor of Vienna and even Paris. Above the confluence of the Neman and the Neris, the city installed a Swiss-made funicular to transport sightseers to an overlook point in Aleksotas, where they could marvel at the old town's Gothic churches and the broad cobbled plaza in front of the archbishop's residence. Jews made up nearly a third of the city's population. Their largest settlement lay on the far bank of the Neris, dating to a time when they weren't allowed to settle in the city proper. The neighborhood was named Vilijampolė, but its residents called it Slobodka.

Lithuania's independence began with a promise of equality for the Litvaks. In 1922, they won a share of cultural autonomy and a role in government nearly proportional to their share of the population. But by the 1930s, particularly after the establishment of the Third Reich and the precipitous rise of anti-Semitism in neighboring Poland, their situation became worse than at any time in their history. Jews were weeded out of government, high-ranking military positions, banking, law and education. Because of pressure from business owners, they were also losing a toehold in most forms of respectable commerce.

For all that, they created a vibrant, cosmopolitan home in the city they called Kovno. It was home to five high schools, a seminary, several vocational schools, an ethnographic society and museum, thirty synagogues, two theaters, five daily papers and three libraries.

Welfare organizations, sports clubs, professional guilds, political parties, an orphanage, a hospital and countless restaurants and cafés rounded out a Jewish communal life second only to the one in Vilnius.

My grandfather enrolled in the university's mathematics and sciences faculty in 1933. Only a handful of Jewish professors remained. During lectures, some students complained openly about the "Jewish problem." Some cracked hostile jokes loud enough for everyone in the lecture halls to hear; they mocked Jewish classmates for speaking Yiddish and for speaking Lithuanian with an accent. Semyon— who spoke German, Russian, Polish and Lithuanian in addition to Yiddish and Hebrew—detested these instigators, many of whom were children of farmers from nearby villages who spoke only their native language.

His best friends at the university remained close to him and to one another for the next forty years. All three were Lithuanians: a towering, prematurely bald pre-law student named Balevičius; the painter Savickas; and Valius, a spindly ornithologist. (My grandfather inherited some of Valius's nineteenth-century German field guides, and as a child I paged through the meticulous hand-colored etchings of gull-billed terns and Eurasian pygmy owls, still the most breathtaking illustrations I've seen.)

Even then, Semyon's friends marveled at his absence of meanness and bitterness, his childlike delight and capacity for surprise, which he retained until the end of his life. I remember him sometimes becoming so overjoyed with an anecdote or a piece of music that tears poured from his eyes. In their capriciousness and bluster, his sudden rages were childlike, too, and could be frightening. He wasn't physically imposing, but he fought often. At the university, when a student standing behind him lisped in a parody of Yiddish, Semyon swung before getting a good look at him, without considering the outcome or the odds. In classrooms, during nationalist tirades, he stood and argued loudly with the startled professors, acts of dissent for which he was reprimanded but never expelled.

I don't know where in Kaunas he lived. His name and the names of his immediate family don't appear in the city's archives. The sole trace of his years there is an entry in an interwar encyclopedia that lists the members of Lithuania's armed forces. Next to the name Semionas Galberstatas there is a scant paragraph of dates and ranks. Thanks to his university degree, he could enter military service as an officer, and so instead of slogging across potato fields with a backpack and a rifle, half-dazed with hunger, he enrolled in an officers' academy in Kaunas. There he was trained to command cavalrymen and, strangest to me, won trophies for his horsemanship.

More than riding, he enjoyed horses. The minute workings of their minds fascinated him; he never tired of watching how his smallest gestures made the animals move. In later years, he kept a graph-paper notebook open beside his reading and sketched page after page of horses, always in profile. When I read his entry in the military encyclopedia, I tried to imagine my grandfather as a slender equestrian in breeches and patent-leather boots. Instead, my mind kept returning to the potbellied Social Security recipient I knew in my adolescence who on most nights fell asleep in a yellow floral-print armchair, a copy of *Chess Life* open in his lap.

He graduated from the officers' academy as a decorated lieutenant. But afterward, when he tried to find work as a science teacher, he discovered that the jobs were open only to ethnic Lithuanians. By happenstance, a friend mentioned a position at a fashionable German gymnasium, corralling the young children of the city's wealthiest citizens. Instead of lecturing on botany and physics, Semyon found himself in front of a room of neatly combed seven-year-olds, singing in Lithuanian about ducks swimming in a pond. He liked children and didn't mind the work. He moved into a small apartment near the city center, and when he wasn't reading, he spent nights walking or listening to the orchestras on Laisvės Alėja. On occasion he took women out on dates, though never too seriously.

These relatively carefree months ended on a warm day in the middle of June 1940. Semyon was walking under the old trees on

Laisvės Alėja when a tank rolled into view from a side street. In a flash of panic he thought the Germans had invaded. Germany had occupied neighboring Poland, and during the past year he'd read newspaper accounts about the Germans' brutality toward Poland's Jews. Litvaks in Kovno talked about little else. But the tank's dull flank wasn't painted with a cross—the Soviets had restored Vilnius to Lithuania the previous autumn, and now they were arriving to collect on the debt. Once news of the invasion spread, some among the Jews celebrated. The Russian tanks, they said, would form a wall between them and the Nazis.

If some Red Army commanders impressed Kaunas's residents with their civility, it didn't last. Bedraggled soldiers pillaged shops, emptying them of men's shoes and winter coats, regardless of size or style, cameras, and bassinets; their families back in Khimki and Tula needed them. Red Army detachments dismantled factories and loaded the machinery onto trucks to be transported and reassembled hundreds of kilometers to the east. A radio announcement declared that all businesses and private homes were now Soviet property, though most of the city's residents continued to live and work where they did before. For the first time, the Russians proved to be more benevolent to Jews than to Lithuanians, their former vassals, whom they suspected of pro-German sympathies. Suddenly high-ranking positions at newly Sovietized universities, ministries and factories were open to Jewish applicants, often at the expense of former Lithuanian bosses. If some Litvaks gloated about these promotions, their gentile neighbors didn't soon forget it.

The new jobs scarcely made up for the Soviet campaign against religion and the shuttering of communal life. NKVD agents padlocked synagogues and churches. In the streets, Red Army soldiers offered chocolate bars to children in exchange for promises to renounce parochial superstitions. "Did Jesus give you this chocolate bar, or did I?" they asked. In Semyon's classroom, Soviet agents plastered Politburo portraits above the blackboard and along the walls, and children came to school with pictures of Molotov and Bulganin pinned to their clothes. Soviet "educators" marched them around the courtyard and taught them to trill in shaky Russian. For Semyon, those days took on a surreal quality, where the boundaries of reality were redrawn every morning while the city held its breath.

The occupation brought new patients to Haskel's dental office: mostly sullen Russian soldiers with abscessed teeth and swollen faces. At home, Haskel persisted in being cheerful and mild; besides an occasional exhaled *"Vey iz mir,"* he smiled away mundane upsets. Roma, who helped out at the dental office, turned into a prematurely graying, timorous man who liked to stay close to the family and smiled shyly in an appealing, hooded way. He spent his private hours in his room painting watercolors or listening to the radio.

One morning in the spring of 1941, Haskel came to the office with a case of indigestion that by afternoon had grown into a throbbing ache. During a break between patients, he told Frida that he was going down the street to speak to a doctor, a colleague to whom he sometimes referred patients. He will probably prescribe bicarbonate of soda, he told her. Haskel was waiting in the doctor's reception room when his expression went slack and he tumbled sideways out of his chair, dead of a heart attack. The funeral was held at the lovely old Jewish cemetery in Žaliakalnis, a neighborhood that owed its name to the green hill on which it stood. It rained while the undertaker patted down the soil with a shovel. Semyon set a wooden marker at the head of his father's grave: according to a Jewish custom, a year must pass before mourners may unveil a tombstone. Dozens of Haskel's patients stopped by the house during shiva. Afterward, Frida took over the dental practice.

In March, a Soviet edict expelled German citizens from the annexed territories. In the two years since Molotov and Ribbentrop, the Nazi foreign minister, signed a nonaggression pact at the Kremlin, the Soviet Union and Germany carved up the land that lay between them. The borders were proving too porous. In Moscow,

Stalin refused to believe that Hitler would violate the pact, yet on the country's western periphery Soviet troops grew restless, sensing the approaching endgame like the smell of rain.

Late on the night of June 14, trucks fanned out around Kaunas, pulling up in front of shuttered houses and apartment buildings. NKVD agents in twos rushed in with carbines raised, ordering the buildings' residents into the trucks. Like elsewhere in the Soviet Union, the arrested were accused of assorted infractions of ideology and class: they were property owners, government officials, the excessively religious, Zionists, Bundists, anyone who'd spoken publicly against Stalin and the Soviets, and, as ever, the merely unlucky. Over four nights across the Lithuanian Soviet Socialist Republic, as the territory was now known, the secret police arrested 30,000. The prisoners included Lithuanians, Poles, Belorussians and Russians, as well as roughly 7,000 Jews. NKVD troops herded them aboard trains—150 to 200 people per boxcar with no toilets and one small window for ventilation—and wound the doors shut with barbed wire. On the sides of the cars, they wrote "Traitors to the Homeland" in white paint. The prisoners were bound for forced labor either in Kazakhstan, in southern Siberia, or at the mouth of the Lena River, near the Arctic Ocean. After the deportations, everyone in Kaunas walked in silence, ashen-faced. The fabric of daily life was rupturing and coming apart. Even the birds, my grandfather said, stopped singing.

Six days after the last of the Soviet raids, on June 22, Semyon awoke in the dark, roused by a blast. It was three thirty or four in the morning. He heard sirens but couldn't figure out their origin and eventually drifted back to sleep. He woke again an hour or two later and opened a window. On the far side of the two rivers, the military air base in Aleksotas was smoldering. Against the lightening early-summer sky—the color of plums, he recalled—a braid of smoke wound its way skyward. Semyon lay down again but couldn't sleep. Some time after six he turned on the radio; the announcer reported that the Reich had declared war on the Soviet Union. The stations were buzzing with the news. The border with occupied Poland lay a hundred kilometers away. Semyon realized the Germans could be in the city in a matter of hours.

Outside, disheveled Red Army soldiers ran through the streets, some barefoot or shirtless. From certain windows, Lithuanian partisans shot at them and, mostly, the Russians didn't return fire. Semyon threw on a shirt and ran to his mother's apartment. In the corridors of her building he saw startled Jewish neighbors, arguing about whether to stay in Kaunas or leave. Everyone had gathered at the apartment: his half brother, Roma; his grandmother Sarah, who had moved with them from Utena; and of course his mother, Frida, who was boiling coffee, unperturbed. Semyon leaned against a wall, panting. Words tumbled out of his mouth. They needed to leave the city in the next hour or two, he said, and when no one in the room budged, he began shouting. Hadn't they read about how the Jews in Poland were dealt with?

"The Germans will behave decently," Frida responded in the definitive tone she adopted during family disputes. She remembered the previous German occupation. General Ludendorff, deputy to Germany's chief of general staff, Paul von Hindenburg, had written a manifesto that began, *"Mein liebe Juden . . ."* "My dear Jews," it read, "we have come to change your lives!" The Germans were no blessing, but they would again behave like civilized Europeans, Frida assured everyone. These were the countrymen of Schiller and Bach. Besides, the Litvaks had endured other occupations, and would again. Sarah, who was 102 years old, laughed in her easy way. She said that she had been on the earth too long to run now and, besides, couldn't bear to be apart from the *Kinder*.

That left Roma. Semyon pleaded with his older half brother, but Roma looked down at the floor miserably. All he could muster was that the dental office needed looking after. Frida had been working there alone since their father died, and he didn't dare leave her. "I will take care of Mother," he stammered, not convincing even himself. Semyon wanted to grab his brother by the lapels, to force him out of the apartment, but he began to doubt himself. Roma was ill-suited for running. He was neither athletic nor comfortable around strangers—a diffident bachelor, the kind of man neighbors gossiped about and women shied away from. What if they became separated? His brother's sheepish, tearful expression filled him with dread. "I might be killing him," he thought. He was lost in conflicted thoughts when Frida stepped in between them and put her hand on her son's shoulder. She said they'd be safe in Kaunas and would see each other after everything calmed down. Semyon wanted to say something else, but the words caught in his throat. He kissed his mother and grandmother, embraced Roma, and ran home. He threw several changes of clothes, a few books and some food into a suitcase; locked his door; and headed for the train station. Others, Jews by the look of them, were hurrying to the station, too, clutching hastily packed suitcases and bags.

The platform roiled with people trying to make their way onto a train that couldn't fit them. Bodies, suitcases and crying children jammed the cars. On the platform, people yelled for those who'd made it onto the train or those they'd lost in the crowd; they wanted to say goodbye or hand someone a sweater or a loaf of bread wrapped in newsprint. Fights broke out. The tougher men simply flung others off the train and climbed aboard in their place. Semyon tried to shoulder his way into several cars, but a wall of bodies pushed him back. He ran alongside the tracks looking for a gap. Finally he clambered up a metal ladder and on all fours shimmied onto the corrugated roof of a passenger car. He lay flat on his stomach and wedged his suitcase under his head like a pillow.

He'd sweated through an already filthy white shirt, a stupid thing to wear, it occurred to him. The whistle blew, and my grandfather watched Kaunas, the city where nearly everyone he knew remained, lurch behind him. A pillar of smoke from the locomotive billowed and dispersed overhead. He was agonizing about his mother and brother when the wooden dwellings on the outskirts gave way to forest, the kilometers of dense, impassable woods Lithuania is known for. The metal roof under him grew warm in the sun, and he stripped to his undershirt. Hours passed while the train rocked pleasantly underneath him.

While the sun flashed through the pines, his panic subsided and his thoughts slowed to a ramble, moving in rhythm with the train wheels. He remembered a story he'd read as a student at the gymnasium in Ukmergė. Empress Catherine's army laid siege to Vilnius, intent on dislodging the Polish rebels. Elijah ben Solomon, the scholarly saint known as the Vilna Gaon, aged seventy-two, arrived at the Great Synagogue, where a crowd had gathered. The frantic Jews inside the candlelit, imposing temple talked of slaughter and enslavement. Amid the wailing, the Gaon opened the ark and led the congregation in a sevenfold recitation of Psalm 20: "The Lord will answer thee in the day of distress." Just then, a cannonball fired from a neighboring castle mount fell harmlessly onto the synagogue's roof; it could be seen there well into the twentieth century. Inside, the Jews shuddered at the impact, but the Gaon announced that the evil had been averted. Soon after, the Poles opened the city gates and ended the siege. It was the fifteenth day of Av 1792. Semyon wondered whether, 150 years later, another miracle would save Lithuania's Jews.

He was thirsty and his eyes stung. In the dusk, he peered over the side of the car and called out to a man in an undershirt leaning out a window. The man and his wife helped him climb down into the compartment. It was jammed with people, and Semyon crouched on the floor between the berths. After some hours, a Red Army cavalry unit halted the locomotive. A low-ranking officer interrogated the able-bodied men aboard the train, conscripting most on the spot. When asked about military training, Semyon lied and said he had none. He doubted that Stalin's officers would deal benevolently with an officer of a foreign army. Besides, having dealt with the Russians in Kaunas, he wanted no part of the political mire of command. He was made a private in the Soviet infantry and issued temporary papers. It would take another two weeks for him to receive his greatcoat and rifle.

. . .

MY GRANDFATHER WAS twenty-five when he became a Soviet soldier. During the next four years, he received no information about his family or anyone he'd known. How did he endure this? I've often wondered. He didn't learn what happened to his mother, grandmother and brother, or to friends and neighbors, until the war's end. The little I've learned about their lives and deaths comes from accounts and rudimentary statistics compiled by SS officers who arrived in Kaunas some days after my grandfather escaped, and from the research and testimony of subsequent decades. Nevertheless, it amounts to more information than Semyon was able to gather about these events in his lifetime.

On Sunday, June 22, 1941—the morning my grandfather left Kaunas—Stalin's deportations were less than a week old. At Catholic Masses across the city, priests urged parishioners to cooperate with the German army. From the pulpits, some called for revenge against Soviet collaborators, and Jews in particular. At nine thirty on Monday morning, Radio Kaunas reported the formation of a Lithuanian provisional government. It played the march from *Aida,* interrupted by announcements that the radio station was in the hands of partisans and that the Bolsheviks had fled. Lithuania, an announcer declaimed, was free at last.

That afternoon, the Lithuanian commander Jurgis Bobelis announced that German troops had been attacked from houses where Jews lived, and warned that one hundred Jews would be shot for every dead German soldier. By the time the Wehrmacht and the first unit of the SS Einsatzgruppen arrived in Kaunas on Tuesday, June 24, a thousand of the city's Jews—one in thirty—were reported dead. The eastbound train that followed my grandfather's by several hours was hit by Luftwaffe bombs. The locomotive and several cars lay smoldering in a clearing. The surviving passengers were arrested and returned to Kaunas, or raped, or executed on the spot.

The White Armbands, as the Lithuanian paramilitaries became known, mobilized on Monday. Students from the university that my grandfather had attended walked alongside them as they crossed the bridge over the Neris to Slobodka. The neighborhood was home to six thousand of the city's poorest and most pious Jews, some of whose families had lived there since the Middle Ages. The Lithuanian throng carried rifles, knives, axes and hammers. They entered Slobodka's homes and herded the occupants into the streets. When a large enough crowd of Jews gathered, they were ordered at gunpoint to run down to the river. There, other men instructed the Jews to remove their clothes and run into the water. As the naked men and women, some clinging to siblings, parents and children, waded into the Neris—the old river that wound past the burial mounds of the pagan Lithuanians, past the mythological stones and sacred oaks— men with machine guns opened fire from behind.

Some members of the mob weren't content with the orderly execution. They burst into Slobodka's houses, startling families, many of whom were sitting down for the midday meal. The intruders dismembered bodies, nailed hands to walls, pushed needles and awls into eyes. They beheaded a rabbi named Zalman Ostrovsky and put his head in a window like a storefront centerpiece. They set fire to hand-inscribed Torah scrolls and holy arks. They cut off beards with broken glass, then doused the men with kerosene and lit them on fire, while newly arrived SS officers snapped photos of the burning bodies. Corpses littered the streets. Men with rifles and turbid eyes, many of them drunk, staggered along bellowing, "Jews! Communists!"

Elsewhere in Kaunas, the White Armbands arrested Jews, sealed the doors of their homes, and transported them to the old tsarist forts, where nearly every one would be shot. On Friday, June 27, a mob seized another fifty or sixty Jews and herded them to a place known as Lietūkis Garage, near the city center. While a crowd watched, several men turned on fire hoses and forced the nozzles into the captives' mouths until their bellies burst. The garage stood on Vytauto Street. It was named after the grand duke whose charters brought thousands of Jews to the land they called Lita, the ruler whom they dubbed the Lithuanian Cyrus after the benevolent Persian king who freed their ancestors from Babylonian captivity.

Exactly how long the Jews had lived among Lithuanians isn't recorded. It is known that the first of them came many years before the priests, in Jogaila's time, began performing mass baptisms in the Neris. Six hundred years of coexistence came to an end in late June of 1941. In the five months following the German invasion, more than 137,000 of the country's Jews were liquidated, in SS parlance, by their co-workers and neighbors. Most were disposed of in hastily dug pits. Another 70,000 were shot or gassed before the war's end.

The dead were cataloged meticulously. In a report dated December 1, 1941, Standartenführer Karl Jäger, leader of a killing squad known as Einsatzkommando 3, claimed somewhat disingenuously that Lithuania was *judenfrei*, free of Jews. To the name of each city and shtetl he appended a liquidation date or dates and a casualty count, tallying not only the executed Jewish men, women and children but also Communists, thieves, grave robbers and the "mentally defective." The mass shootings, Jäger noted, were carried out "on my instructions and orders . . . by Lithuanian partisans."

Fewer than one in twenty Litvaks lived to see the war's end, the lowest survival rate in Europe. My mother's parents were among those who remained. They carried with them vestiges of a culture that would never again take root in the northern country of cairns and Romanesque ruins and impassable forests, where a latter-day Jerusalem vanished like the spring snow.

LIKE MOST SOVIET children, I was nourished on television programming about the Great Patriotic War, as it's still known in Russia. Everyone agreed that the War Against Fascism was the nation's pinnacle, our sacrifice and gift to the world, a time when the Soviet people behaved selflessly and nobly, bound by collective duty. Like most Soviet boys, I preferred war films to musicals and documentaries about Warsaw Pact–region grain production, and watched as many as I could. Naturally I was proud of Semyon's participation in the fighting and asked about it incessantly. He disliked talking about it nearly as much as I yearned to.

On visits to Vilnius, I played with the medals he kept in a bone-colored box. They weren't the important orders, like the Red Star or the Order of Lenin, that I saw on television. Tarnished, clipped to pieces of striped fabric, his medals commemorated battles and anniversaries. One read "For Bravery." Semyon told me that he received it after army doctors removed two slivers of shrapnel from his back. He hiked up his shirt to show me one of the scars, a seamy aperture on the freckled concavity under his shoulder blade. Later, in New York, he joined a World War II veterans' organization: several dozen elderly Russian-speaking Jews in rumpled suits who gathered monthly at a kebab restaurant in Queens. Still, Semyon rarely spoke about his wartime experiences. At the front he saw many dead, mostly boys younger than he, and said that he didn't wish these sights upon me or anyone else. Usually that was the end of it.

On a few occasions, my nagging extracted some facts: He served in the Red Army's Sixteenth Rifle Division, known as the Lithuanian Division because it comprised mostly refugees from the former Lithuanian Soviet Socialist Republic. He operated a mortar used to flush out enemy trenches and blow up defiladed vehicles and troops. In 1944, a commander impressed with his fluency in German began to use him as a translator. Semyon interpreted at interrogations of captured enemy soldiers and members of the Waffen-SS; he translated radio broadcasts, documents and communiqués. Afterward, he said, he didn't see much fighting.

In the early days of May 1945, he entered Berlin with the First Belorussian Front commanded by Marshal Zhukov. Semyon offered few details about what he saw there, and my images of the battle and its aftermath come mainly from photographs and books: Soviet shock armies and tank units entering the ruined capital, lend-lease Buicks and Studebakers towing light artillery behind them, mounted Cossacks with war trophies strapped to their saddles. On the day

after the Reichstag fell, Red Army soldiers posed for a widely repro-
duced photo on top of it, hoisting up their crimson flag. Hundreds of
thousands had been killed and maimed in the lead-up to the final
battle. The victorious Soviet troops pillaged apartments and shops,
shot imprisoned soldiers and civilians, and downed liquor, beer and
laboratory solvents, staying drunk for days. A Soviet army corre-
spondent recounted that "Russian soldiers raped every German fe-
male aged eight to 80."

Although Semyon told me little about those weeks, he let on that
they left him with a lingering sense of horror. The story he did tell
took place on Unter den Linden, the boulevard that passes under the
Brandenburg Gate, where some of Berlin's grandest apartments
looked out onto the old lindens the street was named for. In the last
days of the fighting, residents cut down the trees for firewood.
Semyon said that when he first saw the boulevard, he wept. Soviet
ordnance had reduced some of the opulent buildings to skeletons
standing above a scree of rubble.

But not all were destroyed. Semyon walked into several unlocked apartments and wandered through the abandoned rooms, marveling at the chintz and the marble fireplaces. On a kitchen table he came across a half-eaten breakfast—still warm—left there by the fleeing occupants. He said he spent most of his time rummaging through hundreds of books, rising on shelves that reached the ceilings. On one shelf, behind an early hand-illustrated set of Goethe's Wilhelm Meister books and volumes of poetry, he discovered a banned novel by Heinrich Heine. He crammed about a dozen of the rarest, most valuable books into his backpack.

Semyon told me about the books with more animation than about anything else having to do with the war. Weeks later, his battalion marched east from the German front along unpaved roads trampled into ankle-deep muck by boots, truck tires and days of rain. The straps of his pack cut into his shoulders. Finally, he put down the heavy backpack and set the old books, including the beautiful Meisters, in a pile by the side of the muddy road. He never forgave himself.

He returned home, to Kaunas, in the fall of 1945. He walked along the streets carpeted with dust and rubble, seemingly swept clean of its residents. Nothing in the city worked. Those who remained stood in lines for ration cards. My grandfather walked to his mother's apartment but found a Lithuanian family living there. They claimed to have no inkling about the previous tenants. Frida's things and furniture were gone.

Haskel's dental office stood empty, stripped even of bathroom fixtures. Semyon found few traces of his family and former life. But somewhere near the city's center, he walked past a familiar-looking Jewish woman, a neighbor of Frida's from before the war. Wizened and thin, she turned out to be among the handful of those who survived the Kaunas ghetto. They embraced. She told Semyon that a few days after he left the city, armed men wearing white armbands arrived at his mother's home. The partisans shot his 102-year-old grandmother moments after walking in; Sarah bled to death on the living room floor. His mother and brother were taken to the Seventh

Fort. Along with some three thousand others, they were machine-gunned, their bodies thrown into a nearby pit. They were probably made to dig their own graves, the neighbor added. "Your father was a shrewd man," she remarked. "He was smart to die when he did."

Semyon left Kaunas within hours of meeting her. He couldn't bear any more vestiges of his life there. He boarded the first train to Vilnius, the city of his birth. He hadn't been to Vilnius since he was two, but to his surprise and joy he located Frida's brother Aaron, the dentist; some thirty years earlier, his uncle had lived with them in Vilnius and, later, visited them often in Utena. Aaron was uncommonly lucky: he'd spent the war years deep in the Russian interior, salving oral infections and extracting teeth, and even managed to reclaim his old apartment in Vilnius. After Semyon found him, they moved in together. My grandfather was twenty-nine and relieved to have found a remnant of his family—the last living reminder that he wasn't born in solitude.

Shortages of every kind defined the postwar years in Soviet Vilnius. As an army veteran, Semyon was entitled to more privileges than most and handed over his ration cards to Aaron. Most of the time they had enough sugar, eggs, coffee and butter. But one night at dinner, Aaron came to the table in a foul mood. When Semyon buttered a piece of bread, his uncle railed at him for using too much butter: Didn't he know how difficult it was to get even a hundred grams of the stuff? He continued to fulminate until Semyon flung his plate onto the table with a clatter, stood up, and began to put on his coat. He couldn't believe that after all the displacement and death, his uncle could be so petty. The argument escalated. "I'm all the family you've got!" Aaron shouted. "You won't like it out there on your own, without anyone, and before long you'll come running back." My grandfather buckled his belt. It was a worn pigskin strap with a star on the brass buckle, a holdover from the army days. "Then I don't have a family," he replied, and walked out. Semyon spent several months sleeping on his friend Valius's sofa. He never spoke to his uncle again.

He slept poorly in those years, some nights for just three or four hours. He dreamed most often about his mother and, especially, about his brother. Shy, dark-eyed Roma looked up at him accusingly, and Semyon woke with a start, his heart heaving in his chest. On those nights, he lay in the dark and replayed that June morning in 1941, convinced he could have saved them. He should've demanded, threatened, dragged them out by their clothes and marched them to the train station. Why did he listen to his mother? And how could he have chosen himself over his brother—his gentle, solitary brother whom he'd never heard utter an unkind word about anyone?

His survival, he decided, must have been a matter of blind luck. In the dreams he saw the number of Frida's house in Kaunas—10-9. Despite his scientist's contempt for superstition, he began to avoid the number 19, convinced it was unlucky and possibly lethal. One day, he realized that the catastrophe that befell him was likely preordained. According to the Julian calendar used in the tsarist Lithuania of his birth, he was born on October 9—10/9—which added up to the malevolent number. And so to celebrate his next birthday—his thirty-first, in 1946—he invited a few friends to his apartment on November 15, a date he chose at random. Later, he entered it on documents as his birth date. He was willing to grow five weeks younger if it warded off the misfortune that had left him in the world alone.

IN 1945, SEVERAL months before Berlin fell, Semyon sat eating in a mess hall when he spotted an army clerk with a blond Veronica Lake peekaboo. He realized he'd seen her before, in Kaunas; he even knew her name. She came from Slobodka and had been married to a leader in a Jewish Socialist organization called the Bund. He couldn't help staring. A natural blonde was rare enough among Litvak women, but for her to also be wasp-waisted and slender, and for her eyes to be lambent and blue . . .

He wasn't the first or last enlisted man to proposition her, but there wasn't a more persistent suitor in the entire First Belorussian

Front. That everyone considered her out of his league didn't dissuade him; my grandfather liked to say that a man needed only to be more handsome than an ape. Before the war ended, she permitted him some conversation and even a few kisses. He made sure to impress himself onto her memory, certain that he wouldn't forget her anytime soon.

He saw her again in Vilnius two years after the war ended. She was standing on a corner, looking into a consignment-store window. Consignment shops, where people sold their possessions for badly needed rubles, were the only places to find a decent blouse or a pair of good leather shoes. The former army clerk saw Semyon's reflection crossing the street toward her. "If he sees me, he'll never stop pestering me," she thought, and stared down at the sidewalk, but Semyon had recognized her from across the street. He'd memorized even the shape of her back.

Raisa Mebelis allowed him to take her out on several dates. She was widowed and had seen so many men at the front that she was in no hurry to meet another. Besides, she wasn't the head-over-heels type. Raisa's first husband, a serious political man, was killed in the war's early days. He'd been handsome in a serious way, too, with a high narrow forehead and a prominent brow that suggested principle and high purpose.

Semyon, well, mostly he made her laugh with his corny jokes and constant endearments. He brought her flowers on every date (if only daisies rolled in newsprint), held open doors, appeared behind her whenever she put on or took off her cornflower-blue fox-collared coat. He was dependable and amusing, and tolerable-looking despite the nose. She married him a year later. On their wedding day she snuck glances at her younger sister, Ida, and rolled her eyes. Raisa told Ida before the ceremony that she'd probably stay with Semyon for a year or eighteen months and then get a quick divorce. My grandparents remained married for forty-six years.

As a child, I believed my grandmother to be a perfect woman, a notion I never entirely outgrew. She was tall and slender, with long fingers that made strangers remark that she should have taken up the piano. Semyon liked to say that she looked like Ingrid Bergman. Friends, in the vaguely envious and distrustful way Jews speak about the fair, said she looked "Nordic." A firmness of character complemented her looks. Raisa rarely raised her voice or used more words than necessary, and she faced misfortunes with a calm common sense that reassured others and served as a foil for my grandfather's tactlessness, incessant talk and quicksilver rages.

And so it fell to Raisa to manage her husband's volatility and make the best of his poor decisions. During her visits to Moscow, I was most grateful for her presence in the midst of my parents' arguing. Semyon took my mother's side and inserted himself into the bickering, invariably making things worse. At those moments Raisa took me by the hand and led me into another room. She closed the door and read to me in a steady quiet voice, looking up occasionally to see whether I was paying attention. Before long I fell asleep in her lap.

It didn't occur to me then that she had once been young. I was three or four when her legs began to tremble and occasionally seize up, especially while she was crossing a street. A specialist at the medical school where Semyon taught diagnosed Parkinson's disease. Premature degeneration of the basal ganglia triggered the symptoms, he explained as though reading from a textbook, and prescribed a battery of pills. He told her there wasn't a known cause and that the symptoms would steadily get worse.

Semyon blamed himself. He'd been unfaithful and, worse, indiscreet. A friend of Raisa's had spotted him at a restaurant with a graduate student, a plump brunette. Raisa confronted him and they argued. They were shouting when he shoved her; Raisa hit her head against a wall and complained of headaches for weeks. After the diagnosis, Semyon buried himself in scientific articles about the illness, convinced that his outburst had caused it. Afterward, he became gentler, more doting, and spent more time with her at home.

My grandparents spoke Russian with my mother and me, Lithuanian with co-workers and neighbors, but with each other, at home, they spoke a lilting Yiddish. My grandfather addressed his wife using the familiar form of her Russian name—Raya—but at affectionate moments he used a soft aspirated Yiddish and called her Khayale.

When Raisa first saw me, my mother said, she was surprised and delighted by my blue eyes and blond hair (which darkened as I grew older); she said I looked like her younger brother, Leib. One of my earliest memories is of waking up in my grandparents' apartment in Vilnius and finding my grandmother sitting beside me. Through the bars of the toddler's bed I watched the sunlight's geometry on the parquet and felt safe. Raisa liked for me to keep her company in the kitchen while she cooked and, in late summers, jarred cucumbers, cabbage and preserves.

During my visits, she devised a dish notable for its expense and inconvenience. She sent Semyon to the farmers' market to buy a chicken, singed off the last of its feathers by holding it over a lit range, then boned and cut the bird into sections. She fed the breasts into a cast-iron hand-cranked grinder that extruded noodles of pink meat; she added milk, onion, dill and finely shredded white bread, formed it into patties, and browned them in butter. I sat on a stool beside her and watched. While cooking, she told me about sisters and cousins I hadn't met who now lived in places called Sydney, Be'er Sheva and Tel Aviv, and sometimes she talked about my mother's childhood, or hers. Once or twice, she even spoke about the war. I could tell she believed that reliving the past was an indulgence.

One afternoon when I was seven or eight, Raisa must have been in a peculiar mood, because she took down a photo album with an embossed pink-velour cover and sat me in front of it. She pointed to a small black-and-white snapshot. In it she wore a sheepskin coat and an army belt with a star on the brass buckle. She glanced into the camera with a defiant half smile. The uniform and military insignia excited me, but I couldn't connect that defiant gaze with the kind, frail woman peering at me with rheumy eyes magnified by reading glasses into quivering pale-blue saucers. I wanted to ask about the photo, but something about the way she looked at me made me swallow my words. Raisa returned the album to its shelf and walked back to the kitchen.

UNLIKE SEMYON'S FAMILY, Raisa's boasted no magistrates, no spinsters who matriculated in Germany, and no prosperous businessmen. The shtetl where she was born in the same year as my grandfather was as downtrodden and unremarkable as any across the Pale of Settlement. Kaišiadorys—or Koshedar, as it was known in Yiddish—supposedly got its name after the railroad decided to build a way station there for locomotives to take on water midway between Kaunas and Vilnius. According to this probably apocryphal story, when the prospector charged with the task first approached the spot, a clearing in the woods, he came upon two peasants camped around a fire. "What are you doing?" he asked the men, who jumped to their feet and stood rigidly at the sight of the official's Russian uniform. "Cooking kasha, your excellency," one replied.

Raisa's father, Moishe, a tinsmith with a mop of red hair, roofed the town's rickety homes, working mainly for neighboring Jews. His wife was a shy seamstress named Liba. Neither received much education aside from homespun religious instruction and enough words to read a blessing. My grandmother, named Khaya in Yiddish, was the second oldest of four—three girls and a baby boy. The oldest, Dvoira, was dark like their mother, but the others were born blue-eyed and fair. Gentile neighbors winked at them and asked, "Are you sure you are Jews? Perhaps someone stole you from Lithuanian parents?" At home, there wasn't much ritual or prayer. There was never enough food, money or clothes to go around, and no one could bring themselves to believe that the Sovereign of the Universe took an interest in these shortages.

By fourteen, Raisa had a full-time job as a bookkeeper at a brewery that bottled beer, seltzer and lemonade a few towns over. In a photo dated 1932, a group stands around a truck emblazoned with the brewery's name, Zilberkveito. Raisa, who is sixteen or seventeen, wears a long shawl-collared dress and clutches a ledger. She stands next to an older man in a three-piece suit who appears to wield some authority. Beside him—her expression wary and her shoulders drawn—she looks absurdly young.

She became—because of temperament and necessity—the responsible child. Her older sister, Dvoira—who detested the sound of the Yiddish name and preferred to be called by the Chekhovian name Vera—was obstinate, quick-witted and severe. By the time Raisa began working at the brewery, Vera had already spent several weeks in jail for handing out subversive leaflets. Unrepentant, she kept attending underground Communist meetings; at one of them, she met a straw-haired Lithuanian boy named Jonas and began dating him. When Moishe found out, he disowned his daughter. Vera left her parents' house without shedding a single tear, cursing her father. Neither a church nor a synagogue would marry them, so Vera and Jonas hitched to Klaipėda, a port town on the Baltic, to be married by a magistrate. They named their son Karl, after a Lithuanian revolutionary named Karolis Požela and, of course, Karl Marx. Vera disavowed Koshedar's fearful small-town Jews along with her father; as the Russian saying goes, she put a cross over them. Afterward, she sent news to her mother and siblings in terse, infrequent announcements scrawled on the backs of postcards.

Moishe cursed under his breath when Liba gave birth to a third daughter. He said he needed another girl in the house like a *lokh in kop*—a hole in the head. My grandmother's younger sister, Ida, grew into a smiling, indolent child; she adored dances and parties and spent what little money she had on hair clips and combs. After her bat mitzvah, Raisa taught her the rudiments of bookkeeping, a trade at which Ida made a living for the rest of her working life.

Leib was the family's joy. Everyone remembered when, during a Hanukkah supper, five-year-old Leibele made a roomful of adults double over with laughter when he walked in with a box packed with snow and announced that he was saving it for summer. He was sweet-natured and handsome and at thirteen already taller than his father. When the Mebelis children walked to school, the three sisters flanked him on all sides, to protect and show pride in their boy.

Moishe, Liba and the children left the tin-roofed wooden house in Kaišiadorys in the mid-1930s and, like many other small-town denizens, headed for Kaunas, with its promise of more work and better schools. Like many other Jews of small means, they settled in Slobodka. Two of Raisa's cousins, Alta and Esther, already lived on Veiverių Street, a few steps from the bridge spanning the Neman, with a grand view of the Gothic cathedral on the opposite bank. Moishe went back to roofing; Liba sewed negligees; Ida and Leib enrolled in a bustling Hebrew gymnasium.

My grandmother adored Kaunas. She took accounting classes and found work mainly at factories. There was plenty of work to be had, at least for her: not only was Raisa scrupulous and hardworking, but she showed up at the drab offices of coopers and umbrella manufacturers in strikingly elegant suits and dresses that were slim but never risqué. Slobodka's seamstresses sewed them for half of what the downtown tailors charged. Raisa accessorized them with ivory-and-coral cameos, fox collars, English lace. Men pestered her constantly. She dated several but fell in love with a willowy, ambitious boy active in Socialist circles who had risen to a leadership position in the Bund.

I cannot tell you his name. My mother didn't know that Raisa had been married to anyone besides her father until after she'd left home to attend university. They spoke about him once or twice, and never in front of me. My mother wasn't sure that Raisa had even mentioned his name. My grandmother kept a photo of her first husband in a jewelry box, and some years before I was born the photo went missing, or so she claimed. All that I know comes from gossip overheard at family dinners: the two of them were a dashing couple and lived briefly in a large apartment near the center of Kaunas. They danced in Laisvės Alėja's nightclubs, loved cabaret, dined with friends at posh restaurants and cafés. People joked that someday he would be a government minister or a judge. They married less than a year before the Soviet invasion.

A Russian colonel grew so enamored of Raisa that he found her a senior job at the Finance Ministry; the position had been off-limits to Jews only a month earlier. She now had a small staff and, strangest of all, a driver who every morning waited outside her apartment in an idling automobile. Her Soviet supervisor liked Raisa—every boss did—and during the Soviet deportations in June 1941, when several of her husband's friends were arrested, NKVD agents passed over their apartment. The colonel called her a few days later: If the Germans crossed the border, he said, she and her family would be arrested or worse. At the earliest sign of war, she should leave.

On the morning of the German invasion—Sunday, June 22— the ministry driver waited outside her apartment. She squeezed into the car alongside her parents, Ida, Leib, and her cousin Alta, who sat with her four-year-old daughter, Sarah, in her lap. The passengers wedged themselves in amid suitcases, bags, blankets and a pet macaw. Vera, the disowned Communist, had already left the city with her husband and the rest of the fleeing Reds. Raisa's husband made plans to leave the city with his parents; they agreed to reunite in Russia. As the car pulled away, Raisa watched Slobodka recede in the rearview mirror.

Soviet soldiers halted the car at the Belorussian border. Everyone heading east had to travel on foot. Liba and Moishe protested; they said it was madness to walk for miles with no destination. Alta's daughter began to cry. Everyone stood on the side of the road looking at one another searchingly. Eventually half of them decided to turn back and take their chances in Kaunas. Liba wept when she embraced her children, who handed her most of their money. Raisa watched her parents and cousin disappear around a bend in the wooded road. Then she picked up her things and, along with her younger brother and sister, began walking east.

The suitcases were heavy and their food ran out several days later. The settlements they passed looked half-deserted: houses abandoned in a hurry, broken windows, lowing cattle wandering along the roads. They considered turning back but heard that Kaunas was captured, that the Germans were pressing east, close behind. When their money ran out, they bartered their possessions for food. In churches and barns, beside trucks, by the sides of roads, Raisa traded her cameos and silk slips for a day-old loaf of bread or an apron full of underripe apples. The village women tried on the clothes in front of her, out in the open, and if they didn't fit they usually took them anyway. Raisa bartered away fur-trimmed gloves, two hats, Ida's ivory combs, compacts, jewelry and every stitch of underclothes until the suitcases were empty. Then she traded away the suitcases. Her gold wedding ring was the last item to go.

Three weeks after they left Kaunas they were swollen with hunger. Often they didn't know where they were or the day of the week. One day a man with a buckboard who passed them on a dirt road took them as far as a train station. My grandmother thought it was a miracle. They had just enough belongings left between them to trade for three rail tickets.

There was no food aboard the train, and in any case they had nothing left to barter. On their second day, Ida found a heel of stale bread under a berth. They split it three ways, licking the hard crumbs from their palms. They never asked where the train was going. Somewhere they changed trains, then changed again, and stayed aboard as long as they were headed east or south. The cars were crammed with panicked or resigned refugees. When men sidled up to the girls, Leib played the protector, though he was thin and looked barely older than sixteen.

One night Raisa woke with a fever. She'd sweated through her clothes, and a purple rash covered her arms. Ida pressed a moist rag

to her sister's head, but by morning Raisa was delirious. My grandmother told me she couldn't recall what happened next. She remembered only fragments—a cot underneath her, strange hands taking
the food and tea she couldn't manage to swallow from her bedside,
someone in the night rolling her onto her side to take the sheets from
under her.

She came to in a makeshift hospital room. A nurse told her that
she nearly died of typhus and had been delirious for three weeks—
and that she was in Uzbekistan. When Raisa touched her head she
discovered she was bald: while she was unconscious, a nurse had
shaved her head to contain the spread of typhus-infected lice. Ida
was there, too, also shorn of hair—she had been ill with dysentery—
but their brother was gone. While Raisa and Ida were ill, a Red Army
regiment conscripted Leib and took him to the front. The hospital, a
repurposed collective farm, stank of hungry and ragged refugees,
many ill or dying. There was no bread or meat or anything to eat
besides rice and watery melons. An Uzbek orderly who cleaned the
room propositioned Raisa. "Marry me, I've got a gold tooth," he offered, grinning. She and Ida slept side by side with strangers and
woke in the night from hunger pains. "We have to leave," Raisa told
her sister one morning, "or we will die here."

They boarded a train to the Uzbek capital, Tashkent, where they
heard there was a Lithuanian mission. They scraped together enough
money to get halfway there. In their train compartment, a Jewish
family eyed them warily: two bald women wasted and dark-faced
from illness and hunger, dressed in moth-eaten army greatcoats in
sweltering late-August heat. "Watch out for these two," an older
woman on the opposite berth muttered in Yiddish. "They look like
thieves." Raisa smiled. "We're not thieves, just hungry," she replied
in the same language, and soon everyone in the compartment was
talking and laughing. The woman reached into a bag and handed Ida
a cooked potato. The conductor would be coming through to collect
tickets, so Raisa and Ida lay on a lower berth front to back, like forks
in a drawer, while the family covered them with shawls and dresses.

When the conductor walked in, the Jewish woman hushed him—couldn't he see that her elderly mother was asleep under those clothes?

I don't know what happened after my grandmother reached Tashkent. I didn't ask her in time. I know that some time later the sisters were evacuated to a town near the Urals where they worked on a munitions factory assembly line. Elsewhere, Raisa sold soda water spiked with syrup. Eventually, sometime in 1942, she and Ida enlisted in the Red Army's Lithuanian Division. She was twenty-six. She told me about sleeping in tents pitched on the snow and washing soldiers' underclothes in icy rivers, but because I was a child, she didn't tell me that soon after enlisting she learned that her husband had been killed. Many years later, she confided to my mother that she had a Russian lover during the war, a soldier from Moscow named Vassily. After the war, he came to Vilnius to propose to her, but he was a gentile, and she turned him down.

In May 1944, Raisa finally saw her little brother. It happened in a dream: she was walking in a park on a mild sunny day when she saw a boy on a park bench who was wrapped head to toe in white bandages. She knew with a start, the way you do in dreams, that it was Leib. She screamed and sobbed in the dream and woke panting, her face slick with tears and sweat. That afternoon she told Ida about her dream; a few hours later, a clerk walked into her barracks and handed her a telegram that she opened with trembling hands. It read that on May 1, Private Leib Mebelis, aged twenty-two, was killed in action somewhere near Vitebsk.

Months later a man from Leib's company described the events in detail to Raisa. During a German counterattack, the commanding officer asked for a volunteer to repair a torn telephone line in enemy territory. It was a dangerous mission, and two older enlisted men took Leib aside: You don't have a wife or children at home, they said, you go. The telephone line was used to communicate with the division commander, and Leib was sent to repair it three times before he was hit by mortar fire and killed instantly. A subsequent telegram

declared him a hero and awarded him a posthumous medal, presented to Raisa in a plain cardboard box: a sky-blue piece of satin
clipped to a gold-plated brass disk that read, "For Valor."

After the war, Raisa returned to Kaunas. The army helped her
track down her remaining family. Her older sister, Vera, had spent
the war years sewing scarves on a collective farm near the Urals.
Her little cousin Esther had worked on another collective farm in
Uzbekistan. But her zaftig, cheerful cousin Alta had been a prisoner
in the Kaunas ghetto. Raisa barely recognized Alta. Her face was the
color of tallow. They sat together for a while, holding each other.
"Your mother is dead," Alta said quietly, and began to cry.

Gradually, Alta told Raisa what had happened after they parted
in the woods at the Belorussian border four years earlier. Before they
reached Kaunas, a band of Lithuanian paramilitaries shot Moishe
and arrested Liba and Alta. In the ghetto, the two women shared a
room. Alta described how, sometime in 1944, she watched Liba taken
by guards and forced onto a transport. As it turned out, she was taken
to Stutthof, a concentration camp near Danzig, where she died in the
gas chamber.

Not long after finding Alta, Raisa walked over the bridge to Slobodka, to her family's old house on Veiverių Street. The only person
she recognized there was their former Lithuanian handyman. He sat
on the steps of the house smoking a cigarette; they said hello and he
invited her inside. The man offered her tea, and they talked about
what had happened. "What could anyone have done?" he said sheepishly. After she told him goodbye and walked to the door, Raisa noticed that his mattress was covered in her bedsheets.

Several years later, after she settled in Vilnius with my grandfather, they took a bus to Kaišiadorys, the shtetl where she was born.
During the war, the SS had turned it into a labor camp where prisoners from the Kaunas ghetto dug peat in the boggy woods. No one
there remembered her parents, or they claimed not to; the Jewish
families she knew had vanished. None of the hand-painted Yiddish
signs that once lined the streets remained, and no one was left to call

the town by its Yiddish name, Koshedar, which afterward appeared only in books. The signs had only the town's Lithuanian name, Kaišiadorys. My grandmother walked the streets in silence. Her childhood house stood where she remembered it, and she knocked on the door. A Lithuanian family lived there now. The woman who opened the door wore her grandmother's coat.

Raisa was thirty-four when my mother was born. Semyon wanted a boy but found himself overjoyed when he learned they had a daughter. After that war, he once said, who'd want to be born a man? The time for Hebrew names had passed, Semyon and Raisa decided, and they named their daughter Anna, after Tolstoy's heroine. The three of them moved into a four-story art deco building on what had been Zavalnaya Street but was now named Street of the Komsomol. They shared a two-room cold-water flat on the second floor with another married couple, who worked for the city's opera company, and their children, Alfredas and Violetta, named after the tragic lovers in Verdi's opera. As a young girl, my mother played house with Alfredas: he was the father, she the mother, and her plastic monkey, swathed in a hand towel, their infant.

The three children grew up believing they were Russian and that perhaps everyone else was, too. Russian was the language their parents spoke to them, the language of kindergarten and school, of radio announcements and street signs. Other languages were for private adult conversations. It was Alfredas's grandmother who made my mother realize that they were different after all. The old woman was soaping the boy's head in the communal tub when she remarked, in Lithuanian, that the neighbors were Jews. My mother, standing just outside the bathroom door, asked what Jews were; she'd never heard the word. "She understands," the old woman muttered, and said no more. She was known around the building for her uncomfortably frank and cryptic pronouncements. When they met, she announced to Semyon and Raisa that she was a kleptomaniac; on most nights she could be found skulking around the basement, siphoning kerosene from neighbors' heaters.

My mother was eight when Semyon first took her to Kaunas. (Raisa, who after the war moved to Vilnius with her sisters and cousins, despised and feared the smaller city and stayed at home. The only time she consented to return there was years later, for the unveiling of a monument for the victims of the Kaunas ghetto, for which she and Semyon had donated money.) From the train station they took a bus to the top of a verdant, sunny hill and walked to the Žaliakalnis cemetery, where Semyon planned to finally put a headstone on his father's grave. The groundskeeper said that the cemetery's records were destroyed or lost—Semyon would have to find the grave on his own. For the remainder of the day, Semyon led my mother by the hand past rows of marble obelisks, mausoleums and clusters of granite headstones. He paused at every unmarked grave, trying to remember where he'd stood at Haskel's funeral eleven years earlier, a few months before the Soviet deportations and the German invasion.

The sun was low in the trees, and still he hadn't found the grave. In the end, he narrowed it down to three plots. The following morning, he paid for a simple granite stone with Haskel's name, in Russian, and the dates of his birth and death, to be delivered to the cemetery. The groundskeeper asked which of the three graves he wanted it placed on. "Choose one," Semyon told him, and then he took his daughter's hand and began walking toward the wrought-iron gate decorated with the Star of David.

AFTER MY MOTHER and I checked into our hotel in Vilnius, she wanted to walk to the Gate of Dawn. There, in an open-air chapel high above the cobbled street, a priest was conducting a Mass in Polish. Pilgrims come to see the famous icon of the Virgin, said to be a likeness of Barbara Radziwiłł—a noblewoman who had a secret affair with Sigismund II Augustus, became queen and died shortly thereafter, possibly poisoned by the king's mother. In older times, Jews removed their yarmulkes when passing under the gate. Sometimes, if they neglected to or forgot, my mother told me, Christians would snatch them from their heads and nail them to a wall. In Soviet times the worship of the Virgin was disparaged, but as a girl my mother enjoyed watching pilgrims— mostly elderly women from the countryside—prostrate themselves on the cobbles under the Madonna.

During our visit, several hundred pilgrims were gathered at the gate. They knelt in the rain and at points in the service touched their foreheads to the wet cobblestones. Many were outfitted in leather jackets and boots, some with a Harley-Davidson logo on their backs. They were members of a Christian motorcycle club devoted to Our Lady of the Gate of Dawn and had ridden here from Poland. The club's website address was printed on the backs of safety-yellow rain ponchos. Crowded in the narrow street in their bandannas and aviator shades, the bikers looked at once fierce and misplaced, like the road crew of a metal band that had wandered onto the set of a medieval costume drama. When they bowed to the Virgin in unison, a field of chrome rivets flashed before us.

Vilnius's old city, which resembles a miniature Prague, is as delicate as a woodcut. As we walked down its side streets, I tried to picture what it must have looked like in the years just after the war, during my mother's childhood. Even today, Vilnius has a tendency to peter out: if you walk long enough, a street will unexpectedly become an unpaved road surrounded by low ramshackle wooden houses and courtyards. You might see a water pump or chickens skittering across the grass. The city my mother remembered from childhood was full of crumbling masonry and bulldozed lots where crabgrass and dandelions grew, a place haunted by the war's passage. One morning when she was five or six, Semyon took her to a bookstore. They were browsing the shelves when they heard what sounded like thunder and then saw the windows go black. A five-story building across the street, derelict since the occupation, had collapsed.

As we walked around the city, my mother remarked that hardly anything had changed. It was a peculiar comment. She seemed to barely notice the glass-and-steel office towers north of the river, or the cellular-phone storefronts and European clothing chains that dotted the avenues. Eventually we reached the squat town house where she lived as a child. The street it stood on was named Pylimo now; the building's dirty mustard facade was inscribed with the year of its construction, 1912.

My mother knocked on the door and a startled young man in a white undershirt opened the door and invited us inside, amused at visitors from the distant past. My mother walked around the apartment, her hands in front of her as though feeling her way in the dark. She gently stepped into the doorway of the room she'd shared with her parents. It was carpeted in green shag; beside a futon, a humming computer sat on a card table like an altarpiece.

My mother's earliest memories are populated mostly by cousins and aunts. As a young child she saw her parents infrequently and, for several years, hardly at all. Soon after she was born, Semyon began work on a doctorate at Moscow State University—there wasn't a qualified neurophysiologist to supervise him in the Baltics—and lived in the Soviet capital for months at a time. After attending economics classes at the university, Raisa found a job at a government bureau in charge of food production. She conducted audits at far-flung factories and was rarely home before my mother's bedtime, though she returned from these trips with her blue patent-leather handbag bursting with candy and wafers for her daughter.

After Semyon returned from Moscow, he stayed at home writing the first of his dissertations, and most of the child care fell to him. His childish temperament made him an ideal playmate. He convinced my mother that he'd worked in a circus, and to prove it he performed magic tricks and even juggled, though badly. He composed impromptu poems about a mischievous boy named Vovka and, when my mother was five, taught her to read and draw. They walked everywhere in the city together—to the Pioneer movie theater, to the farmers' market near the railway station, to the chess club on Lenin Square. Sometimes he called her by a boy's name, Andriusha, and wrestled with her as though she were a boy. She sat on his lap while he typed and nagged him to draw horses for her, and usually he complied, whistling Verdi themes while he did it. Instead of fairy tales he told her about his parents' large house in Utena, where Frida put on plays and the cook brought him soft-boiled eggs in the mornings and there were cut flowers in every room.

As a child, my mother spent most afternoons at the homes of Raisa's sisters and cousins, who lived within a short walk of one another near the city's old Jewish quarter. She liked visiting her mother's cousin Esther, who had a son her age, and to play with Ida's friendly, nearsighted daughters. Vera lived in a new cinder-block tower on the city's edge. Her Lithuanian husband had perished with his company in a German blockade and was posthumously proclaimed a Hero of the Soviet Union. As a hero's widow, Vera was awarded a private hot-water flat. Instead of visiting the public bathhouse, where families lashed each other with twigs, on weekends Raisa took my mother to her older sister's apartment on Shevchenko Street for the pleasure of a private bath.

Then there was my mother's childless aunt Alta. She was round and mirthful; she baked and to everyone's delight turned up at family gatherings with warm cookies, cakes, and loud, girlish embraces. When a waltz or a Russian romance came on the radio, Alta capered around the living room, her arms framing an invisible partner, and warbled along in a birdlike, sentimental soprano. The only times she became tight-lipped and glum were around my mother, who for years assumed her aunt simply didn't like her. Alta fed her dutifully and looked in on her from time to time, but did no more, disappearing into her bedroom until Raisa relieved her.

I was already born by the time my mother learned the reason for Alta's aloofness. Three years before the war, Alta gave birth to a dark-haired, green-eyed girl she named Sarah. In the Kaunas ghetto, they shared a bed, sleeping a few steps from Liba, who helped take care of the girl. On the morning of March 27, 1944, armed men arrived in panel trucks to round up the children. The Germans referred to their planned mass killings as "actions," and none became more notorious than the Children's Action. Witnesses recalled that the wailing and screaming of the Jewish mothers could be heard on the streets for hours afterward.

A ghetto policeman came for Sarah that morning, shouting orders in Polish, but Alta refused to hand her over. They wound up on the street, and following a scuffle Alta picked up her six-year-old daughter and ran. The policeman raised his carbine and shot. The bullet pierced Alta's left arm and Sarah's chest. Sarah died instantly in her mother's arms. Alta fainted. She woke in the ghetto infirmary, sobbing and screaming until she vomited and choked; for days she couldn't keep down food or water. A doctor decided that she'd become psychotic and injected her with sedatives for weeks.

In 1971, while my mother was a university student and at home during a holiday, Alta took her aside and told her this story. Alta said it had been difficult for her to be around my mother, because as a child she looked so much like her own daughter.

FROM MY FIRST visit, I was enchanted by Vilnius, with its pygmy churches and gambrel roofs—the first examples of non-Soviet architecture I'd seen. I thought of the city as a Gothic settlement on the border with the mythical West, a place mysterious and spellbinding in the manner of fairy tales. But there was something else about Vilnius that I didn't understand until years later. While visiting my grandparents as a five- or six-year-old, I met a boy my age in their courtyard. "Are you a Jew?" he asked. It wasn't a question I'd heard before, and I said I didn't know. It was the truth. But from my grandparents' reaction I became aware of the undercurrents of fear and hatred that existed between the city's Christians and Jews, which to me—a child of Socialism—seemed as archaic as the city's architecture. And I sensed my mother's dread and unease whenever she visited the city or even spoke about it. She often told me that nothing about Vilnius was magical.

Her childhood stories are inhabited by a free-floating menace. My mother had been too young to remember Semyon being fired from his teaching job at Vilnius University, several weeks before he was scheduled to defend his dissertation. No official reason was given, but it was understood by all. It was 1952, and Stalin had revived the worst of the government's anti-Semitic rhetoric, sparking purges around the country; it was amplified to a frenzy the following spring and summer, when a group of Jewish doctors was accused of a conspiracy to murder Stalin.

Semyon and Raisa feared the worst—a return to the persecution of the war years—and came up with a plan. Semyon's old friend, a tall, bald-headed lawyer named Balevičius, would take my three-year-old mother to live with his elderly parents in the countryside. They'd bleach her brown hair yellow and give her their surname. Balevičius—a Lithuanian who grew up in a shtetl and spoke fluent Yiddish—married a Jewish neighbor's daughter and spent the years of the German occupation teaching math to village schoolchildren and hiding his wife's identity. After the war, when a Russian neighbor called her a *žhidovka*—a kike—Balevičius kicked in the man's basement windows and spent several months in jail for vandalism.

The most unsettling of my mother's stories takes place sometime in the mid-1950s, when the body of a five-year-old Lithuanian girl who was raped and strangled was discovered in a Vilnius basement. During the widely publicized search for her killer, the old talk began to make its way around the city: a Jew had murdered the girl to use her blood in religious rituals. For weeks, a black, retaliatory mood hung over the city's shops, playgrounds and classrooms. It was said the mayor called for troops to be garrisoned on the city's outskirts, in preparation for riots.

The talk died down after the killer was found. He was a troubled twentysomething Lithuanian, the son of a biology professor named Petrila who happened to teach in my grandfather's department at the university. The killer confessed his crime to his father and soon after bled to death in a bathtub, after his mother, the professor's former wife, helped cut his wrists. After Petrila went to the police and his son's identity became public, he was condemned by party officials for failing to turn him in earlier; he was stripped of his apartment and job, and ordered to relocate to a collective farm.

Professor Petrila was a family friend. He came to see my grandparents one last time, to say goodbye and ask for money. After a brief conversation, Semyon left; when he returned less than an hour later, he handed Petrila a thick roll of bills, his entire savings. Not much older than the strangled girl, my mother watched this unfold while eating breakfast. I've thought often about how close she was to the worst of what transpired between the Lithuanians, Russians and Jews in that country, to the rift that will never close, while watching the wretched visitor in her parents' kitchen.

In time, the worst of the foreboding lifted. My mother wasn't sent to the country or made to bleach her hair. Balevičius become rector of Vilnius University's law school. Stalin's death brought an eventual end to the most extreme anti-Semitic propaganda. Several months after Stalin's funeral, in what seems to me now to be an act of astonishing bravado, Semyon sued the university for wrongful termination and, to nearly everyone's surprise, was reinstated. He remained there for another twenty-seven years.

My mother remembers the years that followed as a period of relative plenty and calm, attested to by the details of her stories. There was the boiler Semyon installed sometime in the early 1960s, and the Old Believer women who helped Raisa with the housework, and the cabin in the country they rented every July and August. That cabin near Valakampiai Beach had a vegetable patch, a crank well and an elderly landlady, a Polish woman everyone called Pani Verpakhovska, who made a habit of talking loudly to her five cats. Ida and Esther rented adjacent cabins, and my mother remembers spending the long summer days playing with her cousins in the woods. One summer, after they read *The Last of the Mohicans,* she and her cousin Grisha smeared their faces with shoe polish, made skirts from oak leaves and decorated their hair with feathers pulled from Esther's hat. Then they climbed into an oak and whooped and hollered at passersby, pretending to be Indians.

The extended family gathered for holidays and celebrations, usually at Ida's second-floor apartment. Raisa's younger sister was the family's best cook and had a knack for entertaining, and in those postwar years family celebrations had grown to include my grandmother's sisters and cousins and their husbands and children. Not long ago, my mother told me about a birthday (she didn't remember whose) when she was five or six. It was well after midnight, and everyone had eaten,

drunk, and danced. Not quite ready to say goodbye, the adults sat dozing in their chairs. Only cousin Esther was in the kitchen, rattling the dishes. The children slept in the other room, except for my mother, who fell asleep nestled in the corner of the sofa. Sometime in the night, she opened her eyes; startled from sleep by a sound or a dream, she began to study the room.

Her mother's oldest sister, Vera, sat by herself, already buttoned into her coat with the chinchilla collar, her mouth set in a dour hyphen even in sleep. Ida, the hostess, blinked away sleep while dozing on the shoulder of her husband, Chaim, whom no one considered a genius but who had a fine singing voice and a closetful of rakish suits. Raisa reclined on the sofa beside my mother, who'd laid her head in Semyon's lap. In the middle of the room, two tables had been moved together, covered with a tablecloth and set with the abundance of those years: remnants of herring in sour cream (in Russian, "herring in a fur coat"), Ida's famous gefilte fish, beef stewed with prunes and carrots, horseradish, rye bread, challah, Esther's homemade eclairs, orange rinds cooked in sugar. There was a bottle of vodka and a bottle of red wine. There were teacups on matching saucers, a blue porcelain teapot, a siphon of seltzer, a tiny pitcher of milk, lemon slices fanned out in a saucer, a sugar bowl painted with primroses, two cut-glass vases filled with pussy willows and mimosas. There were framed family photos on the walls, wood carvings decorated with Lithuanian amber, a tear-sheet calendar that was two days late, a miniature menorah, an ugly clock made of fake malachite and brass. There was, perhaps oddest of all, a tapestry on the wall depicting a man in a three-cornered hat gallantly helping a woman in eighteenth-century dress across a stream. There were books on a shelf, homemade sea-green curtains that billowed in the breeze, a coatrack, an umbrella stand holding dried cattails but no umbrellas, and on the wall a pearly oval mirror in which the women took turns fixing their makeup and the men made a point to avoid.

In the corner there was a radio, a blond wooden console on tapering legs topped with a rabbit-ear antenna, the front a panel of smoked glass with two large Bakelite knobs. It was lit and quietly played one of those big-band things still popular in the mid-1950s, maybe "Bésame Mucho" or "Moscow Nights." Alta, the aunt who rarely smiled at my mother, the childless one who lost her daughter in the ghetto, danced by herself in the lamplight. She moved her hips under a heavy pleated skirt, tugging on the corners of an imaginary shawl in time to the music. She kept her neatly penciled eyes closed. She turned slightly on the beat, flinging her skirt behind her. Only my mother saw her. The orchestra played on, the woozy saxophones giving way to trumpets and back again, a drum beating somewhere behind them. Alta danced there, beside the glowing console and the billowing curtains, danced for a long time possibly, or at least until my mother, yawning on the sofa, closed her eyes.

A NEWLY MINTED professor at the university, Semyon managed to find his daughter a spot at the city's top school, among children of local party officials and the well connected. The desk beside my mother's was occupied by the son of Lithuania's party chief. The boy next to him was the son of the commander of the republic's Red Army division. My mother found it lonely and oppressive. Her closest friend was a sharp-featured tomboy named Giedre. In after-school confabs they railed against the cow-eyed blondes who cooked and knit and fantasized about their wedding days. My mother disliked the school even after the other girls were forced to acknowledge that she was pretty, and invited her to parties where the popular couples smoked cigarettes and got drunk on apple wine and danced to reel-to-reel bootlegs of Connie Francis and Paul Anka.

After a drawing of hers won a citywide competition, my mother looked forward most to art class, and spent the rest of her time reading. Sometime in the eighth grade, she also began to attend an after-school literature club overseen by her favorite teacher, a melancholy transplant from Russia with close-cropped hair and thick glasses named Rosa Vladimirovna. In time, Rosa confided in my mother about her own parents, who'd been newspaper editors in Moscow. They were arrested and shot in 1937, at the height of the Great Terror, and she spent the remainder of her childhood in an orphanage in the bleak city of Gorky, named after the author of popular socialist realist novels. In violation of school policy, she made the club read Anna Akhmatova, Marina Tsvetaeva and Osip Mandelstam, the great poets of the silver age who'd run afoul of Stalin. The Vilnius poet Tomas Venclova—already known as a dissident in his mid-twenties, tall and slim, decked out in sweaters and a black beret—visited the club and told a classroom of thirteen-year-olds about Tsvetaeva's suicide and Mandelstam's madness and eventual death in a forced-labor camp. "Have you stopped to consider," he asked the students, "that not one of our great poets has died of natural causes?"

During these after-school meetings, my mother began to sense the weight and darkness of the place and time in which she lived. This realization ignited in her a fierce adolescent contempt for the official Soviet versions of history and culture taught in her classes. Yet she was also learning how fortunate she was. In those years, she thought often about a wartime story her aunt Esther had told her. One day, when Esther was seventeen and lived on a collective farm in Uzbekistan, she absentmindedly doodled a pair of horns on a photograph of Stalin that appeared on a newspaper's front page. After a roommate denounced her, two NKVD agents drove her to a windowless office and questioned her for hours. In the end, they didn't arrest her only because she was an orphan and not yet eighteen. My mother thought about Esther's story while contemplating her own life; she realized how lucky she was to have been born after the purges and the war were over.

My mother was aware of being different, though at first she didn't know why. After all, wasn't the Soviet Union a classless state where everyone had a common nationality, where religion had been discredited as a superstition? Once or twice she heard a classmate mutter that Hitler didn't finish his job, but outright slurs like these were rare. Plenty of subtler clues abounded. She noticed the stares and the silences that greeted her at assemblies and school dances, and later she came to recognize the graver, hooded glances of adults.

She was still a child, and in Vilnius only children had the privilege of not knowing about the past, which lay just below the surface of the provincial city's unhurried daily routines. Hardly fifteen years had passed since the remains of eighty or ninety thousand, most of them local Jews, were buried in forest clearings seven kilometers southwest of Vilnius, in a scenic spot called Ponary, where before the war families came to picnic. The German command chose it because of the deep pits that Russian soldiers had dug there to store their gasoline and diesel. Like much about Lithuania's recent past, everyone knew about Ponary, but now hardly anyone spoke its name. As my mother's understanding of this history grew, she began to loathe the pretty baroque city where she was born, where secrets lay in plain view for anyone who cared to see them.

The dream of the Yiddishists had been discredited. The Jews who remained in Lithuania knew that this country could never again be a homeland. Ida and her daughters were the first members of the family to emigrate; my mother was fifteen when she hugged them goodbye at the airport. Esther and her family followed them to Israel four years later. Soon Vera, her children, and Alta left, too. By the time I was five, my mother and her parents were the last of Raisa's family to remain in the Soviet Union. My mother implored her parents to leave—for Israel or the United States or Australia or, really, anywhere else *out there*. She believed that the answer to her and her parents' unhappiness lay across the closed border where the sun set over the Baltic.

They remained in Vilnius because of Semyon. On weekdays, he sat hunched over stacks of folders, laboring at a postdoctoral dissertation that was ever tantalizingly close to being finished. There were books and scientific papers half-written or waiting to be started, and he was perpetually on the verge of a breakthrough that would mean a more prosperous situation for all of them. My mother argued with him almost daily, furious at him for keeping them anchored in the claustrophobic city, even more than for the infidelities he was inept at concealing even from his daughter. My mother had grown into a stubborn, proud adolescent, and she judged Semyon with the righteous, unambiguous morality of the young.

To make matters worse, as a careerist Semyon was hopeless. The discretion and tact he lacked in youth hadn't come with age. He was incapable of being civil with colleagues he deplored, and spoke to his superiors at the university with a frankness that bordered on rudeness. At a faculty mixer, he drank glass after glass of vodka on an empty stomach and suffered the first of three heart attacks, leaving the room on a gurney. He published constantly—twelve books and dozens of articles—but his bluntness and tendency to veer away from safe topics of conversation kept the promotions and prizes he longed for out of reach.

Semyon was least pleasant around his first cousin, a son of Frida's older sister, who visited several times a year. These visits might have been cheerful occasions, because Valery Kirpotin was among the few surviving members of Semyon's family. He was also, by any measure, important. Kirpotin was a revolutionary nom de guerre; the surname he was born with was Rabinovich. He'd been a frontline believer in the Bolshevik cause, and in the Soviet Union's early years served as a personal secretary to Maxim Gorky, the country's most famous novelist. Later, he became one of the country's chief literary critics.

Though Kirpotin was a Dostoevsky scholar, he numbered among the chief custodians of socialist realist aesthetics and ideology. In official journals, he censured fellow writers and critics for their anti-Soviet tendencies, for praising the wrong authors, and for imitating the bourgeois West. He had solidified his views while taking the minutes at Gorky's meetings with Stalin, and to the end of his life remained personally involved in the production, reception and censorship of Soviet literature.

My grandfather's first cousin lived in a palatial apartment in Moscow and traveled in a chauffeured limousine. His brother, another former Bolshevik named Sergei Dalin, became a prominent economist who studied China and the United States. At the height of Kirpotin's influence, Dalin was arrested and sentenced to twenty years at a forced-labor camp. This was in keeping with Stalin's habit of arresting the spouses, siblings and children of the members of his inner circle and other prominent figures, to ensure they remained pliable and loyal.

My mother looked forward to Kirpotin's visits, because her famous uncle—who spoke to her seriously about authors and books, and encouraged her reading—was the only member of the family who treated her like an adult. There's a photo of them taken in a park in a small town called Ignalina. Kirpotin, holding a wide-brimmed hat, sits beside his wife; his brother Dalin and their aunt Tania sit next to them; my mother stands behind the bench next to Frosia, her parents' blond housekeeper.

Kirpotin was a yeshiva student from a shtetl who rose to become one of the nation's leading official intellectuals, but this was something Semyon chose not to acknowledge, treating his cousin with suspicion and habitual scorn. At suppers, they argued loudly, their two-tiered Levin noses facing off across the table like duelists in a glade. These quarrels lasted late into the night, fanned by Kirpotin's party-line pronouncements, which Semyon dismissed as "Commissar horseshit." In the mornings, the two of them were sulky and avoided each other, the ill feeling sometimes lasting for months. I don't know whether Semyon realized what a grave risk his anti-Communist pronouncements posed to him and his family, but in any case he continued to ventilate them in his cousin's presence, unchastened. "When you see a crowd running in one direction," he once told my mother, "run in the other."

BY THE TIME I began visiting my grandparents, they had moved from the center of Vilnius to an outlying neighborhood called Antakalnis. Their private three-room apartment was located in a cluster of buildings that were designed by a Swedish architect and were therefore considered chic. My mother lived there for several years before graduating from school with a valedictorian's medal and escaping to Moscow, her temporary stand-in for Jerusalem, Sydney or New York.

Semyon turned my mother's former bedroom into a laboratory, and as a child I spent my summer afternoons there, assisting him with his experiments. Most often, he dissected frogs. He made incisions in the animal's dorsal skin, attached electrodes to the two main columns of nerves running along the animal's spine, then prodded the frog with a menagerie of tools. All the while a tremulous metal arm recorded the frog's involuntary responses as squiggles of ink on a rotating paper ribbon. Semyon insisted the experiments were humane. He etherized the frogs before brandishing his surgical scissors and afterward snuffed them by pushing a pin through their brains.

What I remember best about his laboratory are the sounds: the croaking of frogs in their jars along the baseboard, the cawing of birds in their cages, the whir of the steel drums that turned the paper ribbon, the ingratiating chatter of graduate students who always agreed to stay for supper, the white noise of soccer games on the living room television. Sometimes Raisa hollered from the kitchen to ask Semyon to take out the trash or perform some other domestic chore. At these moments he nodded vaguely, without taking his eyes off of his work, and replied, barely loud enough for her to hear, "Dear, I haven't any idea what you're talking about."

His absentmindedness was storied. Every day he lumbered around the apartment searching frantically for eyeglasses that he'd pushed up onto his forehead. In the mornings, he made soft-boiled eggs, which he'd loved since childhood. At least once a month, after dropping the eggs into the boiling water, he began thinking about work and stepped out for a leisurely twenty-five-minute stroll. Walking, he said, helped him think. When he returned, the eggs had exploded in their scorched pot. Once, when he was leaving the apartment on his way to deliver a lecture, Semyon remembered that he'd forgotten to put on a tie and stuck one in his pocket. He knotted it on the bus without the aid of a mirror. After his lecture, a student approached him and shyly asked, "Professor, why are you wearing two neckties?"

Sometimes, when he went to work, he brought me along. By his estimation, he'd lectured to some thirty-five thousand students. This included most of the city's physicians, and he ran into them everywhere. On nearly every block someone would say hello or nod in greeting. Many of Semyon's students, whom I met even after coming to New York, remembered him best for his lack of squeamishness. While instructing a class in drawing blood, my grandfather rolled up a sleeve and laid his arm, palm up, on a desk. He ate a sandwich and paged through a book on zoology while a line of thirty trainee doctors waited their turn to puncture his vein with a jumbo Soviet hypodermic. He looked down only occasionally to offer a pointer.

Inside a yellow neo-baroque building on campus, Semyon operated a small zoological museum. Its three rooms housed a whale whisker, a taxidermied wolverine, a huge spotted crustacean of the genus *Homarus,* some mastodon bones, and a vitrine of humming-birds containing several white-vented violetears from South America, their thumb-size iridescent bodies pinned to black velvet. While poring over a case of glossy bugs, I decided that when I grew up I would become an expert on the Colorado potato beetle. The orange-and-brown-striped insect looked reassuringly predacious and, best of all, came from America. I was seven and told my grandfather about my plan. "Naturally," Semyon replied, nodding. "You're a man, not some chicken-brained woman, and one day you, too, will be a scientist." With this he locked the museum door with an old-fashioned key he carried on a large ring, took my hand in his, and walked with me to the elevator.

ON THE DAY after we arrived in Vilnius, my mother and I located Haskel's office, at 12 Calvary Street, where her grandparents once extracted teeth with cast-iron pliers. A hand-lettered sign in front of the boutique on the building's ground floor announced a sale on women's underwear. We walked past my mother's school, which she said looked the same—the bust of the futurist poet for whom it was named still stood near the entrance. We wandered around the Jewish quarter, along Glassmakers' Street and Jews' Street, then stopped to look at a barely noticeable stone marking the spot where the Vilna Gaon's house had stood.

After the lights went on in the cafés and beer gardens, illuminating their yellow and green umbrellas, I walked my mother to the restaurant where she was meeting her friends. Forty-two years after she graduated from school, she was attending her first reunion. Seeing a group of women standing outside the restaurant, she broke into a run. There was a flurry of kisses and embraces, and then the women stood together on the sidewalk, their arms draped around each other's waists, wiping away tears.

Gradually, they filled my mother in about her classmates. The bright skinny girl everyone liked, who became a television journalist, died of cirrhosis in her forties. Another was homebound with complications from diabetes. The pretty buxom blonde everyone envied in the tenth grade lived in Germany now and had emailed. The women said that the girls had fared better than the boys, more than half of whom were dead—some of alcohol, one by suicide, several from heart disease. And the boy with the sleepy eyes everyone wanted to dance with, the slender one with the straight brown hair, took his boat out on a lake and, after drinking all day, fell overboard and drowned. He was barely forty. Some of the women had been at his funeral. "But it is wonderful to see you," they told my mother, and the tears started up again. At last the women linked arms behind my mother's back and walked into the restaurant. I waved goodbye and headed back to our hotel.

The following morning her friend Giedre took us to the tower overlooking the city. The Lithuanian tricolor waved at the summit, visible for kilometers. According to the earliest histories, King Jogaila's grandfather Gediminas brought a hunting party to Šventaragis valley, as the land around us was called, and killed an aurochs. That night, in a vivid dream, he saw a huge wolf—made of iron, plated in iron armor—howling atop the peak where he had made the kill. It sounded as though hundreds of wolves howled inside it. In the morning, the pagan high priest Lizdeika interpreted the dream. He told Gediminas that a city hard as iron and fierce as the cries of wolves would be founded on the spot. We looked down at Vilnius from the stone tower Gediminas built there; the city, as filigreed as an antique chess set, lay under a low, storm-colored sky.

Below us, we could see the pontifical rectangle of the reconstructed cathedral, the old city's cupolas and spires, mid-rise tenements in the suburban distances, the smoky silver ribbon of the Neris, and on the far side of the river, an implacable cement expanse of a Soviet sports arena. It was raised on the site of the Shnipishok cemetery, a Jewish burial ground dating back to the fifteenth century. Many tombstones there, dotted with Lions of Judah, had grown unreadable. Before it was razed in 1949, Soviet authorities allowed the local Jews to salvage the remains of only seven graves. Naturally, one belonged to the Vilna Gaon. When they opened his grave, members of the Jewish holy society claimed that his corpse had not decayed, that even the hairs on the Gaon's beard remained intact.

They moved his remains to Dembovka, a newer Jewish cemetery in a forlorn section of Vilnius. The Gaon's mausoleum stands there today. The slab over his tomb is littered with moldering notes in Hebrew and Yiddish, beseeching the saint to intercede on behalf of the city's few remaining Jews and visitors from abroad.

The ashes of the *ger tzedek*—the possibly apocryphal Righteous Proselyte—lay nearby. The strange title was given to a Pole, Count Valentin Potocki, who in the mid-eighteenth century committed the unheard-of act of converting to Judaism and took the somewhat showy name Avraham ben Avraham. After he ignored his parents' pleas to renounce the heathen faith—they even offered to build him a castle where he could practice his religion in peace—Catholic authorities sentenced him to death. The Gaon reportedly visited him in prison and even offered to help spring him from his cell. But Potocki decided to die a martyr. The Jews of Vilnius said kaddish for him on the day he was burned at the stake, the second day of Shavuot, 1749. A strange twisted tree, said to resemble a human body, grew up on the spot where he was buried in Shnipishok cemetery. After vandals broke off its branches, the Jews erected an iron enclosure around it. The pious and superstitious claimed that the tree would dry up when misfortune threatened the city's Jews. It could still be seen there in 1941, shortly before the Nazis arrived, when someone cut it down.

When Semyon was a child, cantors wandered the lanes of Shnip-ishok, offering to chant on behalf of visitors' dead relatives for a few groschen. A gravestone there read, "Stop and look! You're still a visitor; I'm at home." After Soviet bulldozers leveled the cemetery, the gravestones were used to build a stairway cut into the side of a nearby hill. If you look at these steps today, you can still read the names of the dead.

And so the metropolis of synagogues, ritual baths and slaughter-houses, Yiddish theaters and cafés—the most thriving Jewish city in the diaspora—gradually vanished. After the Jews were gone, the remnants of their culture were methodically erased. On a side street near the building where my mother's aunt Ida had lived, I was sur-prised to find the outlines of Yiddish letters above the ground-floor windows. They were barely visible, ghostly under a thin coat of white paint.

The staunchest reminder of Jewish Vilnius perches on a hill above Paménkalnio Street. The oddly georgic wooden house looks like a village general store. Most everybody calls it the Green House, though it's formally known as the Jewish State Museum of Lithua-nia. In its handful of rooms, its single permanent exhibit, titled *The Catastrophe*, documents the abrupt end of Jewish Vilnius. Not many original objects are on display at the Green House because of a lack of funding; most of the photographs and documents on the walls are photocopies.

A blown-up reproduction of the Jäger Report occupies an entire wall. When my mother and I visited the Green House, I stood in front of it for a long while and read the actuarial tallies of the dead.

The entry for Utian, the town where Semyon's family lived, enumerated the liquidation carried out there on July 31, 1941: "235 Jews, 16 Jewesses, 4 Lithuanian Communists, 1 robber, 1 murderer." From a week later, another tally: "483 Jews, 87 Jewesses, 1 Lithuanian (robber of corpses of German soldiers)." The entry for Raisa's hometown, Koshedar, was more succinct: "1,911: all Jews, Jewesses, and Jewish children."

Across the street from the Green House, a newish sign points the way to the Museum of Genocide Victims, a far grander institution. It's located in a neoclassical tsarist courthouse that once served as a headquarters of the Gestapo and, after the war, became a KGB prison. The Genocide and Resistance Research Center of Lithuania conducts its work next door. The exhibits inside document the deportation, jailing and political repression of ethnic Lithuanians by the Soviets—the genocide in the museum's name. Among the items on display, there are grainy photographs of protesting dissidents, a collection of KGB pamphlets and correspondence, and a Soviet general's hat. Only a few of the long explanatory placards mention Lithuania's Jews.

The double genocide narrative, as it's become known—the notion that everyone suffered equally during the war—has become the key rationale in the government's refusal to acknowledge Lithuanians' role in the Holocaust or to put Nazi collaborators on trial. In 2007, this narrative sprouted a bizarre appendage. That year, the country's chief prosecutor finally launched a war-crimes investigation. Oddly, its targets weren't local Nazi collaborators but rather Jews—two women and a man in their eighties—who survived the Vilnius ghetto. In the early 1940s, the prosecutor alleged, they'd participated in attacks on ethnic Lithuanians. The accused didn't deny it. During the war they were members of the Jewish resistance, and the Lithuanians in question worked for the SS. One of the accused was a former chairman of Yad Vashem, the Holocaust memorial in Jerusalem. Another was a family friend—a grandmother of six who taught biology alongside Semyon at Vilnius University. Newspaper editorials urged the government to bring the case against the octogenarians to trial. Local news coverage referred to them as "terrorists."

With Lithuania's economy foundering, a mood of asperity hung over the beautiful Baltic nation, a member of the European Union and NATO, now independent for nearly twenty years. In Vilnius, someone spray-painted *"Juden Raus"* on the city's last remaining synagogue; someone else left a severed pig's head on the steps of another shul in Kaunas. In 2009, the country's third-largest daily, *Respublika*, published a front-page editorial. A cartoon that accompanied it showed two men shouldering a globe. One was black-hatted, hook-nosed and fat, the other mascaraed and tan, his muscled body covered only by a thong. The editorial—headlined "Who Really Runs the World?"—averred that Jews and homosexuals were conspiring to destroy Lithuania's economy. Three days later—alleging a groundswell of interest and support from its readers—*Respublika* reprinted the cartoon on its front page.

The cartoon was one of the topics of conversation in the vast book-lined apartment of Dovid Katz, where I came after visiting the Green House. Katz was one of the few public figures in Lithuania who insisted on talking about the Holocaust, and I wanted to meet him. He was an eminent linguist who'd taught at Yale and Oxford, and came to Vilnius in the 1990s to create a Yiddish institute, a major accomplishment for the provincial university where my grandfather had taught. Then, offering no explanation, the university fired Katz. He insisted that he was terminated because he'd written editorials defending the accused elderly Jewish partisans, and lobbied European and American diplomats on their behalf. "The problem is that no one here is willing to speak up against these abuses," said Katz, refilling my champagne flute.

With his ample belly, black wardrobe, and fulminating black beard, Katz looked remarkably like a Russian Orthodox priest; on visits to Belarus and Ukraine, kerchiefed women sometimes fell to their knees in front of him and kissed his hand. He happened to be the son of a well-known Yiddish poet from Brooklyn. At the party he was hosting, he made introductions and waltzed between an official from the Holocaust Memorial Museum in Washington, D.C., a British journalist, and the American ambassador to Lithuania, a vigorous-looking woman in a pleated navy skirt who wore a State Department pin on her lapel. Someone nearby was discussing a pair of laws the government had enacted recently. One punished "denying or minimizing either of the two genocides" with a two-year prison sentence; the other legalized the swastika as a "symbol of national significance."

A German consular worker was telling a pair of visiting Swedes about the recent gay pride parade. It was only the second in the Baltics and prompted the government of Vilnius to cordon the route with barricades and helmeted riot police. About three hundred marchers, mostly women and foreigners, were met by several thousand protesters who pelted them with rocks, raw sausage and smoke bombs. Two members of Parliament jumped the barricades and were restrained by police. Some in the crowd were skinheads; others waved the flag of the Third Reich. Since arriving in Vilnius, I was acutely aware of being in a European capital with a single gay bar, a place where attacks on gay men and women were nearly as common as homophobic jokes at otherwise decorous dinner parties, and this compounded a sensation that many in this city were living in a past they were unable or unwilling to reckon with.

At Dovid Katz's apartment, I stood with the flute in hand and spoke to the U.S. ambassador's husband, a trim man with the blandly handsome face and fastidious manner of a career diplomat. He looked like someone who spent most of his life in a suit. The one he wore looked impeccable. He talked at length about the "situation on the ground." Naturally, he assured me, it was complex. There were geopolitical realities and economic vagaries to consider, and of course the history—that was complex, too. After the humiliation of the war and numerous foreign occupations, he told me, people here needed to feel in control of their destiny. They needed to feel proud. It was a phrase I'd heard often in Moscow, usually attributed to Putin. The people of

Moscow, too, needed to feel proud of their history, even if that history had to be redacted to better accommodate their pride. The American diplomat spoke discursively, in low even tones that made what he said difficult to follow, which I began to realize was the point.

AT THE GREEN House, a squat potbellied man in his late fifties walked up to my mother and me and asked where we were from. He asked this question provocatively and too loudly, fixing us with close-set brown eyes. A T-shirt pulled snugly over his stomach read, "Shalom from New York." His name was Efraim Gartman. He offered it non-committally, along with the information that he was a guide and amateur genealogist from Kaunas. When my mother mentioned that her parents had lived there, he raised an eyebrow and asked, "Jews?" His avidity was slightly off-putting. I nodded and said we were looking for information. "Then it's decided," Gartman exclaimed, grabbing our forearms like a long-lost relative. "Tomorrow you will come to Kaunas." He wrote down a street corner and said to meet him there at ten the following morning.

We found a ride to Kaunas with a nephew of my mother's classmate, an out-of-work economist named Arunas. His reading glasses magnified his eyes into quivering pale saucers over a severely tucked-in short-sleeved shirt. He studied us in his Škoda's rearview mirror, shyly at first but with genuine interest. During the hour-long drive, women standing along the road sold plastic containers of wild strawberries and chanterelles. Somewhere along the way, Arunas volunteered that a friend of his, an internist, had been a student of Semyon's.

"Your grandfather sounds like he was a funny man," Arunas said. According to the friend, Semyon was notorious for a story he told his students about being a soldier in Berlin shortly after the Allied victory. "Your grandfather used to say, 'There we were—Halberstadt, Shapiro and Gutman—Lithuanian soldiers walking through Berlin singing Lithuanian songs.'" With this his shoulders bobbed up and down with silent laughter. "Imagine—Halberstadt, Shapiro and Gutman—some Lithuanians!"

Efraim Gartman stood waiting at the appointed corner, glancing impatiently at his wristwatch. Arunas parked a block from Laisvės Alėja, alongside a concrete cube that housed the city archives, and reclined his seat to take a nap. It was a balmy Friday morning. Inside, the receptionist glared at Gartman, as though expecting him. She informed us that the chief archivist was out with a cold and that we'd have to return the following week. Gartman winked at us. Ignoring the receptionist, he shouldered his way into a low-ceilinged office and sat us down in front of a woman in a mohair cardigan. She looked up at him with the mien of someone who'd long ago given up arguing with his requests. "Hello, Efraim," she said.

Gartman informed the archivist that we were looking for two families who had lived in Kaunas, and reluctantly she agreed to help us. I wrote the names of Semyon and Raisa's parents and siblings on a slip of paper and told her what I knew. She said to come back in thirty minutes and disappeared through a side door. When we returned, she gestured at a tray of yellowing paper. "No Halberstadts," she announced. When they relocated to Kaunas, their records probably remained in Utena, she told us, and nearly all of the small-town ledgers and documents were lost in the war. "But I found some Mebelises."

She handed over a tray with three yellowed identity cards. Filled out in ink, they contained my mother's family's names, addresses

and photos. Raisa's brother—aged eighteen, clean-cut, handsome, in a dark suit jacket and tie—looked intently into the camera. His identity card read, "Mebelis, Leib, store clerk, born April 7, 1922, in Kaišiadorys." Under nationality, "Žydu: Jew." Under the photograph, his signature in loopy childish script.

The other identity cards belonged to Leib's father, Moishe, tin-smith, born in Ukmergė. I recognized his large ears as Raisa's; she was self-conscious about them and kept her bangs just long enough to cover them. A second card was issued six months after the first, after Moishe lost his passport, sometime in 1940. His name also appeared in a newspaper listing of lost and stolen passports, another item in the archivist's tray.

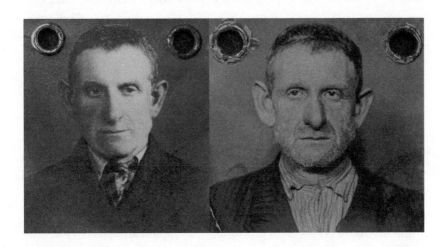

In the earlier photo, Moishe looks composed, even impressive: well groomed, in a knotted cravat and dark coat; obviously, he dressed for the occasion. In the second, taken on the eve of the So-viet annexation of Kaunas, he's disheveled and unshaven, tieless, frowning, looking years older in a dingy jacket and shirt buttoned to the top. What happened in the intervening months? The information on the cards was identical. Complexion, hair color, eye color, occupation. Under height, they both read, "Medium." The police department's blue stamp covers his left shoulder. In both photos he is fifty-nine, a year younger than my mother was on that day in Kaunas. She looked intently at the identity cards and remarked how much Moishe resembled Raisa. It was the first time she'd seen a photo of her grandfather.

She turned the cards over and read an address aloud: "Veiverių 30, apt. 1." "You won't find it," Gartman chimed in, peering over her shoulder. "The streets have been renumbered." He scratched his head, then brightened suddenly and, without an explanation, raced up the stairs. While he was gone, my mother and I strolled under the trees along Laisvės Alėja. The day turned bright and cool; cumulus clouds as white as carnations hovered in a flawless sky. Gartman found us there and thrust a sheet of paper into my hand. He was grinning broadly. It was a photocopy of a prewar map of Slobodka. Number 30 stood at the bottom of Veiverių Street, just a few steps from the Neris. "It's still there!" he said, eyes gleaming under his outsize visor.

The house on the map jutted from the dreary landscape like a stump in an old-growth forest. It stood along what had once been a busy main street. Some years ago, the city bulldozed the houses and shops on the side closest to the river and widened the street into a multilane highway. Cars and tractor trailers heading out of the city whizzed by. A filling station—a few gas pumps on blacktop glistening with decades of spilled motor oil—occupied an adjacent lot. The neighborhood was still the poorest in the city, only halfheartedly modernized. As on many such outskirts of Soviet bloc cities, everything looked as if it were reverting to an agrarian past. Rickety buildings, mostly plank, with additions jerry-rigged onto the prewar carpentry, sprouted along the street like moldering mushrooms. I wondered if Moishe had worked on their superannuated sheet-metal roofs.

The house where my grandmother lived as a young woman was the tallest around—a peeling rectangle of brick and cracked cement with plywood blotting out several windows. In the back, a second-story balcony had fallen down. The building's main function appeared to be holding up a billboard for a French-owned supermarket chain. Incredibly, someone still lived there. Clothes hung on a line over the rear lot, and inside, on a windowsill at the top of a staircase, there was a sardine can overflowing with cigarette butts and ashes. "These people must be destitute," Gartman muttered disapprovingly.

The eelgrass paint on the walls flaked away in spots to reveal French pink and flecks of blue. A padlock hung on the door to apartment 1, the one my grandmother, her siblings, and her parents had occupied decades ago after they moved here from Kaišiadorys. I craned my neck to peer into a window, but there was little to see except for a bare room with several slabs of unpainted drywall propped in a corner. Whatever happened here, whatever this place had been like for them, was now indecipherable. My mother walked down the stairs and stood on the sidewalk, her expression inscrutable, her thoughts muffled by the roar of the passing semis.

Efraim Gartman took us around Slobodka, a neighborhood that had long been known by its Lithuanian name, Vilijampole. On one street we came across a stone commemorating the Kaunas ghetto, a monument that my grandparents had donated money for. It was a bare gray obelisk inscribed with a few lines in Lithuanian and Hebrew and the dates 1941–1944. It looked as unremarkable and homely as a hydrant.

Standing in front of it, Gartman spat on the ground. A small, dogged man in a T-shirt and hat covered in Hebrew script, he looked absurdly defiant in a place now nearly devoid of Jews. A Kaunas native, Gartman said he was a computer programmer who became interested in local history. A local gadfly, he peppered the daily paper with letters and editorials about the city's past; he wrote to the archdiocese about historical errors on a plaque at the main cathedral's entrance. Recently, he even self-published a tourist brochure in French, titled *Les traces de France à Kaunas*, about local vestiges of Napoleon's army. But mainly he worked as a guide for visitors from abroad: mostly American and Canadian Jews looking for ancestors in Kaunas and the surrounding shtetls. "Not really for the money," Gartman insisted. "More out of a personal interest."

He moved through the streets confidently, a fist clenched against the city. Teenagers huddling around a guitar player came up to ask whether he was an "anti-skinhead." All afternoon I tried not to ask the obvious, probably tactless question that occurred to me the moment I met him, but eventually my curiosity won out. We were having lunch at a restaurant in the old city. "Why do you still live here?" I asked. "Why not?" he answered.

After lunch, Arunas drove us to Žaliakalnis, where my mother wanted to look for her grandfather's grave. The cemetery's wrought-iron gate, decorated with a Star of David, hung open, the lock broken. The path leading inside resembled an entrance to a forest. Though some graves there had been dug after the war, the place looked like a figment of antiquity, as desolate as a Roman necropolis. A handful of monuments and headstones jutted irregularly from the ground, barely visible amid a riot of Queen Anne's lace, nettles and scrub maples shading the names of the dead with their leaves. Upturned stones lay on the ground among a carpet of beer cans, food wrappers and other trash. Most of the plots lay bare, their stones and markers removed. The cemetery employed a paid groundskeeper in

Soviet times, Gartman told us, but since independence it's been all but abandoned. There weren't enough Jews left in Kaunas to pay for its upkeep, and locals hauled away many of the marble and granite gravestones; a neighbor of Gartman's used one to make steps for his boathouse. Eventually the cemetery became a hangout for local teenagers, an eerie, romantic spot to come at night, far from the streetlights and police cruisers.

For a while it seemed that we were the only visitors in Žaliakalnis. But in a clearing we came across half a dozen teenagers, neatly dressed and combed, gathered around a middle-aged man sitting on a tomb. A boy in a ski jacket read something in German from a handheld device, and when he finished, the others clapped. I walked over to ask who they were. The teacher, a tall, blondish man in clearplastic spectacles, told me in English that they were a high school class on a field trip from Berlin. They came to the cemetery to "learn about the darker aspects of our country's history." These students chose to come here, the teacher assured me; the remainder of the class went to Morocco. I thanked him, and he shook my hand a touch

too firmly, telegraphing his solidarity. Then he blinked away the tears in his eyes.

Gartman, Arunas, my mother and I walked among the graves for several hours but found none with Haskel's name. My mother had been too young in 1957 to recall much about her last visit here. Besides, Gartman said, the gravestone was in all likelihood missing. We wandered past obelisks—too large to easily remove, it occurred to me—past children's graves that resembled tree trunks shorn of their boughs, past mausoleums of the wealthy and eminent, past inscriptions in Hebrew, Yiddish, Russian, Polish, Lithuanian and even English. No one spoke. On the way back to Arunas's car, near the cemetery's edge, we came across a grave with a name I was surprised to recognize. Nestled in a knoll of trash, the grave belonged to Danielius Dolskis.

Earlier that day, under the elms on Laisvės Alėja, we'd stood in front of a bronze statue of Dolskis that the city had erected several years earlier. It depicted him in tails and a bow tie, and it looked incongruous among the pizzerias and cellular-phone storefronts. The singer once known as Daniel Dolski arrived in his adopted country from St. Petersburg in 1929, just two years before his death at age forty; after learning the thorny language with unusual alacrity, he wrote and recorded a trove of songs that nearly every Lithuanian of a certain age could still hum or whistle from memory. Dolskis filled the cabarets on Laisvės Alėja, places with names like Versailles and Metropolis. Raisa danced at these clubs with her first husband; Semyon brought dates there in the years before the war. Dolskis performed jazzy, sentimental songs called *Schlager* and sang about a summer cornflower that had stirred his heart, and about Palanga Beach, where his love drowned in the cold waves and he stood listening for her voice in eternity.

Dolskis happened to be a Jew. In a clearing of dandelions and sumac, his grave, no grander than the ones beside it, lay amid Barry Beer empties, torn chip bags, candy wrappers and stubbed-out cigarettes, an unlikely resting place for the country's most beloved performer. "A disgrace," Arunas grumbled, picking up the beer cans. Gartman squinted into the setting sun and said nothing. Standing in the tall weeds, he appeared to be a feature of the landscape, unfathomable as the statuary on the decrepit mausoleums. My mother was engrossed in thought, trying to recall the words to a Dolskis melody that Semyon sang to her at bedtime when she was a child. Then she remembered a couplet. "*Onyte, einam su manim pašokti, / Leisk man karštai priglaust tave,*" she sang. "Anna, come dancing," it meant, "let me hold myself warmly against you." She stood there, singing it into the wind.

SEVERAL YEARS LATER, I returned to Vilnius to work a summer job, teaching in a program for Americans and Canadians who wanted to study writing in exotic locales. I spent three afternoons a week with eight mostly adult students in an oak-paneled schoolhouse and had the rest of the time to myself. The program coordinator called me from Montreal a few days before my flight. "We had to reshuffle the accommodations and put you in a different apartment," she said. "Please write down your new address. It is Kalvarijų 12, second floor."

I stared at the notepad for a moment, thinking an errant synapse had fired in my brain. Twelve Kalvarijų Street was one of the two or three addresses I knew in Vilnius. During my last visit, my mother and I had gone to see it—a white art deco–ish three-story house that had been repainted and resurfaced so many times that it appeared to exist in several historical periods. The house had been my great-grandfather Haskel's dental office. In 1916, on its second floor, a midwife delivered Haskel's second son, my grandfather Semyon. No one at the writing program had known.

The house stood on a block just north of the river Neris, separated from the city center by a bridge lined with blackened socialist realist statues of workers and soldiers. When my taxi pulled to the curb, the boutique on the ground floor was open. A fold-up blackboard outside advertised a sale on women's underwear, just as it had several years earlier. The saleswoman, the same one I'd spoken to before, still hadn't gleaned any facts about the building's history. She smiled at me, amused. The house where Haskel and Frida lived—number 13, across the street—had been replaced with the glass-and-steel mid-rise of a Holiday Inn.

The lightless vestibule of my great-grandfather's house had the peaty smell of old Eastern European houses. The apartment, on the second floor, was freshly painted and furnished with the kind of anonymous things that end up in rooms rented by the week: a two-seater sofa, an electric kettle, a framed photograph of a Caribbean resort. The only clues to the apartment's age were the thick plaster walls and the French doors leading onto a wrought-iron balcony overlooking a courtyard. From the balcony, I could make out the entrances to old cellars, where people once kept perishables and coal. Now nearly every part of the yard was occupied by Škodas and Volkswagens parked under a single dusty linden that covered them with its heart-shaped leaves.

Beyond the courtyard, an architectural shambles fanned out to the north. There were squat whitewashed nineteenth-century houses, their facades graying with age; Soviet apartment blocks that encircle every city in the former empire; several wooden houses of uncertain vintage faced with faded clapboard; and the recent translucent towers of Finnish and Austrian banks. Cranes ringed in other-worldly lights were raising a building, and for a while I watched their slow-motion pantomime. A Lithuanian friend told me that because of its jumbled skyline, this section of Vilnius was known locally as "Hong Kong."

July is the loveliest time to be in Vilnius. The nights are cool and the streets smell of lilac. People sit on benches and look at passersby as though it were still a thing to do. The umbrellas of the beer taverns stay out on the sidewalks until morning, and the city center remains crowded at two. After the dark wintry months, everyone basks in the summer delirium of the northern cities, partaking in the manic sociability and carousing you'll find after sundown in Stockholm, Reykjavík and St. Petersburg.

The day after I arrived, I went to a get-to-know-you party the writing program hosted in the city center, and afterward walked along an unfamiliar meandering route, hoping to eventually find myself someplace familiar. How big could the city be? It was my birthday and I was enjoying keeping it to myself. Two writing students, women in their forties from California who were working on novels, walked with me. We stared at unfamiliar shops and high grated windows and monuments to bearded grand dukes and talked about the strangeness of being there. After a while the fiction writers hailed a taxi.

We said goodbye on Glassmakers' Street, at the edge of the old Jewish quarter, beside the small modern monument to the Vilna Gaon, and for a while I walked without paying attention to where I was. I passed a Lutheran church and a Russian Orthodox one before ending up in front of the toylike russet spires of St. Anne's. While passing through on his way to Moscow, Napoleon supposedly said that he wanted to put the church in the palm of his hand and take it with him to Paris, and I could imagine why. Dusk was nearly done when I reached the embankment and walked along the Neris, which shone like a ribbon of blue foil between its dark banks. I was pleasantly lost. It was exhilarating to be immersed in history without being caught in it, to move along the streets as soundlessly as a minnow.

Earlier that day, while passing the Soviet-era train station, I remembered one of my childhood trips to Vilnius. I must have been five or six. I already liked being aboard trains and spent most of the way from Moscow running up and down the corridor, peering into open compartments, asking questions of strangers and watching the landscape move by with my forehead pressed to the windows. The thing I remembered best were the train's curtains. Each had a picture of Vilnius's landmarks connected by loopy lines—a cartoon city map. I was trying to make sense of it when my father walked up behind me. He was in a fine mood. He put his hand on my head and knelt beside me.

He pointed at the curtain, at a point slightly above the city map, and said this is where we would live, at Semyon and Raisa's apartment in Antakalnis. Then he moved his index finger from one picture to the next—a museum, a church, the towers of the university— and explained what each one was. I could feel my father's breath on my neck. Even then I realized how unusual the moment was, and I leaned into him shyly. In my memory of this moment, sunlight beams through the white curtains so brightly that it ignites the motes of dust in the air and the gold of my father's wedding ring. He wrapped an arm around me, pressed a scratchy cheek against mine and kissed me noisily on the ear. I remember excitement welling up in my chest like an inflating balloon; I felt as if I might pass out from its force. Then my father pointed to a picture at the map's center, of a medieval stone fortress on a hill. "If you're good," he said, "we will climb the hill and go up in the tower." I remembered this while standing on the dark street. The sky was clear and the moon was nearly full, and cicadas chirred along the river. Above the rooftops, I could make out the outline of Gediminas's stone fortress.

I walked for hours that night, sometimes not knowing where I was. For a while, I stopped in a brightly lit bar with a carved-wood interior where I lingered over a pint of pilsner and watched couples enjoying the night's last round. They talked and laughed over the 1990s pop songs on the speakers but, in the Lithuanian way, did it quietly and almost shyly. I paid and began walking down a street lined with whitewashed houses, becoming lost again until spotting a sign I'd seen before. Recently applied paint failed to conceal the dark outline of Yiddish lettering. There were only two or three signs like it left in the city, some of the last vestiges of Vilnius's Jews that existed outside a museum.

At some point I must have turned north, because after a while the Neris and the familiar bridge lined with blackened statues of soldiers and factory workers swung into view. Instead of crossing to my apartment on the other side, I turned right and continued walking alongside the river. The streets had emptied out, and only an occasional driver, hurrying home, lit up the scenery with her headlights. I reached a roundabout and passed a late-baroque church. Behind St. Peter and St. Paul's custard-yellow wall stood its cake-like facade, with "REGINA PACIS FUNDA NOS IN PACE" painted on it in large letters. Beyond the church, the old city ended unceremoniously, giving way to a wide street from the Socialist era of urban planning.

As a child, I'd watched this street from a trolley window. It was after midnight now and the trolleys weren't running; their route was traced by twin cables strung above the empty traffic lanes. I walked down Antakalnio Street for the better part of an hour. It was still lined with Soviet-era concrete buildings, but every sign I remembered from childhood was gone. I walked past a pizzeria, a gym, a café advertising chocolate drinks, the green-and-yellow facade of a supermarket. I passed identical apartment blocks for a long stretch and then a concrete box of a schoolhouse in the early-1960s friendship-of-nations style. At the secluded entrance to a research center, I turned left onto a narrow wooded street that rose gradually into the surrounding hills.

I'd walked far from the city center. There weren't many streetlights and I couldn't make out the street signs, but a homing instinct pulled me farther up the hill, though I wasn't sure where. My mind was pleasantly blank. It was a vast, empty night and it felt good to be walking.

The narrow street was named after a Polish composer. Farther up, it passed some of the city's most expensive real estate, villas built into a hillside above the river, but I didn't reach them. I turned left after spotting the familiar outline of what had been my grandparents' apartment building; I wondered whether the metal roof on the shed in front of it was still painted a mottled seaweed color, but it was too dark to see. There, I sat on the edge of a concrete planter, beside a potted palm and some parked bicycles, and looked at the first-floor windows where Semyon, Raisa and my mother had lived, and where I spent several summers. The windows were curtained and dark, except for a bluish glimmer that could've been the glow of a television or a computer screen. There was no one outside. The wind died down and the leaves stopped their clamor.

Sitting there, I remembered a July morning, during the summer I turned eight. I could deduce the year because both of my parents were in Vilnius, during the last summer that all of us would spend together as a family. That morning I woke in what had once been the maid's room, my legs already too long for my child's bed. Because of the reddish glimmerings behind the curtains, I knew it was early and everyone was asleep, and in my socks I slid across the cool parquet into the hallway. Semyon and Raisa had ceded the living room to my parents. The door to it was open slightly, and I looked at my mother and father sleeping on the fold-out sofa: they were entwined, holding each other in the secretive, desperate way they had about them during their last year together. They slept on white sheets, surrounded by hundreds of books on blond-wood shelves—more books, it seemed to me, than anyone could read in a lifetime—while a clock ticked loudly on the coffee table.

The kitchen smelled of rye bread, poppy seed and soap. There was no sign of the solitary mouse that sent my mother into shrieking fits and that Semyon, with a duplicitous wink to me, refused to trap. A string of dried cèpes, for Raisa's mushroom soup, hung from a cupboard knob. Later in the morning, Semyon would walk to the market for the hen my grandmother would pluck and singe over the range, filling the apartment with the pleasant smell of burned feathers.

I slipped into my grandfather's study. Semyon and Raisa slept in a corner. Unlike my parents, they lay on opposite sides of the bed, engrossed in their respective dreamtime obligations. Semyon's laboratory equipment occupied two long tables: gauges, meters, stacks of wax-filled dissection trays, rows of pins, forceps, surgical scissors, ribbons of paper bound with rubber bands, and above this six vertical aluminum drums silvered in morning light, looking like a retro-futuristic Fritz Lang skyline.

Once I made sure they were asleep, I squatted beside a row of jars with holes punched in the shiny metal lids and stared at the animals inside them. A graduate student had brought them the previous afternoon. There were several frogs and a single ornery olive-drab toad that occupied the largest jar by itself. That summer I'd spent hours lying on the floor and staring at the frogs and was under strict instructions not to touch them.

But everyone was asleep, so what was the harm? I unscrewed a lid and set it on the floor, careful not to rattle it, and lifted a frog from its jar, my hands trembling a little from the excitement. I held the animal in front of my face—too tightly for fear it would escape— but when I opened my hand the frog remained sitting in my palm, looking groggy but decidedly alive.

Its compact pebbled body felt unexpectedly substantial. Its eyes—black rimmed with copper—looked into mine. My grandfather snored loudly nearby. Water dripped from the kitchen faucet. Just then I was convinced that in every other apartment in the city, other children slept in beds surrounded by snoring adults and re-assuring furniture and loudly ticking clocks, children who knew even in sleep that they were warm and safe and loved, as I was that morning.

I wondered where the frog came from; I wished I could discern this simply by studying the spots and markings on its body. I knew only that it didn't belong in a city, much less in a crowded apartment— like me, the frog was a visitor here. It was here through no fault of its own, and I wanted to save it from the dissection tray. But I didn't know how to get to a pond, where I believed frogs lived, or even where I might find a pond in this unfamiliar city. Besides (my handling of the forbidden frog notwithstanding), I prided myself on being an obedient child. I didn't yet know that in a year we would leave this country and my father, didn't yet realize that it was permitted or even possible to alter one's life so completely. And so I looked at the frog and it looked at me. Then, grateful for our brief acquaintance, I carefully set it back in its jar.

THE MOTHERLAND CALLS

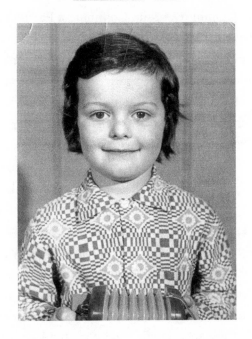

I STAND ON A BASKETBALL COURT HUGGING AN ARMFUL OF CARNATIONS. I don't remember much about what the morning looked like. Recalling it is like trying to study a photograph using only peripheral vision: if I look at it directly, the scene swims apart into a blot of printer's ink. What I can tell you with certainty is that it's the first day of class at a school for the children of diplomats and the well connected in Moscow, and I'm in the first grade, so it must be September 1, 1977. Uniformed children stand in formation on the court, a battalion of blue and brown knit synthetics, each of us clutching a bouquet. On the sidelines our parents holler encouragements; a few take photos. There is a lectern on a riser, and behind it a woman shaped like a vending machine recites a speech in tolling cadences that float above the other sounds; somehow this seems appropriate, because she's the principal. Behind her someone has hung portraits of Brezhnev and Gromyko and other members of the Political Bureau of the Central Committee of the Communist Party of the Union of Soviet Socialist Republics.

I try to stand straight and pay attention, but I can't, because the flowers belonging to the seven-year-old girl in front of me have transfixed me. Each meter-long stem sprouts half a dozen blooms the color of a nosebleed. I seem to know that the word for them is "gladioli." I know, too, that they are expensive and signify status and that my carnations are banal in comparison. The elephantine flowers sway unsteadily above the girl's glossy, pigtailed head, and I stare up at them, aching with envy. She's small for seven, and the gladioli are nearly as tall as she is. The principal drones on. The flowers are too heavy for the girl's thin wrists, and little by little they tilt backward, like a figure skater falling in slow motion, until the gladioli rest on my head and cascade down my shoulders. I can't see my mother and father, who are watching from somewhere on the sidelines. I learn later that they were aphasic with laughter, but I've recently turned seven and my humiliation is sudden and complete on this, the most important morning of my life. I whisper imploringly at the back of the girl's head. I try to bat the flowers aside, to somehow alert the girl without stepping out of formation, but she can't or won't hear me, and under the cover of the sword-shaped leaves I begin to cry.

MY MOTHER WAS the reigning Miss Psychology Department when my father first spoke to her. They met in a student lounge outside her Dialectical Materialism classroom, in the old Moscow State University building on Mokhovaya Street. She was reading a Flannery O'Connor story in an issue of *Foreign Literature*. What she must've looked like at this moment I've reconstructed from photographs: hair that curved in an S across her cheeks and fell down her back, an olive miniskirt, knee-high leather boots with Cuban heels, one leg perched on the knee of the other, a cigarette dangling from a corner of her mouth, no makeup, a face alternately shy or teasing or precocious but invariably self-conscious.

Of course she knew that she was pretty and stylish, and was aware of the status this granted her. She was waiting for class to begin. There would be a lecture on the early writings of Lenin, or a lengthy quotation from Engels to copy from the blackboard and later recite from memory, and sometimes she made the time go faster by staring across the way into the windows of the First Medical Institute's morgue, where on some afternoons students practiced autopsies on cadavers. It was May 24, 1969; three days earlier she turned twenty.

In a library elsewhere in that building, a sallow, curly-haired student named Izya sat in a library and drew a chronological chart of party congresses for my mother's upcoming oral exam. It was the kind of work she detested. Izya was one of several boys whom she permitted to sit beside her in the cafeteria, one among maybe half a dozen who carried her textbooks, plied her with tangerines from the farmers' market, and did her Scientific Communism homework. They tended to be Jews, plainer than she was but resourceful and patient. In exchange for her attention and company they didn't seem to mind being used or, to her way of thinking, being useful. She didn't tell them that she didn't date Jewish boys; to her they seemed too timid, too beholden to their mothers, and reminded her too much of Semyon.

On the commute that took her from the dormitory on Lenin Hills to the classrooms on Mokhovaya Street, she sometimes wore a bell-bottom corduroy pantsuit and a long scarf the color of a revolution-ary banner. The buses were crowded with women in domestic store-bought coats and cardigans who carried groceries in net satch-els; beside them, she looked as if she'd wandered onto the city bus from the pages of *Bonjour Tristesse*. Elderly men with gold-capped incisors and medals spangled across worsted blazers glared at her. One of them demanded, invoking his seniority and veteran status, that she return home and "change into something decent." She pre-tended not to hear him. Some of my mother's girlfriends believed her to be immune to harm. At times she, too, believed she could negate the city's leaden grayness and frigid weather simply by choosing to disbelieve them. Moscow was dreary, but she appreciated its vastness. It served as a temporary solution to Vilnius, a provincial city that she conceived of as existing under the suffocating bell jar of history.

Sometimes her magical thinking made her reckless. During te-dious compulsory meetings of the Young Communist League—the Komsomol—she sometimes stood up and walked out. Her closest friends were exchange students, a Canadian couple named Donald and Faye (every Soviet adult knew that socializing with foreigners from the West was never an entirely safe proposition). The three of them walked to Café Metelitsa on Kalinin Prospekt to listen to the jazz combos, or headed somewhere on campus to listen to the student rock bands, fronted mainly by sons of party officials and diplomats, who could get away with playing "(I Can't Get No) Satisfaction" in public.

With her roommate Beba, a plump Jewish brunette from Beltsy, my mother took the metro to a synagogue near Nogin Square. In front of it, dark-suited men standing in the flatbed of a truck filmed everyone who went in or came out. She was aware that for her ideological transgressions her dorm room and student stipend could be revoked, she could be expelled from the Komsomol and even the university, but she refused to seriously consider these possibilities. Not even after Beba found a hole in the top of their dorm room closet concealing a tangle of wire and a tiny microphone.

My father walked up to her while she read the O'Connor story. A friend had told him, he began, that she had copies of some poems by Joseph Brodsky. Could he borrow them? This wasn't an unusual request. Much of the better recent fiction and poetry was officially banned and circulated as sheaves of mimeographed pages known as samizdat; the pages were lent out sometimes for as little as a day or even several hours.

What gave her pause was his appearance. He looked older than the other students—around twenty-four?—and his cropped hair, starched white collar, expensive suede jacket and sharply creased trousers were a suspicious costume for an undergraduate in 1969. For a moment, she assumed he must be one of those older students who sometimes appeared in classes mid-semester, men who could barely grasp the schoolwork but were there for "social" reasons, meaning that they supplemented their stipends by informing on the other students to the KGB. Worse still, he was enrolled in the philosophy department, which was known to be "ideological," meaning it was off-limits to Jews and other "undependable" people, and his snub nose and gray eyes confirmed him as a gentile. Yet there he was, asking her to borrow banned poetry. Though she knew better, for some reason she didn't send him away. As they spoke, she realized he was articulate and at least passably bright, and that he was flirting with her. His name was Viacheslav, but everyone called him Slava. She thought he looked a little like Steve McQueen in *The Cincinnati Kid*, a movie she'd watched a part of with the sound off.

The following night they met outside her dorm room at the agreed-upon time. She handed him the dog-eared pages of poetry, but he lingered and eventually asked her to take a walk with him, and they spent the early evening strolling along the Arbat. It was still years before the boulevard became a strip of lavender and yellow tourist shops, and the buildings still had the shabby patina of postwar Moscow. Slava spoke about jazz records and foreign films and novels in translation; she could tell he was trying to impress her with esoteric knowledge about the West. He had an animated, expressive face well suited to jumbled outpourings of enthusiasm. But when her turn came to speak, unlike most men he listened without interrupting, giving her the impression that he was thinking seriously about what she said. His manners were appealingly old-fashioned, too: he brought flowers, opened doors for her, held her coat when she stood up in cafés.

They went walking again the following night, and the one after. He was turning out to be unlike the person she'd assumed him to be. He, too, detested the compulsory political classes, and rambled excitedly about the student demonstrations in Paris, Howlin' Wolf and Nabokov. When he found out that she'd studied English in school, he brought an article from *Down Beat* about a saxophonist named Steve Lacy and begged her, with childlike sincerity, to translate it. One morning he took her to breakfast at Seventh Heaven, a café on the seventh floor of the Hotel Moscow, on Manezhnaya Square. After they sat down, he recited a poem aloud to her.

Nearly a month after they met, they whiled away an evening on a park bench not far from the Arbat, under a banner that read, "Lift High the Banner of Proletarian Internationalism." The street was already dark; most of the pedestrians were gone. My father was telling my mother about Vinnitsa and Tamara—he hadn't told her yet about Vassily—when, unexpectedly, he began speaking about a married woman with whom he'd had an affair after moving to Moscow. The story didn't embarrass my mother. She knew he'd spent three years in the army and figured he must be experienced with women. She was a virgin and had nothing comparable to reveal, so instead she told him about the first time she'd been in love, with a boy named Kolya. She was seventeen and still in school. They met while my mother was visiting family friends in Moscow, and after he returned to Moscow, they wrote each other long, romantic letters.

He asked her to come to Moscow and marry him; she said yes, but Raisa forbade it: forget about him, she told her, you're both too young. In the end, Kolya became engaged to a girl closer to home. When my mother glanced over at my father, he was doubled over, sobbing. "I know you'll never love me like that," he said, wiping his face with a handkerchief. She took his hand.

What I've learned about their courtship I gleaned mostly from my mother. On two or three occasions my father spoke to me about it, too, at those unusual times when we were alone and he felt like talking. During one of my visits he and I were walking past the Hotel Metropol when we passed a street corner where he sometimes met my mother in those years. He stopped, made a circular motion with his hand, indicating the city around us, and said, somewhat cryptically, "The only thing we had was our youth."

What I know about the year after they met can be arranged into several scenes, discrete as photographs. Here is one: when the semester ended in late May, they took a train to a vacation spot called Djemete, in Crimea, a student resort with tents, pickup soccer and badminton games, and nightly dancing to somebody's transistor radio or guitar. My father told my mother he didn't dance, so she danced with a few other boys, twisting to a Chubby Checker song she knew from school parties. When she saw him afterward, she discovered that he'd watched her jealously, and he rehashed an argument and sulked.

Another scene: in June or July, she met him at the one-bedroom apartment he shared with Tamara, her husband, Mikhail Mikhailovich, and her mother, Maria Nikolaevna. Tamara was one of the few people who managed to intimidate my mother. Not long after they met, Tamara remarked that my mother's favorite corduroy pantsuit had been cut and sewn shoddily. Style, unlike men, was something Tamara wielded with mastery. She knew that the purpose of clothes was to assert confidence and power, and she designed my father's monogrammed shirts and worsted blazers, looking on while the seamstresses at the House of Fashion stitched them together. Already she wore the bottle-blond perm and rococo accessories I remember from childhood.

On this particular night, Tamara had given them tickets to a Chekhov play, and my mother arrived in a red summer dress with a red carnation in her hair. Tamara declared, in her unequivocal way, that my mother was pretty and had style. It was her supreme compliment. Afterward, when my mother spent weekends at the apartment, she began to look forward to seeing Tamara. On those nights Maria Nikolaevna baked her famous pirozhki and everyone ate around the big table in the kitchen; afterward, my father slept on a folding cot in the kitchen while my mother took the living room sofa. Before long my father asked my mother to leave the dorm room on Lenin Hills and move in with them.

Maria Nikolaevna wouldn't allow it. For decades, she'd watched husbands and lovers—her daughter's as well as her own—appear and vanish just as quickly, and she wasn't about to share her home with some coed a third her age. My great-grandmother preferred children to adults, but not by much. In my earliest memories, she perches on a stool near the kitchen window over a glass of tea, brown-hued and compact, and cracks sugar cubes with a pair of blackened steel pliers, tucking the sugar between her cheek and dentures.

She enjoyed perusing the daily newspapers for political cartoons. A typical one showed a corpulent banker in a top hat and monocle—with "NATO" or "USA" or "IMPERIALIST AGGRESSOR" written across his chest in bold letters—lording over emaciated dark-skinned laborers, and if I happened to be in the kitchen Maria Nikolaevna pulled me up into her lap, pointed to the drawing and read the caption aloud with patriotic gusto. On weekends, she baked apple pirozhki that she doled out with military austerity. "Take one and it'll be the death of you," she muttered when I crept next to the plate. Her peripheral vision was preternatural, and she didn't bother looking up from the newspaper when delivering this warning. If I was feeling brave and lunged, she gave chase, the metal-shod soles of her black orthopedic shoes ringing on the parquet.

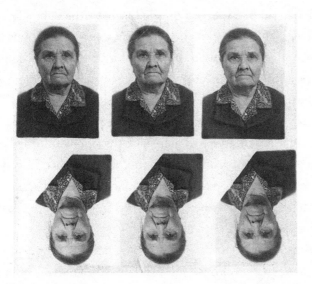

Maria Nikolaevna was unsentimental and believed in the power of unadorned speech. And so she remained suitably unimpressed when she found out, in the late fall of 1969, that my mother was pregnant. "If you push one out, don't think I'm going to watch the brat, because I've got plenty to do without you," she told my mother one afternoon, by way of a greeting. She relented after a two-day argument with Tamara, and my mother became the fourth resident of the two-room apartment. For weeks, my mother's pregnancy was the main topic of conversation around the kitchen table. "You are too young to waste away at home with a baby," Tamara counseled. "You're going to miss the dancing. An abortion takes twenty minutes and doesn't even hurt." The following night Tamara would change her mind and urge her to keep the baby. My father said the decision was hers and stayed out of it. My mother didn't dare tell Raisa; it was bad enough that she was dating a gentile. She was convinced that if Raisa discovered that she was no longer a virgin, her heart would simply stop.

My mother was nearly two months pregnant when, in February, beside a stand of birches by the shore of a still-frozen pond on the southwest edge of the city, my father knelt in front of her and handed her a plain gold band. She'd decided to have the baby. Tamara and Mikhail Mikhailovich took an overnight sleeper to Vilnius to introduce themselves to Semyon and Raisa and to plan the wedding. The ceremony took place several weeks later inside a concrete ziggurat on Leningrad Boulevard called the Palace of Matrimony—in Moscow, nearly every civic function was transacted in a palace—where weeks earlier my mother had picked up a coupon entitling her to buy a pair of white patent-leather pumps at the bridal shop next door. She wasn't yet showing and still hadn't told her mother, but her girlfriend Lyuba ruined the ploy when she arrived at the ceremony with a box of baby toys wrapped with a red ribbon.

Cousins arrived from Vilnius, my father's university friends bought their first neckties, and Mikhail Mikhailovich, the shortest man in the room, wore a suit so shiny that my mother swore it lit up the hall. Even Kirpotin and Dalin, her Bolshevik uncles, came to the ceremony; in their dark wide-lapelled suits, they looked like a pair of Chicago bootleggers. When my mother signed the wedding registry, she held a bouquet of white carnations and wore another in her hair.

Afterward, everyone drove to a banquet hall in the Union of Economic Cooperation, on Kalinin Prospekt; one of Tamara's clients, a vice-minister's wife, had wrangled the reception. Two nights later, Anna and Slava celebrated again with their friends, in a dorm room on Lenin Hills. Everyone gorged on Soviet Champagne and roast chicken left over from the reception while listening to a copy of the *White Album* that someone had traded for a pair of insulated boots.

Semyon, who whiled away his nights in Moscow on predatory games of speed chess with his new son-in-law, remained as tactless as ever. When he heard that my father was studying philosophy, he asked him, amiably and not at all quietly, "How does the son of a soldier and a seamstress become a philosopher?" Raisa hated that her son-in-law was a gentile—in all likelihood a philanderer and a drunk in the well-known Slavic tradition—but, collected as always, she kept these thoughts from her daughter. Semyon was more pragmatic. When he realized his grandchild would be listed as a Russian instead of a Jew in his or her domestic passport, he told Raisa it was for the best. After pogroms and concentration camps, what was the point of bringing more Jews into the world?

Vassily had been conspicuously absent at the wedding. Claiming that his presence would make Mikhail Mikhailovich unbearably jealous, Tamara forbade my father to invite him. He hadn't intended to anyway. When he called his father to tell him about the wedding two weeks earlier, Vassily remarked that marrying a Jew would almost certainly scuttle my father's chances at a government career and party membership. My father hung up. "Everything good in me comes from my mother," he told my mother afterward. Vassily did come to Moscow that fall. According to my mother he looked trim and impressively well tailored and charmed Semyon and Raisa and told Tamara that she looked lovelier than ever. She said he was gentle and affectionate with me, delicately pulling a comb through my wet hair while I sat burbling in the tub.

Afterward, my mother and Vassily drank tea and talked. Though he was articulate and charming, up close he appeared to her somehow blank, wasp-eaten from the inside. Amid the laughter and high spirits in Tamara's apartment, my mother watched her new husband address his father with the brittle formality of a co-worker. My father and Vassily never agreed about what happened between them in the years following this visit. Vassily told me that eventually, out of sheer vindictiveness, my father simply cut him off; my father claimed that it was Vassily who stopped returning his calls and letters, worried that my mother's Jewishness and eventual petition to leave the country would mar his spotless record at the KGB. What's certain is that that day in October 1970 was the last time they saw each other.

I was born six months after my parents' wedding, in July. Minutes after giving birth, my mother straightened out a cramping leg and kicked me off the delivery table. A midwife caught me. The following morning my mother found out that someone had entered a name, Aleksandr, on my birth certificate; it turned out Semyon and my father chose it without telling her. Furious, she announced that because she was the one who gave birth, she would be the one to name her son. She refused to decide for several months, toying with Vadim and Vladimir until one morning, pushing a stroller through a park, she found herself sitting on a bench beside an elderly woman in a kerchief. They began talking, and my mother poured out her indignation over my name. "It must be his fate," the woman said, glancing into the stroller, and my mother relented.

AFTER MY PARENTS brought me home from the hospital, I slept beside my mother on the cot in Tamara's kitchen. Applying for a private apartment in Moscow required a *propiska*, a police permit to reside within city limits. The only way for my mother to obtain one was to register as a resident of Tamara's one-bedroom walk-up. Because she'd neglected to do this, and because of the city's housing shortage, a wait for a new apartment could take years. Tamara's clout proved useful once again: after nine months of living in illegal sublets, my parents moved into a private apartment in one of the new nine-story apartment towers that were going up on the city's southwestern edge. With money Semyon and Raisa gave them, they bought the two-bedroom cooperative—a rationalized loophole in the Soviet ban on private property—while Tamara helped them to the top of the wait-

ing list with a well-placed bribe. The apartment turned out to be decidedly luxurious, with a balcony and an eat-in kitchen, covered in linoleum the tumescent shade of a sore throat. The building, constructed of white cinder blocks that turned gray nearly overnight, stood near the spot where my father had proposed to my mother a year earlier—the pond had been drained and filled, the birches cut down and hauled away. Today these identical apartment buildings are known as Brezhnevki, after the ursine general secretary on whose directives they were built.

Our neighborhood was named Tyopli Stan, which means "warm region," an odd moniker for a hilltop where for most of the year an icy wind blew so hard that it knocked hats off the heads of pedestrians. In the summers, my parents sent me to Tamara's dacha or to stay with Semyon and Raisa in Vilnius, and I remember our Moscow neighborhood mostly as perennially frigid and blanketed with snow. In spring, its streets were caked with ankle-deep mud. The neighborhood's first stores didn't open for another two years; predictably, one was a liquor store. In the meantime, inside a trailer that sat beached on our sidewalk, a woman in a hairnet sold barley, potatoes, milk and semi-cooked meat pucks known as "six-kopeck patties."

Wiring for private telephones took longer still to arrive, and occupants of our building and the one beside it queued up in front of a pair of phone booths on the sidewalk. Long lines for them formed even in freezing temperatures. In our apartment, heat came on and off intermittently. My mother washed my cloth diapers by hand, hung them over the range, and turned on all four burners to dry them. One morning, while playing chess with Semyon, my father began vomiting, moaning on the tiled bathroom floor until paramedics wheeled him out on a gurney. At the hospital he learned that he had been sickened by leaking gas.

The neighbor I remember best lounged on a folding chair on the second-floor landing. He had a convex torso and a face like a ruddy cabbage. He wore training pants and a tank top that held tufts of dusky chest hair in check. Everyone in the building called him

Puzyr—Bubble. From earliest childhood I knew that Bubble was our resident functionary of the *organs*, the term used to refer to the assorted tentacles of the KGB. And so it made sense that Bubble spent his days and nights watching the comings and goings of everyone in the building. The elevator was invariably broken, and we had no choice but to trudge up the stairs past Bubble's landing. Every November 7, Revolution Day, when everyone gathered in front of televisions to watch the holiday variety show on Channel 1, Bubble liked to remind us of his presence by using a passkey to get into the basement and cutting power to the entire building.

One morning, after seeing my father carry some new children's furniture up the stairs, Bubble made a phone call to his superiors. It was sound Soviet logic to assume that where there was new children's furniture, there must also be a stack of samizdat verse or a pornographic magazine or maybe even a shortwave radio used to tune in to the bourgeois propaganda on Voice of America. My father was summoned to Lubianka and questioned by a bored-sounding investigator. After the denunciation, my father harbored a grudge against Bubble, suspecting him whenever the hot water stopped running or the gas flickered out on the range.

As it happened, Bubble had good reason to suspect my father. Like thousands of Muscovites, my father was a *fartsovshchik*—a black marketeer who bartered and sold difficult-to-find or banned merchandise—a contributor to the creeping individualist blight that rotted our society from the inside, as the evening papers insisted. Barter, like unlicensed buying and selling, was an obsession in a country where finding a tube of contraceptive jelly or a well-fitting nylon shirt often turned into a two-month ordeal. The value of an item was measured by its scarcity and the creativity required to obtain it. One afternoon when I was six, my mother ran into a former classmate who managed a store called Gifts of the Sea near the Park of Culture. Right there on the sidewalk, he handed her a plastic bag of frozen Alaskan crab legs that he was carrying home, and she gave him a Lithuanian amber brooch, a gift for his wife. I'd never seen the leg or any other part of a crab, and didn't put much stock in women's jewelry, so when she opened the bag to show me the prickly crustacean appendages, I told my mother that she'd made a shrewd and highly original deal.

My father's business took off in earnest after he found his first job, at the Institute of the History and Theory of Film near Gorky Street. It was the kind of sinecure often awarded to the children of officially sanctioned artists and film directors. It, too, had been finagled with Tamara's connections. My father had been obsessed with movies since watching *Sun Valley Serenade* as a boy in Vinnitsa; the job allowed him to dig through the institute's archives for prints of films by Ford and Bresson that didn't exist anywhere else in the country.

At the institute, my father finally had a chance to write for publication, something he'd always wanted. He was an avid, breathless reader and told stories with color and uncanny timing. But after beginning work on several articles, he discovered that he didn't have the stomach for the kinds of critiques typically published in official journals, articles that parsed films for Marxist themes and images of an ennobled working class. This, anyway, is the reason he gave me for quitting writing. But he told my mother that he didn't think he was as good as the writers he admired, and couldn't stand the thought of being mediocre.

He volunteered instead to work in the institute's modest one-room library (this, again, was his version of events; years later, in New York, a former co-worker of his told my mother that he'd been demoted to the library for failing to publish). It was a lowly job that nonetheless put him in contact with rare books and, more important, with foreign visitors and diplomats who had the enviable ability to travel abroad and pass through customs with little scrutiny from inspectors. For a price, some were willing to bring rock and jazz records from official postings in Germany, France and the United States. In less than a year, my father graduated from a neighborhood *fartsovshchik* to a well-known dealer in musical contraband; records fetched more money than books and soon became his primary merchandise. He told himself he did it because of his love for rock and jazz, but along the way he discovered a talent for making money.

The deals went down in our apartment. The doorbell rang, and on the other side stood a man—it was always a man—with a bag slung over a shoulder and an expectant, twitchy look. My father's favorite bit of salesmanship was to bundle the record a customer wanted with two others he didn't. Typically, there was a phone call from some bearded jazz fanatic interested in, say, a mint copy of *John Coltrane Live at the Village Vanguard* that he'd heard my father had for sale. When the dumbfounded man arrived at our apartment after traveling for two hours on a municipal bus, my father informed him that the Coltrane record was only available as part of a set—along with Bread's *Greatest Hits* and a compilation of Anne Murray singles, all priced stratospherically.

His steadiest customer was a fellow *fartsovshchik* named Gosha, a sharp-nosed wren of a man in a dirty windbreaker. He had a childish weakness for anything American and sported a Muscovite hipster's vocabulary: *shoozi* for shoes, *Frenk* for Sinatra. To Gosha, neglecting an abscessed molar or losing a girlfriend of seven months was a fair price to pay for a lightly scuffed copy of Edgar Winter's *They Only Come Out at Night* or a vacuum tube for an ancient McIntosh receiver that he'd wheedled for some enormous sum from the son-in-law of a cultural attaché to Denmark. Late one night, Gosha arrived unannounced at our door, eyes gleaming with victory, cradling a pair of not-quite-new cordovan loafers. He'd paid a sum for them equal to a surgeon's monthly salary, even though the *shoozi* were three sizes too large. Before a spasm of laughter brought my father to the floor, Gosha, sounding supercilious and hurt, cried, "Can't you see they're from Brooks Brothers?"

In the meantime, more than a year after she completed a thesis on the effects of emotional stress on teams of cosmonauts, my mother still hadn't found a job, though the law mandated it. Stalin had declared psychology a pseudoscience, Moscow State University opened its psychology department only a few years before my mother enrolled there, and the handful of jobs in this new field existed mainly at clandestine government agencies. Back at the university, a man in a gray suit had approached my mother with an offer of a psychologist's job that paid the astronomical monthly salary of three hundred rubles. "The only requirement," he told her matter-of-factly, "is that you have no French blood going back five generations." He had the wrong person, my mother replied: "French" was a well-known euphemism for Jewish. My father wondered aloud why she didn't simply take a job as a department-store counter girl.

She grew so discouraged at one job interview that she began sobbing. "My son is home with food poisoning, and you aren't going to hire me, so let's not waste each other's time," she said to the man across the desk, and began putting on her coat. Either he took pity on her or her frankness impressed him, because the following week she reported for work at the Psychology Institute on Mokhovaya Street, in the department of adolescent mental health. Her supervisor was a psychologist from Tajikistan who'd married a Central Committee member's daughter; he made his rounds with a lit cigarette and a snifter of brandy. In Dushanbe he'd run a school for teenagers with disciplinary problems and had to relocate to Moscow after an underling complained to a local party official that he'd pressured several of his underage students into performing paid sexual favors. On my mother's first day of work, he instructed her to write out a crib sheet for his daughter's university entrance exam.

Still only twenty-three, the former Miss Psychology Department rarely saw friends or left the apartment on weekends. We lived as far from Moscow's center as you could while still remaining within city limits, the Kaluzhsko-Rizhskaya metro didn't yet reach our neighborhood, and friends didn't call because we didn't own a telephone. When my mother returned from work, she often took me shopping. She carried me in her arms and, when I was older, pulled me behind her on a sled; I bounced on the packed snow, sitting on the sled's green and yellow wooden slats while a sack of potatoes, a bottle of sulfurous mineral water and some frozen cuts of veal rattled between my knees.

More often than not, shopping meant locating an intriguingly long line and taking a spot at the end of it. We learned what we were standing in line for some time later. The most commonly heard question at the end of a line was, "What are they handing out?" We needed whatever it was: kitchen stools with faux marble tops, Romanian ladies' hats, grapes from Baku, chocolates from the Red Dawn confectionary factory, compacts of foundation powder that women jokingly referred to as "Lenin's Ashes," leatherette briefcases, bras. Most people bought multiples to hand out or resell to family and neighbors.

My father announced his return from work by bursting through the door and shouting, "Where's supper? I'm starving!" On some nights he did this winningly, with a grin; more often he was merely tired and irritable after an hour on the crowded metro and shuttle bus. My mother took little pleasure in cooking, but like most Soviet wives she cooked every night, washing the dishes afterward while my father discussed records and books with customers or fellow dealers in the study. Sometimes I peered through the crack in the door and caught a glimpse of items disgorged from briefcases and plastic bags and overheard foreign words that I understood to be illicit and therefore desirable: Sansui, Rossellini, Wrangler.

My father turned our apartment into a shrine to the West, filling it with stacks of samizdat verse, drawers of neatly folded blue jeans, and posters of Louis Armstrong and Ella Fitzgerald. My mother had long ago understood the reason for his love of everything foreign and his loathing for official Soviet culture. He'd told her he was ashamed of Vassily, ashamed of carrying the genes of a KGB officer and legally sanctioned killer, and sometimes he seemed to want to disappear bodily into his own make-believe America, an imaginary realm made up of records, books, movies and an ocean of blue denim.

He rarely confided in my mother about his childhood, and didn't believe there was much to be gained from ventilating his fears and doubts. But they visited him anyway in frequent nightmares. On those nights he muttered in his sleep and woke beside my mother, shouting. It was always the same dream: he heard the clanging of large machines, which he said sounded like old-fashioned printing presses. In the dream he was a child, and afraid, but he never told my mother what exactly had frightened him. After a time she couldn't shake the conviction that something at the center of him was so twisted with shame that it broke.

On other nights, my father didn't come home. When I was three, he disappeared for nearly four days. On the first of those nights, after she came home from work, my mother dropped a pocketful of coins into the sidewalk pay phone, calling every one of their friends as well as Tamara, and finally trudged with me to the police station to file a missing-persons report. My father grinned sheepishly when he finally came home; he told my mother that he ran into a friend, and they drove to his lake house in the country to go fishing. How could he call when there was no telephone in the apartment? My mother looked overjoyed to see him and ignored her suspicion that he was lying.

He began to disappear more often. His usual explanations entailed him running into friends who'd returned from abroad with rare records, and listening to the *diski* for most of the night, and eventually having to bed down at the friend's apartment because the metro stopped running at midnight. My mother rarely pressed him. After work, she prepared supper, did the laundry, mopped the floor, stood in lines, but also read to me, stanched my nosebleeds and attended to my constant colds. I'd grown attached to a bulky jumpsuit insulated with wads of cotton, and when I tripped and fell into one of the puddles or mud-filled potholes that crisscrossed the sidewalks in our neighborhood, a walk home in the sodden jumpsuit usually brought on a fever or a cold. It took my mother nearly three days to dry the jumpsuit over the range.

I didn't hide the pleasure I took in being sick. It was an opportunity to stay home from school and to enjoy my mother's ministrations. On those mornings I climbed into bed and my mother rubbed my back with alcohol. She lit a cotton swab tied to a pencil, held the flame inside a small glass cup, and clamped the cup to my back. She repeated this a dozen times. Then she pulled the blanket over me while I lay there with the cups stuck to my back, looking like a pacified lizard. I liked the half-baked mysticism of the routine, and most of all I liked being touched. My reward for enduring the flame's proximity to my skin was two raw eggs that my mother broke into a bowl, mixed with cocoa powder and sugar, and whipped with a spoon—a delicacy called *gogol-mogol*. Being sick briefly made me the center of attention in our apartment—sometimes it even compelled my father to sit on the edge of my bed and read to me—and I registered a rumble in my chest or swollen tonsils with a twinge of expectant pleasure.

I inherited the penchant for frequent illness from my mother. She wasn't prone to nightmares, but reacted to adversity and stress—and especially to my father's disappearances—by developing gastritis, pancreatitis, bronchitis, bursitis, mastitis, skin abscesses and migraines. When I was four, she contracted pneumonia. My father was at work, and Tanya, a friend who lived down the street, came to look in on her. After putting a kettle on the stove, Tanya told my mother that the previous night my father had been to the apartment she shared with her boyfriend, and brought with him a thin brunette named Svetlana. After a few shots of vodka, my father announced that he was going to marry Svetlana. Tanya told him that he was behaving disgracefully—why wasn't he at home with his sick wife and his son? Tanya's story confirmed what my mother had begun to suspect.

I remember my parents' arguments with unnerving clarity. What I found peculiar even as a child was my mother's unwillingness to get angry about my father's infidelities. Instead, as new ones surfaced, she grew increasingly inward and remote, as though she believed herself to be culpable in his disappearances. After a while, she wore her depression like an overcoat.

Not long ago, she told me a story I hadn't known, about her difficult labor. When she delivered me she tore and bled badly; a young obstetrician stitched her in the delivery room. The tear took months to heal, and even after it did, intercourse remained painful. After I was born, there were nights when my father behaved as if he'd been spurned, storming out of the apartment and slamming the front door so hard that it rattled on its hinges. My mother, who lost her virginity two months before becoming pregnant with me, blamed herself.

I've wondered often what made my father vanish with the Irinas and Svetlanas he'd met at train stations and in ski-resort cafeterias. I guessed that it allowed him to forget, for several hours or days, about the man he was descended from and the country where he lived—and to forget, too, the unhappiness awaiting him at home. "It was never the same after you were born," he told me once, about his marriage to my mother. During their first year together, he thought that in my mother he'd found a fellow traveler—someone with whom he could stay up listening to Otis Redding records and arguing about *A Man and a Woman,* someone who'd translate passages from American magazines and liner notes from the backs of LPs, someone like him. But after I was born, by nightfall my mother was too enervated from work and hours on the metro, as well as the housework and parenting my father wouldn't do—cooking, cleaning, reading to me and trying to corral me into bed. Besides, being a parent proved to be less stimulating than my father expected. "You've become interesting," he told me one night when I was eighteen and visiting him in Moscow. "Now we can talk about poetry and jazz. You weren't very much fun when you were five."

When I was five, I thought of my father as an antagonist in a novel who appeared infrequently but had a pivotal dramatic role. When he was away, I pressed my face into the sleeve of a herringbone blazer I admired and inhaled the aroma of his filterless Turkish cigarettes. Sometimes I crept into his study and ran my fingers along his ink blotter and ashtray, or lay on the red plaid blanket on his bed and buried my face in his pillow.

I'd been attending kindergarten for nearly two years when my father first came there to take me home. Like most children, I disliked kindergarten, with its rows of tiny wooden beds and a caged guinea pig that lived under a poster-size portrait of Lenin, whom we were instructed never to draw, lest our childish technique distort his immortal features. The bunker-like building of the kindergarten sat low in an earthen depression—the foundation had been dug too deep—and when the children were set loose to play outside, every one of us became so spattered with mud that soon we resembled a tribe of fierce equatorial aborigines. When my father took my hand and began to walk toward the door, our *vospitatelnitsa*—the word means "upbringer"—grabbed my other hand and jerked me free from his grasp. She wasn't going to allow a stranger to walk out with me, she said, and my mother had to come and vouch for my father's identity.

I remember my father most vividly slumped on the sofa—even our sofa was upholstered in denim—listening to headphones that looked like grapefruit halves clamped over his ears. The curly cord snaked across the floor to his pride, a German Telefunken receiver with dozens of knobs and switches, the faceplate glowing with foreign promise. A floor lamp bathed his face in reddish light. If I walked into the living room while he was listening, I stepped deliberately, trying to set my feet soundlessly on the linoleum and make sure that my plastic sandals didn't squeak, because my father listened with his eyes closed and, when he sensed my presence in the room, his eyes sprang open and looked at me, muddied by the music, with an expression of both mild kindness and mild disappointment. I froze, embarrassed to have disturbed him, embarrassed to be someone he found childish and uninteresting, knowing as I did the look of animation and sly pleasure that brightened his face whenever he sat in his study with friends, fellow connoisseurs of the Paul Butterfield Blues Band and Wranglers and Antonioni.

And so I attempted to immerse myself in my father's things, especially the one he was proudest of, the stereo. One day when I was five and he was away, I lifted the turntable's plexiglass lid and, imitating him, lowered the tonearm onto the spinning plastic mat. My aunt Lyusia, Tamara's half sister, stood over me. I assured her that I knew how the turntable worked, but she watched anxiously, unconvinced, nattering at me to be careful. Lyusia had been a methamphetamine addict and spent five years in a prison somewhere along the northern reaches of the Volga (she even had a safety-pin tattoo on her shoulder to prove it), but the actions of a five-year-old petrified her. As it happened, I'd neglected to put a record on the turntable. As I ran over to one of my father's Latvian speakers, each the size of a bread box with a silver plastic sailboat tacked to the grilles, all I heard was a loud pop. The plastic mat had sheared off the stylus; my father was inconsolable. For weeks he called *fartsovshchik* acquaintances on our new shiny black telephone, searching for a replacement and telling them in a resigned yet demonstratively loud voice that his five-year-old son had "fucked up the stereo."

I sensed the loss of my father's approval and set out to right myself in his eyes. I decided that, like him, I would become athletic, and one day he pulled me on a pair of children's skis toward a ravine that split the treeless expanse in front of our building. It was a frigid and bright Sunday morning. Neighbors and their children careened down the slopes on sleds and skis. Every winter my father boarded a flight to the Caucasus to ski down steep, dangerous slopes (and, I realized later, to meet women) and kept a pair of beautiful Finnish downhill skis propped beside the coatrack in the hallway. Hands on hips, he watched me go down my first hill. I pointed the skis toward each other for fear of accelerating too quickly and slid to the bottom haltingly, as though in slow motion. My father shimmied down the slope after me. After another timorous slide, he clambered away, saying that he had to meet a friend and would return in fifteen minutes, twenty at most. "Enjoy yourself," he shouted, receding, "you look fantastic."

I tried to climb back up the hill the way he showed me, putting the skis perpendicular to the slope while pushing away with the poles, but the incline was too steep, and after twenty minutes of backsliding I gave up. From the bottom of the ravine I watched the sun set, tinting the sky a dramatic red, maroon, violet. Then it was dark. The other children had gone inside. Several parents asked where mine were, and I replied that my father had gone to meet a friend and would be back soon. Eventually I was alone. Strapped into overlapping skis, my arms poking diagonally out of the bulky cotton jumpsuit and my face swaddled in a wool hat, I clutched the poles stiffly at my sides. I wasn't sure how many hours had elapsed by the time my mother appeared over the rise and towed me up the hill, livid with anger. She walked inside cursing at my father; that night they argued past midnight. I sat in his study listening to the sounds coming from behind the locked door: shouting, the clatter of the occasional overturned pot and, once or twice, a gasp—it sounded like a sharp intake of breath—that meant he'd shoved her.

Afterward I began to think of my father with a hot, irremediable hatred. Inside me, this hatred was engaged in an ongoing argument with a craving for physical closeness, for any pretext to be near him. All the while I realized I was blowing it, that the project was hopeless. My father never hit me; in his mind, that would've made him too much like his own father. Instead, he rarely touched me at all. What I remember most was his mild yet persistent annoyance: because I spread too much butter on my bread, because I couldn't head a soccer ball, because I hadn't learned to read until I was five (he'd done it at four), because my love of his Creedence Clearwater Revival record wasn't rooted in the music's technical merits.

I felt as if I were treading water on the periphery of his awareness, unable to swim closer. I think I would've preferred him to shout. That my parents were very young, that their marriage and experience of adulthood felt to them strange and barely manageable, were things I didn't yet understand. To me they seemed like the petty deities from the illustrated and highly expurgated book of Greek and Roman myths my father gave me, clashing above me for capricious, unknowable reasons. At three or maybe four, I inflicted my revenge on them by dipping my index finger into the toilet bowl and smearing shit on our bathroom's canary-yellow floral wallpaper. I varied the direction and impasto of the strokes like a coprophilic Kandinsky. One night my mother discovered me in the kitchen, playing in the dark. When she turned on the light, she saw me sawing off the head of a male doll with a bread knife.

The respite from my parents' unhappiness was my grandmother's two-bedroom cooperative, a showcase of Tamara's ever-larger hegemony at the House of Fashion. I adored everything about it. A pair of crystal chandeliers lit the living room; the toilet seat, made of plush burgundy plastic, made a deflating hiss when I sat on it. Tamara had a taste for late-baroque splendor: a dinner table with hooves for legs, floral chintz wallpaper and curtains, oil landscapes in elaborate gilt frames, and my favorite, a set of impossibly thin china teacups and saucers that a TV anchorwoman had given her. When you held a cup to the light, its bottom glowed with the likeness of Queen Elizabeth II.

Tamara's husband, Mikhail Mikhailovich, managed a fruit-and-vegetable warehouse near the city limits. Like a typical Soviet manager, he rarely left work without filling the trunk of his Fiat clone with fresh inventory that he'd written off as rotten. In the refrigerator, his haul mingled with gifts from Tamara's clients. I liked to stand in front of it and stare at cans of crabmeat ringed with Vietnamese script, Hungarian cervelat, smoked whitefish, bunches of grapes. Tamara socialized with a coterie of baronial women in middle age with immaculate eye makeup and entertained them on Saturdays. Before they arrived, she led me into the kitchen and hoisted me onto a stool in front of a paper coffee cup filled to the brim with beluga caviar. She handed me a soup spoon. "I don't want to see you until you've finished it," she said, and left me in the kitchen to ponder my task.

A night at Tamara's revolved around her color television, the only one I'd seen. Tamara lounged on the couch in a fur-lined crepe de chine robe and paged through an Italian *Vogue* while Mikhail Mikhailovich drank bottle after bottle of beer and gnawed strips of *vobla*, a salted dried fish known in English as roach. When Tamara wasn't looking, he slipped me scraps of roach and a sip of beer. I jumped up and down on the sofa whenever my favorite movie, *Tractor Drivers*, showed on Channel 4. A Stalin-era musical set on a collective farm, it followed a cheerful couple who denounce a layabout in their barracks while celebrating the titular farm equipment in song. On Sunday mornings I woke early to watch *Alarm Clock*, a children's variety program, followed by two uninterrupted hours of armed-forces montage called *I Serve the Soviet Union*. In addition to entrancing me with footage of sheared-headed, muscular men traversing obstacle courses and fueling armored vehicles, the program fed my fevered fascination with military trivia in segments that diagrammed hierarchies of shoulder boards and medals, or told the history of the Kalashnikov family of assault rifles.

My companion during episodes of *I Serve the Soviet Union* was a custard-filled puff pastry the size of a tennis ball covered with butterscotch and crushed walnuts called the Little Nut. Tamara picked them up by the box at a kiosk near the Belyaevo metro station. The Little Nut precipitated shouting matches between my father and Tamara. He insisted the pastries would turn me into a "fat pensioner." Tamara replied that because he and my mother couldn't take the time to feed me properly, she had to. Listening to the arguing from her kitchen stool, my great-grandmother Maria Nikolaevna winked at me, grinning over the teakettle and the sugar bowl.

Returning home from Tamara's meant riding the metro to a shuttle bus, then walking about a kilometer home. On the bus, elderly women cooed at me and sometimes pinched my cheeks. When I was a toddler, some of them had told my mother approvingly that I looked like the baby Lenin, probably owing to my stern expression and large head of wavy yellow hair. By the time I was five, I had a shoulder-length blond mane and a variety of white cardigans from Finland that Semyon and Raisa had mailed me, and a woman in a park once remarked to my mother that I looked like a child who belonged astride a pony. One winter night on the shuttle bus, a fatigued-looking passenger was so taken with me that she reached into her coat and handed me a ripe pear. There was an audible gasp. Fresh fruit was unheard of in winter. Though I know my recollection must be faulty, I remember the event as a kind of secular Nativity. In the dark shuttle bus, surrounded by commuters in their felt boots and damp parkas, the yellow fruit lit up a circle of surprised faces, emanating rays of golden light like a halo in a Botticelli canvas.

ONE OF THE first stores to appear in Tyopli Stan was a poured-concrete bunker that sold vodka and Moroccan port. The port left a black film in a glass; an urban legend claimed that the sweet wine had been transported from Africa in the hold of an oil tanker. A supermarket arrived next. Day and night, on the expanse of already-cracked concrete in front of it, you could spot men in threes huddling around a trash can they'd set on fire, passing around 750 milliliters of vodka. Inside, the aisles were mostly empty. To relieve the emptiness, a single canned product—say, bream in tomato sauce—came labeled in various bright colors, and in the aisles the stock girls built pink, blue, and turquoise pyramids of canned fish, conspiring to create an illusion of choice.

My friend Vova, an army lieutenant's son who lived on the sixth floor, was a scrawny boy with sulfur-colored hair and a stutter. In winters I pulled him alongside our ravine in a sled, and afterward we dug tunnels in the snow. When the Arctic fronts receded we built bonfires and tossed in old perfume bottles to make the flame flicker green. Once, when we found a handful of unfired handgun cartridges, we tossed them in the fire, too, then hid in a swale for hours, waiting on our bellies for the bullets to come whistling over our heads.

Most of our neighbors were newlyweds or young parents, and no one owned many toys, so on Sundays Vova and I climbed the flat-roofed shed that housed the fuses to the power grid and leapt into a row of dumpsters. Trash was our porthole to adulthood, a storehouse of otherwise unobtainable information. There were dish detergent bottles to convert into squirt guns, ball bearings, books illustrated with pictures of train cars and subtropical birds, tangled panty hose, used condoms tucked into folded-over paper bags, tattered handbags and wallets, too-large cavalry-style boots that we pulled on and marched around in, pretending to be on an episode of *I Serve the Soviet Union*.

When the dumpsters failed to regurgitate something useful, we set fire to piles of dry grass by dragging a chunk of flint across the edge of a license plate to produce sparks, or else Vova and I tore a piece of bark from the solitary fir behind the liquor store and carved it into a sailboat with one of my father's spent razor blades. We fashioned a keel from a toothpaste tube, made sails from *Izvestia* newsprint, and set it afloat in the drainage ditch or on one of the colossal puddles that ringed our building. When the boat shot away from us on a fast current of meltwater that ran alongside the curb, we straightened our backs and saluted.

I GREW UP an only child in a country of only children. Among my parents and grandparents, only Raisa could claim a full-blooded sibling. A survey published the year I turned three found that 64 percent of Soviet women of childbearing age had one child, while another 17 percent were childless. Nearly every woman surveyed said that she would have preferred two or three children but that the demands of a full-time job, housework, an unhelpful husband and constant shortages made this untenable. Like most children in Moscow, I wanted a sibling—someone to relieve the hours spent playing alone, but also another body to deflect my father's anger and my mother's unhappiness. I recall imploring my parents to "make me a brother or sister," and their laughter.

I was nearly six when my mother, recovering from the flu, missed her period. The first pregnancy test came back negative, the second proved inconclusive. The physician who finally examined her said that she'd been pregnant for over three months—two weeks past the legal limit for an abortion. She was struggling to get out of bed before work, fighting off hopeless, guilty thoughts, and the prospect of another child terrified her. She woke several times a night, wondering what to do. Finally, she brought her dilemma to Tamara, the person she knew who was most adept at solving unsolvable problems, especially when they required circumventing the law. As it happened, the chief obstetrician at a clinic for KGB employees was a client of Tamara's. In exchange for cash and a favor, she'd dispense with the paperwork and hospital stay and perform the abortion at home. Neither my mother nor Tamara told my father about their plan.

It happened at the apartment of my mother's girlfriend Lyuba, a funny, boisterous blonde whom my mother had known since their first year at the university. The obstetrician turned out to be a capable-looking fiftyish woman who wore her gray hair in a tight bun; she introduced herself and changed quickly into a white coat. My mother lay on her back on a sheet that Lyuba threw over a coffee table. The procedure was supposed to be routine, but because of the poorly stitched tear from my mother's first pregnancy, the doctor struggled with her instruments. My mother began to worry only after she saw the color drain from Lyuba's face. She looked frightened. Blood had soaked through the sheet and run down the table legs onto the floor. There was too much of it. The doctor worked silently, her breathing rapid. Two and a half hours later, with her patient sedated and asleep, the doctor lit a cigarette and confided to Lyuba that my mother had nearly bled to death.

My mother told me about this many years after we came to New York. I'd already learned that in the Soviet Union abortions were far more common than they were in the West; my mother knew women who'd had six or seven by the time they were twenty-five. Diaphragms were difficult to find and unreliable, and condoms so thick that men often refused to wear them, and for many women abortion became a form of birth control. Even after learning these facts, and knowing about my mother's pain and fear, I still catch myself wondering, always guiltily for some reason, about the random arithmetic decreeing that I was born while my sister or brother was not.

AFTER TWO YEARS at the Institute of Psychology, my mother worked up the courage to file an official complaint about her supervisor, who promptly fired her. She landed a new job almost immediately, administering psychological tests at Kashchenko, a three-thousand-bed psychiatric facility known before the revolution as Alexeevsky Hospital and before that as Kanatchikov's Dacha, after a Moscow merchant who built it as a sanatorium for his disturbed daughter. The hospital was a purgatory for the rebellious, the indiscreet, the weird and the merely unlucky. The Soviet academician Andrei Snezhnevsky famously wrote that schizophrenia caused most forms of political and social dissent, and refuseniks were merely the most notorious among a patient population that included Baltic nationalists, Christians, drag queens, vegans and a smattering of the actually ill. Among the incoming patients who landed at my mother's desk was a butcher who intentionally mislabeled cuts of meat, a high school student who lay down on the floor in class and refused to stand up, a police trainee who wandered off into the woods for days, and a prisoner who, in an attempt to get transferred to a ward for the criminally insane, nailed his scrotum to the floor.

An adjacent, decidedly luxurious wing of the hospital housed the psychologically disturbed party elite. On cigarette breaks, my mother watched their mistresses and wives march up the sanitary-green staircase for conjugal visits, trailing their furs on the cement steps. Her favorite patient was an oddly personable sex offender named Antosha. She medicated his habit of grabbing women's breasts at public beaches and sometimes, after she put away the inkblots and the questionnaires, they talked for a while about their lives. "I'm thirty-four," Antosha confided to her once, "and no one has ever loved me back."

My mother said that in those years she developed what Soviet diagnostic manuals termed "anesthesia dolorosa"—a sensation of looking at the world through a pane of dirty glass. Eventually, she stopped asking my father about his disappearances, and he no longer offered explanations. Sometimes, in repentant moods, he told her that "these other women aren't worth your little finger." Still, after he bought a winter coat for a girlfriend, a clothing-catalog model from Kiev, he asked my mother what she thought of it. "You have such excellent taste," he added. My mother and I spent New Year's Eve of 1976 in front of our black-and-white television, listening to the midnight announcement and chimes over a static video feed of the Kremlin while my father took his girlfriend to a kebab restaurant called Baku. When he was home now there was less shouting, but the tense silences—charged with unspoken recriminations—eventually saturated every cubic centimeter of the apartment.

Where once I wished for my father's disappearance, now I avoided him, because I realized that the problem between us was me. After all, *he* was adept at seemingly everything: he'd come close to playing soccer professionally, skied the most dangerous slopes in the Caucasus, fished expertly, looked dashing in Tamara's bespoke blazers and suede jackets, read long difficult books in translation, and could open a beer bottle with his bare hands. One summer, when he took a job felling trees near the Arctic Circle, he hacked into a hornet nest and survived sixty or seventy stings. In kindergarten, I'd met other, visibly inferior fathers—balding men with comb-overs and beer bellies in boxy suits and op-art polyester shirts—and knew that any boy would be lucky to have mine. It was equally obvious to me that my father deserved a son who was smarter, cleaner and better-looking, as well as more athletic, masculine and self-assured, but no amount of trying would change me into that boy, so our stalemate persisted.

By the time I was seven, my mother and I had grown inseparable. At nights we cooked together or waltzed clumsily on the living room rug to a scratchy record of *Die Fledermaus*. After supper, we went walking past the outdoor flea market, where neighbors sold and traded their possessions, then up the hill to the new glass-recycling station. We strolled past a store called Jadran, its windows decorated with gleaming Yugoslavian dinner sets and mohair scarves that were priced well out of reach of most Muscovites. Our destination was the lobby of the local movie theater, home to the claw machine, which I attacked every time with a fistful of coins. I never managed to extract from it the stuffed rabbit, much less the miniature bottle of Armenian brandy that men coming out of the screenings tried to free from its glass prison. On the way home, I plied my mother with promises of devotion, like the oaths to Lenin and the party I'd soon recite every morning in school. "We're going to get married," I promised. "I'll wear a necktie and my father will visit us, but not very often." I was secure in our bond and never wondered whether my mother wanted a six-year-old for a confidant, though sometimes, in her blackest moods, she asked which of my parents I loved more.

Her inability, or unwillingness, to tell her parents about her unraveling marriage deepened her misery. Semyon and Raisa had had her uncommonly late, in their thirties, and even as a child she thought of them as middle-aged and fragile—orphans worn down by the war who couldn't endure more shocks and disappointments. She was aware, too, that her mother's sisters and cousins and their Jewish

friends rarely divorced, and considered divorce a form of moral failure, and shameful. Like other children of Holocaust survivors, my
mother thought of herself as an embodiment of her parents' aspira-
tions. The tragedies they endured before her birth bound her to
them. She thought often about the families each of them lost in the
war. How could she tell Semyon and Raisa—who fought and suffered for their families' survival, and made a fetish of survival
itself—that she wanted to break up *her* family, and that she'd chosen
to end her unborn child's life?

Ironically, the one person she trusted with her misery and her
loneliness was her mother-in-law. Tamara became my mother's closest girlfriend and good fairy. She cheered her with gifts of frilly un-
derthings, cut-glass flasks of eau de cologne, and hard-won lessons
in a homespun feminism. Tamara viewed lovers and husbands, and
men at large, dialectically, as either a convenience or an annoyance:
they might be recipients of judicious affection or even love but
weren't allowed to dictate her behavior or become proprietors of her
well-being. Her low opinion of men didn't spare her son, whom she
scolded regularly for his infidelities. So while she sympathized with
my mother's distress, she couldn't bring herself to regard the behavior of any man too seriously. She believed firmly that it was more
important to look good than to feel good and that the latter flowed
from the former. "When I feel frayed," she often told my mother, "I
put on a layer of foundation and something *gorgeous*."

Tamara, who filled out in her fifties, considered my mother's slender figure and high cheekbones an ideal canvas. She designed her
wedding dress—a floor-length peau de soie gown accessorized with
long white gloves—and later made her a raft of miniskirts to make
sure her daughter-in-law stood out from the other coeds with their
prêt-à-porter Warsaw Pact Pucci knockoffs. When my mother was
at her lowest, Tamara sat beside her on the sofa, asked her to pick out
a camisole or a blouse from the latest issue of *Cosmopolitan*, and
promised to make her a copy. When even this failed, Tamara whisked
her away on vacations she took with Mikhail Mikhailovich, the three

of them sharing a room at a resort in Sochi or Yalta. I waited for their return with Maria Nikolaevna, who sometimes said that I couldn't stay at home with my father because he, too, was traveling. I never asked where he had gone.

During one of these peculiar family vacations, at a resort on the Black Sea, a man struck up a conversation with my mother at a beachside café. A dark-eyed architect who spoke with a slight Georgian accent, he sat close to her and looked unabashedly into her eyes, making no attempt to hide his interest. Mid-conversation, my mother spotted Tamara and Mikhail Mikhailovich strolling down the boardwalk toward them. When Tamara looked up and spotted my mother and her suitor, she grabbed Mikhail Mikhailovich by the elbow, spun him around, and began walking in the opposite direction. Later, Tamara put an arm around my mother's shoulders and gave her an appraising look. "Dear," she said, "why don't you take a lover. No one will know."

WHEN I WAS four, a Boeing jet with a beautiful aqua stripe brought Gerald Ford to the far-east port city of Vladivostok. He came there

to meet the Soviet premier Leonid Brezhnev and to discuss the finer points of an arms control treaty called SALT II. Prior to Ford's arrival, the city's party boss transformed the center of Vladivostok into a spotless, freshly painted film set. Apparatchiks stocked local restaurants with chefs and waiters flown in from Moscow. Men in buses rounded up drunks and the homeless and drove them outside the city limits for "treatment."

The talks took place at a sanatorium in a nearby village, Okean-skaya. The party boss decided that the road from the sanatorium to Vladivostok—the route along which Brezhnev and Ford's motorcade would travel on a sightseeing trip—would reflect the city's rebirth. In a matter of days, police turned out families living in cabins and lean-tos along the road and burned down their homes. Crews of workers cut down several hundred of the Primorsky region's tallest, straightest firs, trucked them in from the surrounding forests, and stuck them upright along the road in freshly bulldozed banks of snow. It was a variation on a time-honored tradition. Some historians claim that when Field Marshal Potemkin lined the desolate banks of the Dnieper River with hollow, elaborately painted facades during Empress Catherine's visit to Crimea in 1787, he did it not for Catherine's benefit but to impress the foreign emissaries in her traveling party.

In Russia, appearances always mattered more than reality, and judged by appearances, we lived in a Socialist Arcadia that our grandparents sacrificed themselves to build. This is how I thought about our country even after we left it. It was a conviction instilled, nearly from birth, by cartoons and coloring books, by upbringers who taught us that "the General Secretary is the children's best friend" and, more explicitly, by our teachers. My mother and father regarded my patriotism ironically but knew better than to contradict it, lest I repeat their private comments and jokes in class.

As far as I could see, the Great October Revolution obliterated centuries of class warfare and inequality, the Great Patriotic War was won, and the Great Terror was renounced by Khrushchev and mothballed by Brezhnev. Did anything Great remain to be done? The Soviet economy was the world's second largest, after the United States'. In 1974, an average Soviet worker made as much as an American at the outset of the 1920s and lived on a per capita floor space of seventy-two square feet, one-seventeenth that of his American counterpart. Yet our upbringers and teachers reminded us weekly that our country boasted advances the United States could not: free medical care and education, gender equality, near-total literacy, and vending machines in every one of the country's regions that dispensed a mixture of seltzer and fruit syrup, to be partaken from a shared glass. Meat prices were stable, the consumption of alcohol had increased fourfold since the war, and half of the nation's households boasted a refrigerator.

Nowhere was this new opulence more evident than on TV. The unrelieved programming of documentaries about urban planning in Bulgaria, Stalin-era musicals and World War II dramas built gradually toward the New Year's Eve broadcast, a postprandial ritual in nearly every Soviet home, the colored lights and tinsel on the New Year's trees brightening the notables on screen. These programs resembled award shows for the elderly. Party *nomenklatura* in black suits and ties—bow ties had been nixed as bourgeois decades earlier—and their wives (some in Tamara's gowns!) sat at round tables, dutifully applauding domestic stars of song and screen. Usually this meant a film montage about nationwide overfulfillment of the Five Year Plan followed by a bass baritone belting a Glinka aria and finally a medley by Alla Pugacheva, our state-sanctioned lite-rock songstress. Her tropically mascaraed eyes and synthesizer-heavy ABBA pastiches—about sun-dappled spring mornings and guileless young love—bleated from millions of television screens across eleven time zones.

Many Muscovites didn't like to even speak Brezhnev's name aloud, instead swiping a finger over their eye, a reference to the leader's massive brows. The holiday broadcasts offered a chance to see our head of state in a decidedly more genial guise than his usual setting atop Lenin's mausoleum, where on high holidays he stood waving at a procession of intercontinental ballistic missiles rolling by on tractor trailers in slow motion. Leonid Brezhnev's head looked as if it were chiseled from a block of knotty pine. He appeared fully rectangular from every angle—his wife, Viktoria, was equally substantial—and moved with the languor of a pachyderm moments after it's struck by a tranquilizer dart. He was the first head of state to shrug off Bolshevik austerity and adopt the splendor of his counterparts in the Philippines and Uganda. Away from the Kremlin, he traveled in a Maserati, a vintage Lincoln and a Rolls-Royce Silver Cloud. In an official TASS photo, he appeared near one of his five dachas dining al fresco with a boar-hunting party, decked out in the loden jacket and feathered hat of an Alpine outdoorsman, a pair of ornate revolvers dangling in tooled-leather holsters from his hips. At televised party congresses and Central Committee meetings he read speeches with the animation of a ventriloquist's dummy, hence the following well-known Brezhnev joke:

> There is a knock on Brezhnev's door.
>
> He heaves himself up from the sofa, ambles to the foyer, puts on his glasses, takes a card from his shirt pocket and reads from it haltingly:
>
> "Who . . . is . . . there?"

Beauty flowered all around us in Moscow. Far below the streets, metro stations' walls and colonnades delighted me with bronze relief figures of veal farmers and welders. I asked Mikhail Mikhailovich to take me to the Exhibition of the Achievements of National Economy Park, to see Vera Mukhina's monumental sculpture *Worker and Collective Farm Woman*. I knew it as the revolving center of the Mosfilm logo that preceded *Tractor Drivers* and other favorite films; I thought I detected something undeniably erotic in the way the powerfully built worker and buxom farm woman held their hammer and sickle so close together. At home, I paged through picture books of monu-

ments. To me, none compared with *The Motherland Calls* in Volgograd, formerly known as Stalingrad, the site of some of the Great Patriotic War's deadliest fighting. At eighty-five meters it was one of the world's tallest statues, a figure of a woman thrusting a sword into the air and striding across an expanse of manicured grass with an expression of martial ecstasy.

I stared, too, at the interiors of bakeries and furniture stores, featureless rooms plastered ceiling to floor with identical group portraits of the Politburo—all reassuringly male, elderly and white—as though we were an island nation that had launched a single pop group into the world's consciousness. The Politburo was our Menudo. The only spot along the walls of our shops not covered with printed matter was the perch of a bulging plastic-bound tome called "The Book of Complaints and Suggestions." A pencil stub tied to a string dangled beside it. If it were intended to entice customers into complaining about the endless lines, or suggesting that the store stock more than a single variety of processed cheese, no one took the bait. These books, with their reassuringly blank pages, became the subject of hundreds of private jokes.

Prior to national holidays, I watched Mikhail Mikhailovich grimly slip a bottle of brandy and some wrapped packages into a briefcase to present to his boss, a regional director whose name was never spoken aloud in the apartment. Mikhail Mikhailovich communicated it instead with a subtle movement of the eyebrows. I understood that without this man there would be no daily trunkful of produce nor even a car to load it into, that in our country the contours of most lives were determined by an immediate superior.

I experienced this firsthand after enrolling in first grade. Tamara made sure that I ended up not at just any school, but at an academy for the sons and daughters of apparatchiks, diplomats and high-ranking officers in the *organs,* where English instruction was mandatory. Six mornings a week, Mikhail Mikhailovich dropped me off in front of the school's Doric facade. My uniform—a blazer and slacks of ocean-blue polyester, with a patch depicting a sun rising over the pages of an open book sewn halfway up the right sleeve— was freshly ironed. Pinned to my lapel was a red star with the face of the child Lenin, rendered in gold relief, peering serenely from its center. The star signified my membership in the munchkin division of the Communist brotherhood—known as October's Children, *oktyabryata*—the duty and privilege of every boy and girl aged seven to nine.

Like the Shriners, the Soviets were an insignia-mad people with a taste for commemorative pins and buttons, *znachki,* a mania that reached its apex during the 1980 Moscow Olympics. I was no different. Early on the morning of March 8—International Women's Day—I shook my mother awake to surprise her with a homemade gift. I'd pinned a tiny rectangular portrait of a teenage Lenin to a dry-cleaning receipt and stuck a sprig of baby's breath on each side with clear tape. She managed to thank me before tears welled up in her eyes and she turned her face away so I wouldn't see her heaving with laughter.

On Saturdays, I brought our first-grade teacher cut mimosas; an apple struck Tamara as down-market. The teacher's name was Nina Petrovna, and she partitioned our days into penmanship, memorization, and the rote copying of text from the blackboard. Sometimes we scribbled in our graph-paper notebooks for several hours in silence, something that pleased her as an example of age-appropriate behavior. She warned us daily about the dangers of smudging ink in the margins and walked up and down the aisles to make sure that our hands were spotless. *"Povtorenye mat uchenye,"* she liked to say: repetition is the mother of learning. She composed her face in an expression of mournful dedication—we hadn't yet learned to differentiate seriousness from unhappiness—expected of a Socialist educator.

"Children, what is the most aggressive country in the world?" Nina Petrovna intoned in singsong cadences at the beginning of the history portion of our class.

"Israel!" we shouted in unison.

The first textbook I remember—about children who'd committed extraordinary acts of courage—was titled *Young Heroes of the Soviet Union*. Chapter 1 was the apocryphal story of Pavlik Morozov. During collectivization, he turned his father over to the Reds for hiding several sacks of grain, a crime for which the father was shot. Later, Pavlik's own family murdered him. For a textbook written for six- and seven-year-olds, this one was remarkable for its abundance of torture, vengefulness and killing, illustrated in the saturated colors of a nightmare.

The image I remember best showed a Gestapo officer interrogating a straw-haired adolescent girl with pigtails. Her name was Zina Portnova. In the illustration, the officer is momentarily distracted, and Zina snatches his pistol from the desk. There is a rope around her neck—possibly because she tried to kill the Germans by poisoning a pot of soup, which she was made to eat herself. Though in photo-

graphs Zina looked like a pretty, fairly ordinary adolescent, in the drawing she has bulging heavy-lidded eyes and a fierce, almost demonic expression. The text beside the image informed millions of Soviet children that in the moments immediately following the scene depicted in the illustration, Zina "shot the Gestapo man dead" and was later tortured to death "animalistically." For their patriotic acts, most of the children in *Young Heroes of the Soviet Union* were punished: hanged, shot, immolated, poisoned, left to freeze in the snow. Their courage wasn't remarkable in itself—only in dying did they become heroes. Death made them beautiful.

It was while poring over a drawing of a teenage revolutionary hero—this time a boy—that I sensed the first hot-and-cold jolts of sexual desire. They were followed swiftly by panic. I told myself that it was the boy's bravery that made my face hot. But it happened again several weeks later at the Pushkin Museum, where I saw a small bronze of a naked, slender Prometheus chained to a rock, a bird of prey feasting on his liver. This time I wasn't so sure. Something about men's bodies and death was coalescing in my brain and trig-

gering electric shocks in my solar plexus. I understood, in some in-
choate way, that this attraction made me different from, and possibly
objectionable to, my father, and all I could think to do was look away
before my mother could catch me staring.

In the meantime, our first-grade textbook instructed a class of
unnerved seven-year-olds how to set fire to a stable, lest the horses
fall into the hands of the Whites, and how to halt a train laden with
Nazi munitions by throwing yourself under its wheels. The meaning
of these stories was difficult to miss: the will of the collective mattered more than the welfare of the individual, and our best destiny
was to die for that collective. "An individual, who needs him?" wrote
Vladimir Mayakovsky, whose poems we recited, standing pole-
straight beside our desks. "A single voice is smaller than a squeal."
There was a monument to Pavlik Morozov in nearly every Soviet
large town and city.

And there was also this: we were taught that the time we were
living in mattered less than the past. The golden age we were too
young to experience was a period not of peace but of war. We learned
that conflict gave our lives meaning—that meaning flowed from the
bearing of, and preferably dying from, intense suffering and strug-
gle. Unfairly, our time—the relative peacetime of the 1970s—didn't
offer us opportunities to die for our country by the millions, but it
remained our duty to behave as selflessly as the child martyrs in our
textbook. And so our sense of pride was to come not from material
abundance, or even personal accomplishment, but from a series of
national abstractions—the nuclear arsenal, space exploration, collective farming, the construction of dams and severe monuments—
that had nothing to do with the often miserable reality of daily life.
The worship of these abstractions is what in Russia was called spiri-
tuality.

For all the indoctrination we faced in school, the boundaries of
our behavior were not yet clearly demarcated. One morning, while
walking to class, I whispered the word *khui* (cock) into another boy's
ear. I'd heard my father say it when he was angry or joking with

friends, and I decided to try it out. A teacher walking in front of us whirled around and demanded that I repeat it. I don't recall what I mumbled in response, but minutes later I was sitting in the principal's office and waiting for my parents to arrive; they were telephoned at work and summoned to an emergency meeting. Later that afternoon they sat beside me and listened contritely while the principal lectured them about a zero-tolerance policy for foul language, about adolescent delinquency and the threat of narcotics, about "parasitism," about rough schools on the city's outskirts for children who'd been ruined with lax discipline.

The most dreaded day on the school calendar was the quarterly dentist's visit. A nurse called us one by one out of class and took us to an examination room in the basement. Inside, a chipper middle-aged woman in a lab coat drilled and tugged at what remained of our milk teeth without even a thought of anesthetic; Novocain had apparently been deemed as bourgeois as a bow tie. Even my father feared the dentist's office. The drills were slow and smoky, painkilling injections were reserved for root canals, and he had a habit of passing out in the dentist's chair while getting his molars filled. I talked up the terrors of the dentist's office to my best friend, Kyrill, trying to impress him with my stoicism. He was small for his age, with a mouthful of shiny braces and a flap of blond hair that fell over his left eye, but he was popular owing to his ability to draw an eerie likeness of a ZiL dump truck, especially after our teacher hung his drawing on the bulletin board beside a portrait of Minister of Foreign Affairs Gromyko.

Kyrill's mother had died in childbirth and his father worked at the Soviet consulate in New York, and he spent most of his time with grandparents. When his father returned on holidays, the three of us spent evenings at their cavernous apartment in the city center, playing with the plastic cowboys and Indians he'd brought from abroad. They had no peers among domestic toys, and my admiration for them must have been naked. A few days before New Year's, before being driven home in Kyrill's father's Volga, I found a cowboy tucked into my yellow rubber boot. The cowboy had a lavender shirt and a black lariat coiled above a black Stetson. The realization that he was mine to keep made me nearly sob with happiness. I slept with the cowboy facing me on the nightstand and fantasized about towering saguaro cacti, tomahawk-wielding Apaches and skilled craftsmen who made tiny, miraculous action figures. When I spoke up about my love of America over supper at Tamara's apartment, Mikhail Mikhailovich guffawed. He said brusquely that the United States existed to undermine the Soviet Union and oppress workers, and was not to be admired, despite what some Jews would have you believe. Tamara elbowed him and Mikhail Mikhailovich quieted down. Maria Nikolaevna chortled and turned back to her cold pork in aspic.

BY THE TIME Semyon and Raisa came to visit with us in Moscow, during the last days of 1976, they'd sussed out their daughter's unhappiness. My mother didn't dare tell them, of course, but a downstairs neighbor came up while my mother was at work and filled them in on our familial dramas. Later that day, Semyon told my father curtly that he wasn't about to go on speaking to a philanderer, and true to his promise didn't say another word to him during their stay. Still, neither could bring himself to give up their nightly chess games, and they spent the early morning hours in my father's study chain-smoking around the board, their silence interrupted only by the methodical tapping of the chess clock.

On New Year's Eve, we took a taxi to Tamara's. Mikhail Mikhailovich had dragged an enormous fir up the five flights of stairs, Tamara and I had decorated it with bells, tinsel and porcelain stars, and finally everyone gathered around it, toasting with Soviet Champagne and, in my case, tomato juice in a teacup. Later Tamara brought out a miniature songbook bound in red plastic, and she and

I performed several songs about the Great Patriotic War to scattered applause. My favorite was called "The Bells of Buchenwald." The entire night I kept glancing over at the presents under the tree.

Earlier that week, Tamara took me to the city's most splendid toy store, Children's World, to pick out a construction set and a children's microscope, to placate my budding interest in science. Waiting for Tamara outside the store, I recognized the figure of Feliks Dzerzhinsky—the nation's first secret police chief—snowbound on a pedestal in the middle of the square, and got a first glimpse of Lubianka's stolid facade looming behind him. I didn't know yet that in Moscow, "Children's World" had become an ironic euphemism for the KGB headquarters and prison, so that a Muscovite might say, "Two agents detained Olga for selling hard-currency certificates, and she spent three days at Children's World."

On our way home from Tamara's, we passed a Grandpa Frost, his fake beard sagging, the sack tossed over his shoulder, climbing into a dark sedan. He looked tired and cold. Inside the car, he took a swig from a vodka bottle. Still, I persisted in believing in our Socialist Santa Claus until a few months later, when I was sitting beside Tamara in the backseat of Mikhail Mikhailovich's Zhiguli sedan and mentioned Grandpa Frost for the last time. "You're too old to believe in that nonsense!" she snapped. "*I* buy your presents. The man you saw was an alcoholic in a red hat."

My mother left my father in February. I didn't know that the previous September they met at a courthouse near the Novye Cheryomushki metro stop to sign a divorce decree—a judge ordered child support to be paid equally—and afterward walked to a restaurant called Minsk to share a meal. Nor did I know that they'd long planned to separate, but because of the city's housing shortage, the sole available option would have been an apartment swap. This meant that my mother and I would move into a one-room apartment, while my father would have to take a room in a communal one, a possibility he refused to consider.

I did notice the increasing presence in our home of my father's friend and former university classmate Volodya, a fellow *fartsovsh-chik* from the far-east city of Ufa. He usually showed up while my father was away. My mother detested him, at least at first—she was convinced that he kept my father embroiled in his illegal business—and told my father that she didn't want him in the apartment. Nonetheless, Volodya continued dropping by. When she was home alone, he spoke to her in a low, consoling voice, letting slip details about my father's girlfriends and their whereabouts, and telling my mother that she deserved better in a tone that suggested barely suppressed outrage. "If he doesn't love you," he told her, "he should let you go."

Volodya was plainer and stockier than my father, but he understood the uses of patience. Eventually he confessed to my mother that he loved her, that he'd loved her from the moment they met, that he longed to raise her child, that he was ready to rent an apartment and move in together if only she'd accept him. The night she left home, another of my father's friends waited for him in our living room, chain-smoking on the sofa until well past midnight. He made her remember her twenty-seventh birthday party the previous May, when my father spent the night playing chess on the balcony with a downstairs neighbor and ignoring her. She remembered, too, that weeks earlier, when she dropped by my father's office at the film institute, she walked in on him kissing a younger co-worker.

While my father's friend waited in our living room, smoking unfiltered cigarettes and clutching a bag of Elmore James records, my mother threw some of our clothes into a suitcase, grabbed the electric light-up globe Tamara had given me for my seventh birthday, and pulled me and our things in a sled to a girlfriend's apartment down the street.

Three days later, my mother and I stood in an unfamiliar, twilit room. She was trying to persuade a hollow-cheeked woman in her late eighties to move in with her daughter and illegally sublet her one-bedroom apartment to us. The apartment looked haunted. A cloudy mirror with most of the silver backing flaked off hung in the hallway. The woman wore a too-large beret and looked as frail as a neglected fern. While she and my mother discussed money, I sat down on the edge of a chair; it disintegrated under me as though it were made of sawdust, sending me tumbling to the floor. The old woman apologized and brought out another chair, but it, too, buckled under my weight, its legs sliding out from under it like a fawn's. We moved in the following morning. Volodya and my mother claimed the bedroom while I bunked on the sofa.

Sleepless and giddy in the living room, I wondered whether I'd finally beaten my father. We lived now in Moscow's northwest quadrant—on the Voikovskaya stop of the Zamoskvoretskaya metro line—half a city away from him, and my mother had chosen me over him, just as I knew she would. I'd have done the same for her. Each night before bed, Volodya read to me; at supper he told me that I didn't have to eat the hot cabbage soup I detested. He'd never paid attention to me before, and I knew he indulged me only to win over my mother, but I liked him for it nonetheless.

Our Stalin-era building had high plaster ceilings and an enclosed courtyard shaded by old oak trees, and I made a posse of new friends. Dina, whose right hand was amputated at the wrist, lorded over us. The flesh of her stump curled in on itself like a bun and she kept it wrapped in a dirty green scarf. Several times a day she whipped off the scarf and brandished her stump like a pistol, all of us laughing and squealing, scattering in every direction, Dina laughing hardest of all.

My perfect new life didn't last. Volodya's young wife, Marina, showed up at the psychiatric hospital where my mother worked and threatened to kill my mother and herself. My father called, too. He'd forgive my mother anything, he said, "except Volodya." My mother knew she didn't love Volodya. Four months after we'd left, she met my father at a café. After they finished their coffees, she walked with him to our old apartment in Tyopli Stan and stayed, eventually moving back in. I felt betrayed, but Tamara was jubilant. She wanted to give my parents time alone and spirited me away to her dacha for an entire summer.

The flawless ribbon of asphalt that led to the village of Stepanov-

skoye was the same road that ministers and academicians took to
their sumptuous dachas in Zhukovka and Usovo, the same road that
led to Kuntsevo, where Vassily spent nights patrolling the lanes of
Stalin's dacha. Stepanovskoye was smaller and homelier: a dirt road
lined with prewar wooden houses, two shallow ponds, some woods,
a corrugated-metal shed of a store that sold condensed milk and cigarettes, and on a hill a whitewashed church denuded of its domes and
crosses, where on Saturday nights the entire village watched movies
from rows of folding chairs. In summers, Stepanovskoye was populated by other children of well-off Muscovites: Mitya, whose musi-
cian parents toured Europe with the Moscow Philharmonic, and had
outfitted their bathroom with a bidet; and Lionya, a child of diplomats who enthralled the younger children when he spoke the non-
sensical words "Chevrolet limousine" as though they were an
incantation from *The Arabian Nights*.

Maria Nikolaevna and I lived in the front half of a low green
house with blue shutters; Tamara and my parents visited on weekends. The summer I turned five, my father ran along the main road,
his hand on the back of my new bicycle seat while I pedaled furi-
ously. He'd taken off the training wheels that morning. When I
glanced over my shoulder and saw him standing six houses behind
me, I rode into a woodpile and opened a gash in my forehead.

In the mornings, I lugged water from a crank well in a plastic bucket, and Maria Nikolaevna fired up the samovar. We had weak instant coffee with buttered white bread and then set off for the woods. Maria Nikolaevna knew the good trees. Tufts of mushrooms sprouted among the moss and dry leaves near the roots, and she bent down to cut the stalks of the larger ones, the ones we kept, with a penknife. If you left the roots intact, she explained, they'd sprout new mushrooms the following morning.

She taught me the hierarchy of scarcity and flavor: crunchy *siroezhki* (genus *Russula*), with their russet, green and yellow caps, were the most common; slimy *maslyata* (slippery jacks) were better; then chanterelles, called *lisichki,* which means "little foxes"; and finally dense, bulbous *boroviki* (King Boletes), the rarest and most delicious. We carried home the day's haul in wicker baskets. While Maria Nikolaevna fried potatoes in an iron skillet, I cleaned the mushrooms, sliced them, dropped the pieces in water to dislodge the bone-colored worms, then dried them before she tossed them, along with half of a chopped onion, into sizzling butter. This was supper, seven nights a week.

After the evening meal, Maria Nikolaevna sent me down the garden path to the outhouse. Inside, the walls were hung with plastic toilet seats belonging to the landlady's family and boarders. Mine was the smallest, the color of buttermilk. While sitting on my seat and "minding my business," as my great-grandmother insisted on calling it, I listened to the night wind whining through the unfinished wooden slats, the soft rustle of the wheat field behind the fence, the buzz of bluebottles in the pungent dark. After Maria Nikolaevna banked the fire and climbed up to her sleeping loft above the *pechka* (a wood-burning stove built into a wall), I lay in bed and stared at our landlady's red corner: three icons under an eave, a pair of saints around an Ethiopian-brown Madonna and child robed in gilt, a piece of day-old bread tucked into a frame's corner. I spent hours looking up at the mysterious figures, wondering who they were.

·   ·   ·

BACK IN MOSCOW, something in my father changed. He was quieter, more attentive, less liable to leave without an explanation; sometimes I noticed that he was sadder, too. Though I didn't know why, he and my mother seem to have fashioned a truce that at times gave way to a cautious tenderness. Later, she told me that during those months his nightmares visited him more often, sometimes for several nights in a row.

It astonished me when my father began to spend time with me. He took me to the House of Film, to watch a screening of *The Stunt Man*, a thriller with Peter O'Toole that hadn't yet been released in the United States and that scared me out of my wits. He asked me to walk with him to a friend's apartment or to the corner kiosk for cigarettes. We spent an entire afternoon in the film institute's cramped library, where he showed me rare prerevolutionary books and cans of foreign films, and he introduced me to co-workers in the cafeteria. At home we sat up late watching movies on the black-and-white TV and later play-fought with plastic toy sabers he'd bought for us, my father finally allowing me to defeat him. I was unnerved by the change in him but enjoyed and accepted the attention. I came up with theories about his metamorphosis. What I didn't know is that he was saying goodbye to us.

My mother made up her mind that autumn, when meat began disappearing from stores. One Sunday, she'd run out to the supermarket for a second time in two hours, after Tamara called to say they were "giving away" frozen cuts of beef. She returned home clutching three bags of groceries, her hair and coat plastered with November snow. My father was away. Raisa, visiting from Vilnius, looked up at my mother. "We have to leave this country," she said quietly. Her sister Ida, the last of her family to leave, had been living in Haifa for years. Her other sisters, nephews and nieces now lived in Sydney and Tel Aviv.

In the coming weeks, my parents spent nights locked in my father's study, negotiating out of my earshot. He couldn't decide what he wanted. At times he seemed to be coming apart. "I don't want my child to grow up in this country," he told her. He said he'd decided to leave the country with us, then realized he couldn't go through with it. "If I come with you, I'll only end up lying on the couch in my one pair of jeans and listening to the same old records." And: "If I were a Jew, I'd leave in a minute, but I am Russian and will always miss this country." And, once: "After you're gone, I'll hang myself."

Tamara bargained with my mother. She pleaded with her to leave me in Moscow, promising to quit her job and devote herself to raising me. Once, she offered to leave the country with us. When he found out, Mikhail Mikhailovich exploded, accusing my mother of stealing me from them. "How can you lousy Jews do this to us?" he shouted before locking himself in the bathroom.

My mother applied for an exit visa to Israel—our only legal route for leaving the Soviet Union—in November 1978, a week after Semyon and Raisa filed their applications in Vilnius. Ida had mailed the required invitations and support voucher from Haifa. My mother knew a little about life in Israel and worried about the compulsory military draft, about her not-quite-Jewish son becoming a second-class citizen, about being judged a lapsed, self-hating Jew. She imagined Israel as a larger version of Vilnius's Jewish community, with its provincialism and gossip, its narrow-minded grudges and fears. And so she decided we would go to New York.

When she filed the application at the visa agency, my father signed a form authorizing my mother to take me permanently from the country, with no possibility of return. In exchange, she signed away all future claims to child support. Neither thought that telling me any of this was a good idea. Mikhail Mikhailovich continued to drive me to school Mondays through Saturdays; in second grade, I began studying English. On Sundays, I still woke at dawn to have breakfast with Tamara and Maria Nikolaevna and to watch *I Serve the Soviet Union* on their color TV.

On the day after my mother filed her exit-visa application, the hospital director fired her. There'd be no income while she waited to find out whether her petition was granted, a process that could take several years, and little by little she sold her Finnish sheepskin coat, most of the crepe silk blouses and skirts Tamara had made for her, her two pairs of Levi's and nearly all her jewelry and books. In the mornings, a black Volga sedan idled outside the doorway of our apartment building, and later in the day it reappeared across the street from the film institute. The *organs* now took a pointed interest in my father's private commerce; he didn't yet suspect how intrusive this scrutiny would become.

My memories of the summer I turned nine, my last in the U.S.S.R., are as disordered as a shoe box of postcards. Tamara and Mikhail Mikhailovich took me on a meandering road trip to Yalta, on the Black Sea; for some reason the moment I see most clearly is my crying jag somewhere near Kiev, after Mikhail Mikhailovich ran over a duck. Yalta was the first place I'd seen a palm tree or denim-blue seawater. I never knew Tamara's moods to be anything but buoyant, but on Yalta's white-sand beaches I noticed her looking intently at me, her expression perplexed and lost, as though she were trying to solve an equation. It was the first time I saw her look helpless. When I asked whether something was wrong, she waved away the question and smiled. On the drive back to Moscow, she hardly spoke to Mikhail Mikhailovich.

The letter from the visa agency arrived in July. My father brought it up from the mailbox with tears in his eyes, or so my mother said. I don't recall being asked to choose, or even questioning whether I'd be going to "the West" with my mother. She told me we would be gone for a while only, that before long we'd return and I would again see my father and my friends. I don't remember feeling much besides a numb excitement. We had three months to leave the country.

I shared the news with my upstairs friend Vova. He blinked at me, confused, while I pressed some green plastic soldiers and a ball bearing into his palm. At school Nina Petrovna had told us that emigrants were traitors to the motherland, but when I blurted out that my mother and I were leaving for the United States, the capitalist superpower, she merely sighed and tousled my hair. Even though I was a traitor now, she allowed me to remain an October's Child and wear the star on my lapel until my last class. Kyrill and I said our goodbyes in the school cafeteria. We'll never be Pioneers together, he said, wiping away tears. I'd never wear the red kerchief around my neck and give the vaunted salute, hand above head, symbolizing the will of the many over the one. Kyrill's hand was on my shoulder and he was crying. "Now you will never be able to die for your country," he said.

Semyon and Raisa's visas arrived a week before my mother's. Semyon decided to take with them every last object they owned: a maple-veneered bedroom set, spatulas and spoons, the hand-cranked meat grinder, a Grundig radio console from the 1960s, and 450 kilos of books he packed into more than a hundred boxes. He followed these sundry things to a customs checkpoint in Brest, from where they would be shipped to Vienna and eventually to New York. My mother and father met him there. They waited for several weeks in a run-down hotel while customs agents combed through Semyon's boxes, tearing them open and dumping the contents on the floor, leaving the three of them to pack everything again. The exit visas were about to expire, and my mother took the train to Moscow to petition the visa agency for a two-week extension. In Brest, the wait continued. Tamara suggested that my mother apply for another extension, but she was afraid. My mother had a dream in which she was waiting in line at the visa agency, and one of the women who worked there tore up her documents and told her that her exit visa had been revoked.

On the day my mother and I arrived at Sheremetyevo airport with our suitcases, we had twenty-four hours left to leave the country. Our plane tickets to Vienna had cost two thousand rubles, roughly fifteen times my mother's monthly salary. My father had given her most of the money in exchange for her share of the apartment. She paid another, smaller sum to renounce our Soviet citizenship and internal passports. After selling nearly everything, all she had left were two sweaters, several blouses and skirts, several pairs of underwear, a winter coat, two pairs of shoes, a portable camera, three jars of osetra caviar that someone said she could sell abroad, and a hardbound book of poems by Anna Akhmatova.

The memory of that last morning in Moscow has the sickening vividness of moments after one is struck by a car. Mikhail Mikhailovich drove in near silence. There are times when I believe I could retrace that drive to the airport, turn by turn, even today. My father sat stiffly in the passenger seat. I sat in the back sandwiched between my mother and Tamara, who didn't let go of my hand until the air-traffic-control towers came into view. That morning Maria Nikolaevna refused to say goodbye to us and shut herself in her room.

At the airport, a uniformed woman led my mother and then me into separate cubicles for a final customs inspection. I dropped some coins onto a tray. My mother recalled that we were allowed to take with us one photo album, no art or antiques, no more than five grams of gold, and exactly 137 U.S. dollars. Before they said goodbye and embraced, my mother handed Tamara the gold watch that Tamara had given her as a wedding gift. Another customs officer, a man, ordered my mother to strip while yet another tapped the heels of her boots to check for precious stones. She was trembling because she'd heard that some women were subjected to gynecological exams at the airport. A week later, Semyon and Raisa would stand in a similar room at another airport while a customs agent slit open the soles of their shoes with a razor and then unceremoniously threw the contents of their suitcases onto the floor. "Tell the Jewish professor to remain calm," the agent barked at the soldier at the door.

For a few minutes after our luggage was returned to us, my mother and I stood in a featureless hallway outside the customs area and stared through glass at the jet that would take us to Vienna. The fuselage was marked with Aeroflot's winged hammer and sickle. The morning was bright and cloudless, and my mother and I lingered by a window at Sheremetyevo airport in the Union of Soviet Socialist Republics, though we no longer counted among its citizens or those of any other country. On the way to our gate, we took a wrong turn into a diplomatic lounge furnished with Scandinavian leather-and-chrome furniture. The moment had a dreamlike quality. No one spoke to us or asked to see our documents. We wandered out onto a glass balcony overlooking the waiting area. My father and Tamara stood below us. They looked up and spotted us, and they waved. My father was crying. They'd been there for more than two hours, unable to make up their minds to go home. I waved back for what seemed like a long time, standing there in my puffy nylon jacket and wool hat. My mother held my hand. "Take a good look at your father," she told me, "because you will never see him again."

. . .

THE FLIGHT WAS smooth. Aboard the Tupolev Tu-154 we were served an unexpectedly luxurious meal of baked chicken and mashed potatoes and a triangle of soft processed cheese in a foil wrapper that read "Progress!" I remember my mother slipping the metal forks and knives into her coat pockets. An hour into the flight, the pilot announced, in German and then Russian, that the plane had left Soviet airspace. *"Meine Damen und Herren . . . ,"* the announcement began, and when it was finished, one or two passengers, the boldest ones, clapped. I looked out the window, but the sky and the rectangles of earth below looked exactly as they did a moment earlier. After landing, I sat on my suitcase and saw the pilot walk out of the gate, his hat embroidered with the six-sided star of the Israeli air force. "Is Austria a capitalist country?" I asked my mother, suddenly spooked. Years later, she told me that I looked "as scared as a rabbit."

For a week we lived in a ramshackle inn on Vienna's outskirts— I can recall only that it had *Grüner* in its bucolic name—that abutted a small, walled-in urban park. The proprietor was a fattish ginger-haired man with a glistening black leather coat and a black Porsche parked in the courtyard who made a habit of rolling his eyes and spitting on the floor and sometimes shouting at the Soviet refugees. He made it clear he disliked having us in his establishment and did it only for the money. I suppose his attitude was understandable; we were a panicky, haggard cohort, families of three or four in nylon slacks and overcoats stuffed with wads of cotton. No matter where we went, we insisted on taking our suitcases, some held shut with tape, afraid of leaving them in our rooms for even a few minutes. In our rooms we attempted to cook with hot plates wired for the wrong voltage and blew the fuses.

From a pay phone in the lobby, my mother placed calls to Moscow at agreed-upon times, when everyone gathered at Tamara's apartment. She punched in a series of codes from a mimeographed sheet, spoke a few words into the receiver, and handed it to me. She said I had one minute. I quickly said hello to my father and asked to speak with Mikhail Mikhailovich. "On the way from the airport, we rode in a Mercedes-Benz!" I shouted into the receiver when I heard his voice. "It was so much nicer than your Soviet shitbox!"

The moment that most of us talked about for years to come was our first visit to an Austrian supermarket. The first glimpse of beautifully designed, brilliantly colored packaging, the absence of empty shelves, and above all the coexistence of multiple brands of the same foodstuffs was a revelation of almost unpleasant intensity. All of us remember it. Walks through downtown Vienna, with its palaces and topiary-lined gardens, presented other, milder shocks. I watched a newspaper boy leave a hat full of money and a stack of newspapers on the sidewalk and walk away, while pedestrians, on their way to work, picked up the papers and dropped exact change in the hat. Also: pristine rectangles of gelatin-topped pastry inside gleaming vitrines, in brightly lit shops that were perversely empty of customers. And, on a city bus, speaking to my mother at a conversational volume and after a few moments realizing that nearly every head had turned to glare at us with Germanic expressions of reproach.

Our stay in Vienna lasted all of ten days; the next stop on the refugee caravan was Italy. We slept through the border crossing, traveling aboard a bus with no signage and windows tinted so dark that we could barely see the passing scenery. It had departed Vienna at four in the morning: a precaution, the driver told us, against a potential terrorist attack, like the hostage taking of Soviet refugees carried out six years earlier in Austria by a group calling itself the Eagles of the Palestinian Revolution. This also explained the submachine-gun-carrying soldiers in flak jackets who sleepwalked past our gate at the gloomy poured-concrete bus terminal.

The first walk my mother and I took after we arrived in Italy was along a gravel path lined with cypresses. In between their regularly spaced trunks we could see verdant olive groves. We were staying at the Hotel Flamingo, on the Via Flaminia, not far from Rome. A Persian cat sauntered alongside us and rubbed its flanks against the cypresses' dusty bark. It was the middle of November, maybe an hour before dusk. The landscape looked like a scene from a travel brochure, and had I seen one, I'd have recognized its studied showiness. But I was nine and told my mother breathlessly that this was what paradise must look like.

After forty-eight hours in Italy, we remembered Vienna as someplace fretful and twilit, like a late Shostakovich quartet. It was warm in Lazio; the palette brightened. The gravel path led to a building that from afar looked like a castle but turned out to be a fifteenth-century convent. Around it grew rosebushes and persimmon trees and clusters of oleander. We were walking past it in pleasurable silence when a door of a wooden cabin on the property sprang open and a wiry dark-haired man in an apron emerged and started toward us. My mother grabbed me by the shoulders and pulled me toward her protectively. She assumed the man was a groundskeeper who'd come to tell us we were trespassing, but instead of shooing us away, he beckoned us into the cabin. Inside there was a woman and another couple; they spoke a few phrases in melodious incomprehensible Italian and invited us to sit at a long wooden table and put in front of us a plate of bread and cheese and a bottle of red wine. I sat at the table and gnawed on a hunk of hard cheese while my mother conversed with the couples. They spoke no Russian, French or English, and we spoke no Italian, but everyone made do with hand gestures and a handful of shared geopolitical terms. That foreign strangers brought us into their home and gave us food and wine left my mother and me dazed; the quattrocento landscape compounded the sensation. Before sending us back into the oleander-scented dark, the woman handed my mother an armful of tangerines still swaddled in their glossy leaves.

The Flamingo was a peeling box of pink stucco built sometime in the 1950s and wasn't particularly popular with tourists, which is why it was being rented out as temporary lodging for refugees. The morning after our walk to the convent, we came downstairs for an early breakfast of coffee, a few plastic packets of butter and jam, and a basket of rolls that turned out to be mostly hollow. At our table, a man from Odessa in a sweater pulled snugly over a hemispheric belly took a salami out of a briefcase, laid it across his plate, and began sawing at it with a butter knife.

The most communal events at the Flamingo were the bazaars the Soviet Jews organized in the hotel's parking lot. On card tables covered with fabric, our fellow refugees laid out dainty theater binoculars, amber necklaces, and whole cities of teacups painted with primroses. My mother sold her camera and, in spite of my fit of howling and crying, two silver-and-enamel teaspoons—their handles shaped like a cockatoo and a bear—that Tamara had tucked into a rubber galosh when we packed my suitcase in Moscow. The Italians sniffed and haggled over the merchandise and unfurled rolls of colorful lire. I turned over one of the bills and was startled to discover a picture of a bearded Leonardo da Vinci; it was the first money I'd seen without a profile of Lenin.

The hotel felt like summer camp, even in late fall. Everyone kept their doors open. They dropped in on one another, marveled at the still-life-perfect fruit sold at roadside stands, complained about failing dental work, debated Boston versus Sydney versus Tel Aviv. My mother flirted with a confident-seeming man with curly black hair and a leather jacket whose face and name I no longer recall, probably because at the Flamingo there was no shortage of men with curly black hair and leather jackets. Our stay in the idyllic countryside lasted less than two weeks. A worker from the Hebrew Immigrant Aid Society (HIAS) announced that while some from our group were being settled in a town called Ladispoli, our family was being relocated to Lido di Ostia, a beach resort about thirty minutes from Rome. He handed Raisa an envelope filled with lire—our allowance for the following two months, most of it earmarked for rent. There, by the Tyrrhenian Sea, we would await our U.S. visas.

Ostia looked nothing like a travel brochure. Its seaside trattorias catered to working-class Romans, day laborers, soldiers and fellow migrants who arrived aboard the train from Piramide carrying folding chairs, transistor radios, plastic bags of sunflower seeds and tanning lotion, even in December. The town was founded on a malarial marsh. Four years prior to our arrival, one of my father's heroes, the film director Pier Paolo Pasolini, was killed on an Ostia beach when a seventeen-year-old hustler ran him over several times with Pasolini's Alfa Romeo. Several years later, the Red Brigades kidnapped and murdered the former prime minister Aldo Moro. One of the Marxist-Leninist faction's hideouts was nestled among the tenements that fanned out from Ostia's beaches, and shortly before our arrival, carabinieri raided it and confiscated a truckload of guns and thirty kilos of explosives.

Our one-bedroom apartment, furnished with wobbly chairs and floored incongruously with real marble, was situated on the third floor of a tenement in the Communist quarter. Neighbors called the other, tonier side of town the fascist district. On our first day in Ostia, my mother watched a procession of elderly men in short-sleeved shirts carrying red flags down our street and singing "Bandiera rossa," a Communist anthem she'd learned at a Lithuanian pioneer camp in a flourish of international solidarity. Behind our building there was a concrete path lined with potted palms and a seawall covered in graffiti. Someone had written "Viva Stalin, Viva Brezhnev!" on it with crimson spray paint.

In Vienna, many in our group had compared the handful of countries that were accepting Soviet refugees—our future homes. What I recall about these discussions in other people's hotel rooms are the protracted silences, sighs and exchanges of faulty or incomplete information; many Russians agreed that Canada and Australia were most desirable by virtue of accepting the fewest immigrants, having the lowest levels of air pollution, and boasting the smallest populations of blacks. But Canada and Australia didn't admit refugees with chronic illnesses like Raisa's Parkinson's, and most American cities required a written invitation from a family member residing there. Fortunately, our chosen destination—New York—was one where the large Jewish community was willing to take in the ill and the unattached. We spent a number of weeks in Rome awaiting medical examinations, interviews at the U.S. embassy, and the perpetual signing and countersigning of documents. In 1979, more than fifty thousand Jews left the Soviet Union; so many families from Sochi and Ufa crowded the waiting room at the resettlement agency in Rome that when someone opened the door, half a dozen people had to shift position. Sometimes, after waiting from eight in the morning to six at night and failing to see anyone, we were told to come back the following morning.

During one interminable afternoon in the HIAS waiting room, a bearded man reached into a cardboard box and surreptitiously handed me a book with a blank red cover. "Free of charge," he whispered in Russian. The book narrated the life of Jesus in line drawings and balloon-encapsulated dialogue. I'd never seen a comic book, and I reread it until the pages were dog-eared and stained with food. Afterward, with a set of color markers from Children's World, I made drawing after drawing of the Crucifixion. I lavished the most attention on Jesus's pectorals and lats, and on the details of the halo, which I colored an electric orange.

My mother and I had been living in Ostia for several weeks when Semyon and Raisa arrived from Vienna and moved into our marble-floored apartment; a few days later, I surprised them with several dozen drawings of Jesus on the cross. I'd never seen my grandfather turn pale so quickly. He began shouting. Did I realize that our food and rent were paid for with money lent to us by the world's Jewish community? It will be taken away immediately, he bellowed, if the caseworker discovered my blasphemous, ungrateful drawings. He snatched the sheaf of drawings from my hands and tried to throw it away, but I blocked him; we careened around the room, tugging at them, until Raisa took them from us and hid them at the bottom of a suitcase.

Our caseworker in Rome warned us about street crime and counseled my mother to carry jewelry and cash in her boots or brassiere. Raisa was terrified of burglars and insisted on keeping nearly all of our valuables in a sky-blue patent-leatherette purse with a gold-plated clasp that she clutched beneath her breasts with both hands.

On a sunny morning in February, my mother and I stood by the kitchen window and watched Raisa take an unaccompanied stroll down the sidewalk. Going outside on her own made her anxious, but my mother and I encouraged it, urging her to be more independent. From the sidewalk, Raisa looked up at us and smiled, taking a few tremulous steps. Suddenly a moped with two teenagers on it turned the corner and sped down the street toward her. With a single graceful motion, the boy on the back of the moped bent at the waist, looped a metal hook around the handles of Raisa's purse, and whisked it from her hands. Raisa let out a terrible cry. She bounded after the moped but after a few tottering strides fell to her knees. My mother and I ran downstairs, but the *ragazzi* on the moped were gone.

In the purse, Raisa had kept her gold engagement ring, Parkinson's pills, and most of our documents and money. My grandmother wasn't given to self-pity; I'd never seen her cry, and I never would again. But there, on a sidewalk in Ostia, she wept inconsolably, smearing lipstick on her cheeks with Semyon's plaid handkerchief. "Why is life so cruel?" she remarked to no one in particular. She was disconsolate until a caseworker helped us file a police report and returned to us part of our stolen allowance.

As a university student in Moscow, my mother had known a classmate whose parents were high-ranking party officials; during a visit to their colossal apartment, she came across a stack of American Spiegel catalogs. She told me that while looking at the models on their pages, she got the impression that while life in the Soviet Union transpired in black and white, people in the West lived in full color. Our weekly trips to Rome bore out her suspicion. Though it was balmy that November, women strolled in full-length furs and men wore cashmere coats. My mother and I stopped for *tramezzini* near the Fontana di Trevi, for gelato on the Piazza Navona, then continued on various daylong excursions: to the Gallery of Maps at the Vatican, to the Church of St. Peter in Chains on the Esquiline Hill to gape at Michelangelo's horned Moses, and to the Villa Borghese, where we sat quietly for an hour in a room of mostly black Caravaggios. My mother was dating a man from St. Petersburg, and the three of us spent an overcast afternoon feeding the feral cats among the crumbling masonry of the Colosseum, where a passerby snapped a photo of us, squinting into the setting sun.

My mother looked elated in Rome. She adored the city's palms and squalid antiquities. Amid men who propositioned her on city buses and fashionable women who clicked through baroque plazas on high heels, she caught the first glimpses of what felt to her like authentic freedom. At a café near the Pantheon, she ran into her former classmate Izya, the one who did her homework at Moscow State University and planned to become a lecturer of Marxism and Leninism. He was coming out of a bus with his pregnant wife. He and my mother embraced. "We're going to New York!" he told her.

Two weeks later, visas in hand, we boarded an Alitalia jet bound for John F. Kennedy International Airport. Families from Tula and Bukhara, some of whom hadn't been aboard an airplane before, roamed the aisles. Within half an hour, the 747's toilets were clogged with food wrappers and diapers. The overhead luggage bins sprang open when the plane hit a patch of turbulence over the Atlantic and nearly everyone gasped. Nine hours later, my grandparents, my mother and I walked out into a room where officers from immigration, customs and the New York City police waited for us impassively. Someone had strung a paper banner across a bank of metal detectors that read, "Welcome to the United States of America!"

My mother spotted Lyuba, her best girlfriend from the university, waving at us outside the baggage claim. She'd been living in Queens for a little over a year. It was already dark when an unmarked bus carried the six of us through the wastes of Queens toward Manhattan, letting us off at Ninety-first Street and Broadway, in front of a residential hotel called the Greystone. With its hot shower and clean sheets, our small room seemed needlessly luxurious. Later, when my mother and I walked down the hallway, several old men lingering in open doorways glanced up at us with a mixture of curiosity and apprehension.

The following morning my mother wrapped a scarf around my ears and took me on a walk in our new city. Manhattan's Upper West Side had neither palm trees nor baroque fountains. It was March and upper Broadway was mired in sleet. The weather was the same, my mother remarked, as it had been on the November morning we left Moscow. Rectangles of overcast sky were visible between nondescript apartment buildings; pedestrians slogged by in rubber boots, nylon jackets and parkas. I peered at the city timidly over my scarf. My mother put her hands on my shoulders. "You see," she said reassuringly, "America isn't that different after all."

OUR CASEWORKER AT the New York Association for New Americans insisted that we rent an apartment in Brighton Beach, the oceanside neighborhood where about a third of New York's Russian-speaking population lived, most of them Soviet Jews. And so on a sunny afternoon my mother and I rode the subway to the end of the line, across the whole expanse of Brooklyn. We walked under the elevated train tracks in a state of astonishment. Many of the shop signs on Brighton

Beach Avenue were Russian; a particularly odd one read, "Books/ Dry Cleaning." There were produce stands on nearly every corner encircled by open crates of ripe fruit in saturated colors. There were specialty food stores with vitrines containing *pelmeni,* smoked sturgeon with the skin on, butter from Sweden and Poland, garlands of sausages. There were shops selling Russian-language books, records and cassettes alongside nesting dolls and Soviet military hats. There were banquet restaurants where dancers in sequined leotards high kicked, amid tables laden with crown roasts of lamb and bottles of Smirnoff, to the music of live pop bands with singers who sang in Russian, English, Yiddish and French. Brighton Beach was not the West, not exactly. It was a fantasy of the West, a corrective to every major Soviet shortage by virtue of offering a practically unlimited supply of pop music, meat, tropical fruit, alcohol and soft-core nudity.

Nearly everyone on Brighton Beach Avenue spoke Russian. Women wore mohair hats and men wore felt caps with short visors, as they had in Minsk and Odessa, but mixed with items that signified the West, if mostly to us: leather jackets, blue jeans, digital wristwatches, aviator sunglasses. My mother and I sat on a bench on the boardwalk and watched the strolling couples. It was still too cold out to catch a glimpse of the style that would become synonymous with Brighton Beach; in warmer months, middle-aged women promenaded in formfitting low-cut tops in jungle-cat prints, Gucci-style glasses with gold decoration at the temples, patent-leather stilettos and permed hair dyed a worrying shade of orange.

But we'd arrived in New York only weeks earlier—what did we know about Brooklyn? Other Soviet refugees we met in resettlement agency waiting rooms described the neighborhood as either a wonderland of economic opportunity and Jewish culture or a haven for uneducated men from Soviet provinces who ended up driving carservice limousines and committing Medicaid fraud. And then, of course, everyone talked about Brighton's fabled Russian gangsters, always going to great lengths to point out they weren't Jewish. In the end, none of it mattered— my mother had made up her mind. While we sat on the bench and stared out at the Atlantic Ocean, I asked my mother whether we'd be moving to Brighton Beach. She looked at me and replied, "We didn't come to America to speak Russian."

She wanted to live closer to Manhattan, and a week later she put down a deposit on a three-room walk-up in Long Island City, Queens, a block and a half from Lyuba's apartment. Like most of Queens, Long Island City was a lower-middle-class neighborhood teeming with people from other countries, none of whom seemed terribly excited to be living there. The three rooms in our new home connected to one another through a series of doorless doorways; even when the sun was out, the apartment's interior looked twilit.

Lyuba brought over some pots and pans and told us about Garbage Day. One night a week, Lyuba, my mother, Semyon and I headed out to surf the neighbors' trash. Within weeks, we had furnished our rooms with a sofa, a kitchen table, a mattress-and-bedspring set, and a black-and-white television. The furniture sagged, lacked knobs and gave off odors of food and mildew, but it was mostly functional and free. Someone had snapped off the TV's rabbit-ear antenna, and when I turned on the set, it rustled with angry static. In the name of science, I twisted apart a wire hanger and stretched it between the antenna stub and a rusted shopping cart, another Garbage Day find, and when I rolled the cart around the TV, the pattern on the screen shifted and danced until eventually there was a picture on channel 2.

Several nights after I hot-wired the TV set, we sat around it holding plates with bologna sandwiches and dollops of applesauce on our laps, feeling like genuine New Yorkers. Channel 2 was showing *Love at First Bite*, a film about another immigrant from Eastern Europe: George Hamilton plays a vampire who comes to Manhattan from Transylvania. In one scene, he changes into a bat and flies into a low-rent tenement apartment much like our own, where a Puerto

Rican family chases him, waving a skillet and a broom and yelling, "Flying chicken." None of us got the joke, but we laughed ourselves nearly sick.

At PS 166, the elementary school on Thirty-fifth Avenue where I enrolled a week later, most of the other students had Greek surnames. My English was threadbare and demanded constant vigilance. I tried to keep important terms like "lunch," "auditorium" and "bathroom" mentally handy at all times and mouthed them several times before pronouncing them. For a while I wasn't sure I'd get the hang of English, and on some days questioned whether I even wanted to, daydreaming about Brighton Beach with its kvass stands and Russian signage. I was content to daydream in Russian, until one day I spotted the blue-and-red cover of the novelization of *The Empire Strikes Back*—the first movie I'd seen in an American movie theater—on a carousel in our school library. The dog-eared paperback filled me with the desire to read English, and I kept it at my bedside all spring.

Our new language, currency and transportation system left Semyon and Raisa alternately nonplussed or dismayed. They also struggled with the national holidays. Independence Day upset them the most—Semyon took to calling it "Indoor Day." My grandparents celebrated the Fourth of July by drawing the blinds. After dark, our neighbors poured onto the rectangle of grass under our windows, to set off fireworks. Fireworks were illegal in New York City, but everyone seemed to have plenty. Entire families came out first, the grown-ups sipping from cans of beer in brown paper bags and lighting sparklers and Roman candles that rose with a soothing whoosh. After the adults and small children left, the teenagers ignited their ordnance well into the morning. The cherry bombs and M-80s went off so loudly that I felt the blasts in my solar plexus. Semyon and Raisa huddled on the sofa, our shopping-cart TV turned up as loud as it would go. Raisa said the blasts reminded her of German shelling.

After less than a year, my mother realized that the rent for our walk-up was too high, so the four of us moved a few blocks away, to a ground-floor one-bedroom apartment in the Ravenswood Houses—housing projects that offered heavily subsidized rent for the lower-lower-middle class and the poor. Semyon and Raisa slept on a fold-out sofa in the living room while my mother and I shared the bedroom. The linoleum there was a shade darker than it had been at our apartment in Moscow.

There was only one other Russian-speaking family in the building and I was self-conscious about my English, but my mother insisted that I try to make friends with the neighbors. On the playground, I fell in with Jason and Junior, brothers who lived on the sixth floor and liked to refer to themselves as J&J; they were roughly my age, owned several baseball bats and gloves, and began teaching me the drawn-out, complicated rules of the sport. We pitched and hit right on the playground's concrete, and once, after Jason lined a pitch through a second-floor window, we ran inside and hid in a stairwell, laughing until our bellies hurt.

A few weeks later, on the playground, I was riding a yellow-and-purple three-speed Ross with a banana seat and riser handlebars that I'd rescued from the Sanitation Department on Garbage Day, when Jason and Junior rode up to me on their Schwinns. They were with a group of older boys I hadn't seen before. Like J&J, these boys were skinny, black and wore T-shirts. They rode behind me for a while and eventually I stopped, straddled my bike and waved. "What's up?" I hollered, proud of the newly learned neologism, and smiled a smile that was meant to telegraph approachability. One of the older boys made a circle around me and then rode his bike, hard, into the side of mine. I fell and scraped my elbow. The boys laughed and circled me, like a posse of ranchers. Before they pedaled away, one of them yelled, "Communist!"

It was a name I'd been called before in school. The social economy of elementary school left no personal liability unaccounted for: the overweight, the acne-ridden, the fatherless, the foreign and the noticeably poor weren't allowed to forget this. The verdict was usually spoken through a set of braces and accompanied by hooting and laughter. In my case, "Communist" was sometimes followed by the oddly retro "better dead than Red" or, more often, "Go back to your own country!"

I knew that being a Communist was bad. It followed me like an embarrassing smell. My former homeland darkened the culture with its mushroom-cloud shadow. In a speech he delivered before a convention of evangelicals in Orlando, Ronald Reagan called it an "evil empire"; according to news programs I watched on TV, the U.S.S.R. had enough ICBMs to destroy the United States eleven or fifteen or twenty-two times over. Even worse, in film after film, Americans took pleasure in defeating hulking, emotionless Soviet villains. After Soviet paratroopers invaded Colorado and murdered Patrick Swayze's father in *Red Dawn,* someone behind me shouted "Go home, you fucking Communist!" loudly enough for everyone in the school cafeteria to hear, prickling the back of my neck with dread.

My Redness and foreign accent weren't my only obstacles to acculturation. In school I spent most of my time around boys, and once, while saying goodbye to a particularly handsome one named George Kaklamanis, I must have hugged him for a beat too long. Because afterward, Denise DiNunzio—pigtailed, pretty, given to dotting all three *i*'s in her name with loopy purple hearts—walked up to me and said, not at all quietly, "Are you gay?" "No, of course not!" I shouted, startled by the question. "How do you know?" she shouted back mockingly. "Have you been to a doctor?" I was trembling from the surprise and the buried awareness that Denise was right. I wasn't entirely sure what being gay entailed, only that it was socially undesirable and possibly catastrophic. I knew then that my name and past—and the things George's feathered bangs and Windex-blue eyes made me feel—were problems requiring a vigorous solution.

And so I made it my mission to become permanently, irrefutably American—which is to say normal. I managed to get rid of my name soon enough, just like other boys I knew who came from the S.S.R.s

(Soviet Socialist Republics): many a Vladimir, Ilya and, worst of all, Vadik (a name that American children pronounced, with pitch-perfect cruelty, *va-DICK*) became a Steve, a Jason or a Bruce. We scowled at our parents for speaking Russian to us in front of class-mates, and in supermarkets, and in Laundromats. With each other, we conversed in accented but loud English, as though to assure native-born onlookers of our America-love. We wanted nothing to do with Russian, with the past, with the sighing grievances of our grandparents in their mohair cardigans and berets and waterproof astronaut boots who sat all day on Housing Authority benches and complained that the cheap, abundant strawberries at the Rego Park A&P weren't as sweet as the ones they bought at the outdoor mar-kets in Gorky.

Like the latter-day Jasons and Steves, I practiced speaking En-glish in front of a mirror, molding my lips and tongue into the pre-scribed shape and embouchure, lowering the pitch of my voice to make it more masculine. Someone told me that to speak a language perfectly, you had to think and dream in it, and nearly every night in bed, before my consciousness grayed into sleep, I rehearsed mental monologues in English, hoping they'd percolate into my dreams. When this didn't work, I relied on rote mimicry. It took me three years of saying "dist a minute" in a chipper voice before I wondered what "dist" actually meant.

After crawling through the *Empire Strikes Back* paperback with the aid of a dictionary, I spent hours motionless on the floor in front of the television studying baseball telecasts, with their odd stretches of stillness and barely comprehensible rules; I marveled at the impro-visational genius of the dwarves and giants wrestling on channel 9, their faces caked with real blood; I thrilled at Alexis flinging Bacca-rat stemware at Krystle on *Dynasty*. I drank in Americanness like water from a faucet, my thirst never subsiding.

One night when I was twelve, a graying fifty-something Jewish man in a leather bomber jacket came to our apartment; Gordon had met my mother through a classified ad in the back of *New York* magazine and was picking her up for their date. He said he owned a record-and-tape warehouse, and before they left, he handed me an armful of cassettes by Waylon Jennings, George Jones and Johnny Paycheck; it was the most American music I'd heard, sung by real men, and for months afterward I listened to little besides honky-tonk and outlaw country.

Away from home, I disavowed everything and everyone Russian. When Semyon fulminated about my spending habits at our local supermarket—"Put back those Jeno's Pizza Rolls," he declaimed in the frozen-foods aisle, "we're not millionaires!"—I pretended not to hear him and moved subtly away, giving his shopping cart a wide enough berth to suggest to everyone at Met Food that we weren't related. The part about my past I hated most was my father, and eventually I told everyone in school that he was dead, in hopes that killing him in effigy would kill my need for him and my shame about his voluntary absence from our lives. In my stories, I made him a cancer victim and eventually a high-ranking army officer who perished heroically in the Soviet-Afghan War. Killing him helped me to care less about the fact that during our second year in New York my father stopped writing and then calling us; it helped me forget that whenever I checked the time, I habitually added seven hours, to account for the time difference between New York and Moscow, and that I still started when the phone rang in the mornings.

I didn't yet know that trauma is perpetuated by repression. I didn't understand that the nightmares that visited me several times a week might have had something to do with my radical makeover into someone seamlessly, if blandly, American. And I tried to ignore the happier dreams, in which my father stood watching me trying to swim in the dark water of the pond in Stepanovskoye, hollering at me to kick harder.

AFTER I GRADUATED from PS 166, my mother decided to pull me out of New York's public school system—she'd heard stories about gangs, teenage pregnancies and marijuana—but she could scarcely afford private school tuition. As a social worker at a mental-health clinic for Soviet refugees on Coney Island, she was earning $12,400 a year, and expenditures besides groceries, rent, utilities, subway fare and occasional furtive purchases of deep-discount women's wear were out of the question. Then a girlfriend told her about a small yeshiva that catered to the children of the moderately religious rich, attached to a stately Moorish Revival synagogue uptown; Soviet refugees were a popular cause in the Jewish community, and the school was looking to enroll one of us, presumably on full scholarship. Neither my mother nor I was excited about the religious part of the bargain, but I knew that to go to school in Manhattan was a chance to advance my Americanization, to distinguish myself from the children of other immigrants surrounding us in Long Island City—there was a reason, after all, why Russian speakers referred to Queens as *Svinsk*, or Pigtown.

With my tuition reduced to a mere hundred dollars per semester, I became a seventh grader and token Soviet refugee at the Park East Day School. I attended Talmud classes taught in Aramaic beside teenagers with good haircuts, expensive orthodontics and Lacoste polo shirts in every conceivable shade who were picked up after school in chauffeured Town Cars with electric windows. My payback for the school's generosity was exacted at weekly assemblies, when the principal, Dr. Smilowitz, asked me to say "a few words" about my experiences as an oppressed Jew living behind the Iron Curtain. I stood behind a lectern, faced my classmates and said in my still-accented English that everyone in Moscow hated us, that we had to list our Jewish nationality in our passports, that my mother was the best student in her school but still couldn't get admitted to the fine-arts institute, because these were things my mother had told me to say, but what I was thinking was, in Moscow my grandmother had a color TV and a sedan and teacups with the queen of England on the bottoms, and personally I never met any Jew haters, and in any case it was a hell of a lot better than living in the projects and being beaten on for being foreigners. At least in Moscow, everyone knew we weren't Communists.

On Fridays, everyone dressed up for the Sabbath—the girls in long-sleeved dresses, and the boys in natty suits and ties, mostly from Brooks Brothers. And so after I enrolled at the Park East Day School, my mother took me shopping at one of the discount stores on Steinway Street, where she bought my sub-Wrangler dungarees. As usual, she came up to the attractive teenage girl behind the counter and asked to be directed to the boys' husky section. The girl glanced at me and snickered. My mother bought me a billowy white dress shirt and a pair of navy polyester slacks that made a swooshing sound when I walked. The following Friday, Dr. Smilowitz walked up to me in the cafeteria, which went quiet. Cutting his eyes at my outfit, he said that if I couldn't wear something appropriate on the Sabbath, I shouldn't come to school. With this he sent me home. I rode the subway back to Long Island City, delighted to be leaving early and looking forward to the afternoon Mets game on channel 9.

For a brief time, my favorite teacher, Rabbi Steinig, also became my best friend. He tutored me in Hebrew after class and made me a mix tape by the Mamas and the Papas. He told me often that if I wanted a meaningful life, I had to learn to live like a Jew. Initially I resisted the notion, being brought up in a proudly atheist country, but the patient, affectionate way he spoke to me weakened my resolve. Little by little I became convinced he was right—the Jewish community helped bring us to America, and who was I to say that there wasn't a ledger of *mitzvot* and sins presented to you after you died, like a bill at a restaurant? At home, during a weekend breakfast a few days before Passover, I told my mother that we were going to be righteous: in accordance with Jewish law, for seven days we'd eat no leavened bread nor have any in the apartment. To underscore the point, I opened a box of matzos I'd been given in school and began spreading butter on a large square of the stuff. My mother nodded absently, paging through a *Cosmopolitan*.

On the night before Passover, I put on a yarmulke and flung the tassels of a tzitzit over my Waylon Jennings T-shirt; I gathered the Wonder Bread, my mother's cornflakes and my Franken Berry, and tossed them in the trash. I recited the prescribed Hebrew prayer. Then I walked around the kitchen with a lit candle, opened the cupboard doors, and with a long goose feather Rabbi Steinig had given me, I swept out crumbs of leavened bread. My mother returned from work and walked in on me ritually cleansing our kitchen. "We're going to be good Jews," I said by way of a greeting. The candlelight flickered across her face. She looked mortified. "No, we're not," she replied finally, putting down her grocery bags. "Put this candle out before you burn down the building and stop throwing away our food."

Across East Sixty-seventh Street from the school stood the gray brick box of the Soviet mission. I stared at it often during classes. It was nondescript except for a man with binoculars and a walkie-talkie who paced slowly across the roof. He looked lonely and bored, and I felt sorry for him. Once a week, teachers handed us construction paper on which we wrote messages to the Soviet government. Some of us drew the blue-and-white flag of Israel; some wrote, "Let Our People Go"; and then the teachers taped these messages to the windows, facing out toward the lone man on the rooftop.

If I needed more motivation for my de-Russification project, I got it when one of my mother's ex-Soviet friends came to visit. These adults seemed to occupy a peculiar outpost between a culture they were beginning to forget and another that they were unable, and sometimes unwilling, to navigate. In ungenerous moods I pitied them and, I think, feared them a little, because they regarded me with equal reproach, especially when I ventured an opinion or memory about the old country. "What can you know about that, you were only a child," they'd say, demonstrating, in the quintessentially Russian way, their expertise in every field and a knack for making pronouncements that ended conversations.

These adults only convinced me further that my past was of no use here; in the United States, they put no stock in dying for your country. The whole notion sounded morbid. From what I could tell about the cultural texts of my tweendom, what mattered in America was a creative overcoming of personal limitations. Like Luke Skywalker and Waylon Jennings, my prospects were limited only by my imagination. And I knew that to become more American was also to become less of what I so obviously was: suspiciously foreign, unathletic, poor and poorly dressed, accented, cowardly, tainted by Communism and uninterested in girls. I could barely wait for the tidal wave of my transformation to wash away the flotsam of history.

ONE NOVEMBER AFTERNOON I was walking home after school when one of the three boys huddling on the corner of Crescent Street asked me the time. I absentmindedly glanced down at the Swatch my mother had bought me at Gimbels. "Three thirty-five," I said. Just then I realized that we were standing under the clock of the Long Island City Savings and Loan, and that the boys wanted to see whether I had a watch on. This wasn't unusual in Ravenswood, and I knew that the appropriate reaction was to shrug or spit on the sidewalk and keep walking, making sure not to look back.

They followed me. I'd recognized one of them from the adjacent building. My heart drummed in my ears, but I was nearly across the street from my building's door, which required a key to open. I knew I could beat them there. I slipped the key out of my pocket, stepped off the sidewalk onto Twenty-fourth Street and broke into a run. I heard them running behind me. As I got closer to the door, I saw a piece of duct tape covering the lock and an out-of-service sign, written in marker, taped above it. I ran into the lobby and leaned against the wall, panting; I knew they had me.

The boys were around my age. They surrounded me holding scalpels—rusty blades with blue plastic handles—that they must've salvaged from the dumpsters on Thirty-fourth Avenue. One stood lookout in the lobby while the other two pushed me into the hallway, out of sight, and shoved me against the door to apartment 1D.

"Empty your pockets," the taller one instructed with surprising professionalism. I remembered that his name was Wayne.

I turned out my pockets and opened my hands; in one palm there were two pennies, all the money I had. Wayne, whose thick prescription lenses shrank his eyes to furious raisins, smacked me across the head so hard that my left ear wind-tunneled. "The watch," he said. I arched my back, trying not to press the doorbell with my backpack, because I was standing against the door to my grandparents' apartment. I could hear the faint sound of the television and knew that Semyon and Raisa were watching it on the fold-out sofa. If one of them opened the door, I was afraid Wayne would work up the nerve to rob them, too. With a twinge I thought about the stuffed waxbill on the dresser—a present from Semyon's zoology students— and beside it the cigar box with his medals, heart medication, Raisa's Parkinson's pills and their bankbook, which had twenty or twenty-five dollars tucked into it.

In an inside jacket pocket I carried a folding knife with a fake mother-of-pearl handle that I'd bought in a head shop on Fourteenth Street. I realized that trying to pull it out and open it would take too long and probably get me stabbed. I wished that my mother had let me buy the switchblade I'd seen at a street market in Mexico the previous summer, during our first and only getaway from New York, when we spent half a day in Tijuana with a university friend of my mother's who lived in Los Angeles. I also wished, for the first time, that I had a gun. Wayne peeled the Swatch off my wrist and smacked me again across the head. It rang as though it were made of brass. "Later, faggot," he said, then ran into the lobby and out the door with the others.

After glancing into the lobby to make sure they were gone, I rang my grandparents' doorbell and told Semyon and Raisa about what happened. I expected them to look dismayed or at least worried, but instead they stood around me and smiled. "You're not hurt," Raisa said, tousling my hair. "Everything is fine." I was grateful for their equanimity but felt sick. When I sat on the sofa, a low guttural wail came out of me. Semyon sat down beside me, patted me on the back and said, "You're safe now, stop crying."

I went upstairs and called the police. My mother was at work, and I waited in the kitchen in my jacket. Twenty minutes later, a Housing Authority officer rang the doorbell, sat down on the sofa and took notes in an oblong black pad. He looked up at me from time to time while I spoke. He had receding red hair and a paunch; the silver name tag on his uniform read, "O'Malley." "We can get into the cruiser and drive around, and you can point them out to me," he said after I was done. "But they'll spend a few hours with a social worker, and afterward the little niggers will be out scot-free and come after you."

I looked away. That word—"niggers"—made me understand that the cop was powerless and corrupt, and I felt alone and scared. He fixed me with a knowing look and said, "I advise you not to press charges."

A few days later, from my window, I watched Wayne and his two friends riding their bikes on the sidewalk. It was Saturday and I wanted to be outside, too, but I was afraid, and the shame that came over me felt worse than the fear. Just then I wanted more than anything to hear my father's voice; I was convinced that he'd know what to do, but I hadn't spoken to him in almost a year. When my mother came home, I told her what happened and asked her to let me buy a gun.

Afterward, I developed a routine: at school, I waited until it got dark to come home, then scoped out my block under the cover of darkness from behind the clipped bushes surrounding the Queens-view co-ops, the more upscale housing development across the street, where security guards puttered along the paths in three-wheeled golf carts. Once I made sure that Wayne and his friends were nowhere in sight, I quickly crossed the street and covered the fifty feet to the door.

Around this time, my mother was dating a mild-mannered Israeli chemist named Tzvi who took her on a vacation to Belgium. They returned from Europe with presents: a framed etching of a canal and, surprisingly, a nineteenth-century double-barreled pistol. "You keep asking your mother for a gun," Tzvi said with a wry wink, "so I bought you one." For a moment I stared at it, goose bumps roiling my flesh, but then I saw that the gun's barrels were plugged with lead. It was a non-firing antique—two triggers with traces of verdigris, two hammers, two powder reservoirs, a knurled walnut handle. In the bathroom, I pointed it at myself in the mirror, covering the hammers with my left hand in a Clint Eastwood flourish. From the front it looked like a sawed-off shotgun.

I took it to school every day. I knew that if a teacher saw the gun she'd have to call the police, so I kept it in my backpack all day. When I got off the subway in Long Island City, I waited for the platform to clear, transferred it to the pocket of my baggy winter coat, and walked home with my hand wrapped around the handle. I never thought clearly about what would happen if I pulled it out and pointed it at someone, but I fantasized about this constantly, practicing drawing it like a border-town sheriff in the bathroom mirror. I carried it with me nearly everywhere, having discovered that it made me less afraid. The metal and wood felt warm in my hand.

One night after school, I was standing at my usual lookout behind the bushes of the Queensview co-ops, scanning the sidewalks on Twenty-fourth Street. Suddenly my face went cold. By the light of the bulb above our building's doorway, I saw Raisa standing alone, clutching her handbag with both hands. She shook lightly, as always. Semyon, who took her out for walks several times a day, must have gone back inside. Several yards away, Wayne and another boy stood crouched behind a parked van and watched her, inching closer. She didn't see them. I knew they were about to make a grab for the bag.

What happened next was instantaneous. I tossed my backpack on the ground and charged from behind the bushes. I sprinted toward them, closing the distance between us, my hand clutching the gun in my coat pocket. I must have been yelling because Wayne turned around. I can only guess what the expression on my face must have been, but to my amazement he elbowed the other boy and they broke into a run, disappearing behind a row of parked cars. Just then Semyon walked outside. I ran up to him and doubled over, breathing hard, disappointed to have lost my chance to draw the gun. Semyon looked me up and down quizzically. "What's gotten into you?" he said.

WHEN I WAS fifteen, my mother took me to a reading at a high school auditorium in midtown Manhattan to hear Joseph Brodsky, the great poet of her youth; like us, he now lived in New York. His poetry, my mother reminded me, was the pretext for her meeting my father. A prematurely gray-haired man whose shirttails poked out from under a shapeless sweater, Brodsky stood behind a lectern and read in rushed drafts of breathy Russian, pausing only to announce the poems' titles. Afterward, when someone in the audience asked about the Soviet Union's most famous poets—Yevtushenko and Voznesensky—Brodsky replied, "They are second-rate poets and second-rate people." My mother looked enthralled. After the reading, she waited in line to speak to Brodsky, and afterward the two of them lingered by the lectern after nearly everyone had left. A few days later he called and invited her to dinner.

They saw each other on and off for several years. When my mother took the subway to Manhattan to visit Brodsky at his garden apartment on Morton Street, where she often spent the night, she wore outfits she'd bought in Upper East Side boutiques and often paid for in installments—a poppy-colored crepe sundress, a bluish-gray trench with a man's fedora. On his desk, Brodsky kept a framed photo of Billie Holiday and another of his cat. Brodsky asked my mother to read a play of his and spoke to her about Anna Akhmatova, his former teacher. Best of all, he put her in touch with his friend Tomas Venclova, the Lithuanian dissident poet who visited her high school literature club in Vilnius and who now lived in a professor's cottage in New Haven. Brodsky could be imperious and remote, and my mother was aware of his reputation as a womanizer, but she didn't seem concerned about it. When she came home after seeing him, she hung her coat over a chair back, closed her bedroom door behind her and wrote down the things they'd said to each other in a notebook.

One night, before returning from Brodsky's, my mother called to ask Semyon and me to meet her at the Broadway subway stop, because she didn't want to walk home alone in the dark. While we walked home three abreast, she told us that she'd gone to a Japanese restaurant with Brodsky, his friend Mikhail Baryshnikov and Baryshnikov's ballet-dancer girlfriend, and that all night people kept approaching Baryshnikov for autographs. I asked my mother whether it felt strange, eating in public beside a famous poet and a Hollywood actor. "No," she replied without giving it much thought. "It didn't feel strange at all."

At home, she liked listening to a warped ten-inch record of Akhmatova reading her poems: a weary, melancholy voice barely audible under a storm of pops and scratches. She kept the record in a cardboard box beside several Beatles cassettes, Ray Charles's *Greatest Hits,* and an old Melodiya LP of sad songs about trolley cars and the Great Patriotic War by Bulat Okudzhava, which she played whenever other former Soviets came to visit.

One night, while she was playing the Akhmatova record, something in me snapped like a worn-out fan belt. I couldn't stand another second of the scratchy record, with its suffocating nostalgia and colossal sadness, which I believed to be the primary emotions of our former homeland. "How can you listen to this?" I shouted at my mother. "It's so fucking depressing!"

She was making dinner and stopped her chopping, looked up and said, "You're ignorant and it would do you good to read Russian. You know the language, so why don't you use it?"

"Because it's worthless," I shot back, suddenly enjoying making her angry. "Did you bring me to America so we can listen to old Russian records and feel like shit all the time?" I tried to take off the record, but she came out of the kitchen and pushed me away. Our cat, a tabby from a shelter, darted under the sofa.

Now my mother was shouting, too. I'd never seen her so furious and it exhilarated me. "Why do you hate what you are?" she shouted. "I hate *you!*" I shouted back, and believed it, thinking suddenly about her leaving me in the apartment alone to spend nights with Brodsky. She picked up one of her leather boots—her favorite cream knee-highs with the Cuban heels—and came at me. She swung and missed, but the second swing caught me across the back. The boot's heel clattered onto the floor. My mother looked at it incredulously. "You broke it," she wailed. I fell on the floor, laughing. "I wish you were never born," she said quietly, then sat on the couch and wept into her hands. The following morning she apologized and said she didn't mean it, but I stayed in my room and milked it for another day and a half.

THE PREVIOUS YEAR I'd begun attending Stuyvesant, a math-and-science magnet high school in Manhattan's East Village. Admission was determined by a citywide test, and getting in counted as a victory: Stuyvesant was forty-five minutes away by subway, but it was free.

More than a third of the students were immigrants who, like me, commuted mostly from Queens and Staten Island. The native-born tended to be chess whizzes or sci-fi aficionados and children of academic sociologists, documentary filmmakers, managing editors of left-wing political journals and other members of the city's middle-middle class who lived on the Upper West Side. Stuyvesant was also home to a small but highly visible population of well-dressed, smartly groomed white teenagers, many of whom lived on the Upper East Side or in midtown Manhattan and ate lunch at Stavy's, a diner on the corner of First Avenue and Fifteenth Street. They had names like Tinsley, Blair, Preston and Cole and had the bemused easy manner of coming from money. They sported skateboards and real Ray-

Bans, accompanied their parents to free-Tibet rallies in Battery Park, spent summers in Amagansett and Sag Harbor. It was clear to the rest of us that they were having sex. They belonged to an unreachable caste, and to conceal our inferiority and envy, my friends and I avoided them at all costs.

If my mother had begun to wonder why I didn't spend much time with girls or date any, she mentioned it only once. It was a weekend, and she stood surveying the wilds of my bedroom. The linoleum was hidden under a moraine of paperbacks, baseball cards, half-open *National Geographics* and dirty laundry. "I've wondered sometimes whether you prefer boys," she opened, framed by the doorway, and her words made the breath catch in my throat. "But I've realized," she continued, "that you are too messy to be gay. I mean, look at this room!" I sniggered awkwardly—I meant it to sound like laughter, and maybe it did—and replied that she was definitely right. She told me to clean my room, something we both knew I wouldn't do, and closed the door.

Of course I hadn't told her about Luka. An ancillary member of our group of outer-borough nerds at Stuyvesant, he was a quiet, bookish immigrant from Yugoslavia who lived with his parents in Fort Greene. I was smitten with him almost instantly—Luka was lanky, doe-eyed and oddly graceful—and after our last classes of the day, we spent several hours sitting on windowsills in empty classrooms, discussing Hermann Hesse and William Burroughs. Luka spoke in slow thoughtful sentences, knees tucked under his chin, from time to time glancing up at me with a faraway, kind expression, which made my cheeks flush. For a while we were together nearly every day, and I began looking forward to seeing him, then thinking about him, with an unfamiliar possessiveness. That he was pining for a girl in his homeroom, and talked about her more and more, was something I refused to consider.

It was while debating *The Glass Bead Game*, which I found interminable and boring but pretended to enjoy for Luka's benefit, that we broached how Hesse wrote about love—love for God, or universal love, or some other soupy, chaste variety. I must have sensed an opening, because I told Luka that I thought I loved him and reached up to touch his face. An aperture ratcheted down in his eyes, and I knew instantly I'd made a mistake. He thanked me for being honest and said he had to go. A few days later he asked me to meet him after school in the East Cafeteria, where he was waiting with our group of friends. Somberly, one of the other boys announced that I was no longer welcome to eat lunch at their table, on account of being a "homo."

Then there was Hector. I can picture him now standing in the school's second-floor hallway in his tight Lee jeans and Run-D.M.C. T-shirt. He was scrawny and had a comically deep voice; his favorite possession—plastic-framed Cazals that were too large for his face—made him look a little like a menacing insect. Hector's swagger was a pantomime of a larger, older man. He'd grown up in Haiti and lived in the Bronx with a strict Catholic mother and a series of brutal step-fathers from whom he occasionally ran away.

My other friends, who aspired to early admission to Cornell and Dartmouth, considered Hector seedy, weird and possibly dangerous. Aside from enumerating fictitious acts of street justice in which he starred, Hector loved discussing the exploits of Run-D.M.C., Kurtis Blow and other favorite rappers. After watching *Knights of the City,* a drama about a rapping street gang that tries to score a record con-tract, he came to the cafeteria with a portable cassette recorder, which he used to tape the entire film. His bluster could be unnerving. Once he took two crack vials out of his jean jacket that he said he was carrying for a friend; he stowed them in the same pocket as a switch-blade that he liked to take out and jab in the air. If Hector had friends besides me, I didn't know them.

Why I became friends with him I can't quite remember. Maybe it was his hangdog look, or the comedy of his machismo, or the step-fathers whom I joined him in hating. After he ran away from home and slept for a night on a bench in Union Square, I told him he could spend the weekend with us in Ravenswood. I knew my mother probably wouldn't approve, but she and a girlfriend of hers were spending the weekend in Montreal, and the apartment would be empty. Hector arrived too early, when my mother was getting ready to take her things down to the car. She made small talk with the two of us and asked him a few questions. I noticed that his hands trembled while he offered inarticulate answers. Before she left, my mother said, "That boy gives me a bad feeling."

Hector and I watched *Friday Night Videos* and shared a can of corned beef hash I heated on the stove, then sat on the couch and took turns drinking from a flask of Cutty Sark that he claimed to have shoplifted. "Which girls do you like?" he asked. I named a few that he thought were okay. He said he liked a red-haired girl in his homeroom named Megan who had "really huge tits." "I'm going to fuck her," he said. The boast sounded so inane that both of us laughed. It might've been the late hour or the scotch, but I blurted that when I changed in gym class, sometimes I looked at the boys. Hector said it was cool. He looked at the boys too—sometimes. But mostly at the girls.

We undressed under a blanket. The lights were out and I felt his breath on my neck. We touched foreheads and thrashed, all elbows, at each other's bodies until we were done. We lay quietly for a while until Hector wrapped himself in a sheet and walked to the bathroom. I heard the shower running and turned on the light. The cot I'd set up for him stood expectantly beside my bed. It was three or four in the morning. Awkwardness, or maybe something worse, congested the air.

I lay on the bed and waited. Hector came out of the shower wrapped in a towel. The triangle of his torso, chestnut brown, looked boyish and small. He flipped off the light. Without saying a word, he walked past the cot, took off the towel and got into bed beside me. He wrapped his arms around my chest and pressed his cheek against my neck. His skin smelled pleasantly of soap. His breathing grew deep and slow, and he drifted off to sleep.

I lay beside him, stupefied with happiness. Somehow I knew even then that sex, no matter how truncated or temporary, is a bid to be loved. And now I realized that there were sources of love besides those I'd been born to. And this one was unmarked by the past, by distance and rage, and belonged entirely to me. I put my hand on the back of Hector's neck and listened to him breathe, trying to stay awake for as long as I could.

FOR REASONS THAT are still unclear to me, I began playing my mother's scratchy Akhmatova record, then reading from the small hardcover volume of Akhmatova's poetry that she'd brought with us from Moscow. Eventually I memorized about a dozen of her poems. I did this furtively and never told my mother. After she was asleep, I sat in the living room with the TV on quietly and began writing my own rhymed, metered poems in English—sentimental, oddly Victorian versions of Akhmatova and Brodsky—and wondering what it might be like to be a writer.

I suspect that I began writing as a kind of magic ritual used to ward off evil. On most nights, I still kept a knife under my pillow, to protect against not just frightening dreams but a peculiar waking belief that the door to our apartment might burst open at any moment, smashed inward by a malevolent force I couldn't name. It was when I began writing—and taking, for the first time, an inventory of who I was—that it occurred to me that the malevolent force might be the past that I'd been trying diligently to disown. As I wrote to the soothing burble of nighttime TV, there were moments when it felt possible to allow the past inside me without a concomitant feeling of violence, without the need to efface it, so that in my imagination I could finally lay claim to several times and places at once, which is to say the full span of my memory.

Years later, as a student at a graduate writing program in Manhattan, I translated several of Akhmatova's poems into English, including my mother's favorite—part 5 of *Northern Elegies*. It's narrated by a woman forced to live a life far different from the one she intended to. Akhmatova wrote it during the war, after having been evacuated to Uzbekistan, where she became ill with typhus, while her son was imprisoned and her work banned.

> This hard age bent me
> like a river.
> My life was replaced with another.
> It flowed into a tributary
> and I don't know my shores.
> I missed so many sights,
> the curtain rose without me
> and fell without me.
> So many friends of mine I never met.
> So many cityscapes never drew
> tears from these eyes—I know only one city.
> Asleep, I could find my way there by touch.
> There are so many poems I never wrote.
> Their secret chorus stalks me, and maybe
> someday will strangle me. . . .
> I know beginnings, I know endings too,
> and life after death, and something I shouldn't
> now recall. Another woman took my place,
> my name, and left me with a nickname
> with which, perhaps, I've done the best
> I could. Even the grave where I'll lie
> won't be my own. . . .
> But if I stood outside myself and saw the life I have,
> I would at last know envy.

I'D LIKE TO be buried on Staten Island, at the United Hebrew Cemetery on the corner of Clarke Avenue and Arthur Kill Road. Raisa and Semyon are buried there in adjacent plots, but that's not the only reason. It also happens to be the most untroubled place I've been.

Many cemeteries are peaceful, but this one feels like a remote and wooded place, miles from a city, and there's nothing to hear but birds and wind rippling through the elms. A distant thrum barely registers as the sound of cars.

Raisa was buried there in 1992, three years after suffering a series of strokes that left her unable to speak in full sentences and, at times, to recognize any of us. Those years followed a pattern: She was discharged from a hospital, moved to a nursing home, then returned to a hospital several days or weeks later. There'd be a doctor on the phone to my mother or me mentioning fevers and bedsores, and a room number at the hospital where an ambulance had taken her. The strokes rendered her mostly immobile, and afterward her movements resembled palsied responses to discomfort or pain.

Semyon visited her every day. He didn't miss a single afternoon, not because of illness or a holiday or inclement weather. On these outings he wore one of the two suits he'd brought from Vilnius and the fedora with the scarlet feather in the hatband, and he carried a plastic bag with the Russian-language newspaper and the *Times* folded into eighths. After an hour on two trains, he walked to Beth Israel on Sixteenth Street and First Avenue. He spent his afternoons sitting beside Raisa's wheezing, beeping hospital bed; he read and talked to her in a low, solicitous voice, bargaining with her to swallow another spoonful of applesauce, even when she didn't answer or seem to know him. Sometimes she smiled, broadly and with her whole face, looking for a few moments like the person we knew. Several dozen times I accompanied my grandfather to Beth Israel, walking to the bank of elevators past the emergency room where I'd volunteered as a high school student. I don't think I ever admired my grandfather more than I did during these visits.

One spring, while home from college, where I decided to become a photojournalist, I took a photo of Semyon and Raisa in her hospital room. In the photo, he sits beside the bed in the pin-striped suit and rests his hand on Raisa's head in an odd gesture that I think he intended to be affectionate and protective. One side of him is distorted by the wide-angle lens. A large black-and-white print of the photo won second place in a local art contest in the Ohio town where I was attending college, and some months later I decided to frame it and make a gift of it to my mother. I regretted it as soon as I handed it to her. She glanced at the photo for a moment, stricken, I think, by her mother's withered appearance, and then put it back in its box and stuck it in the closet, where it remains to this day.

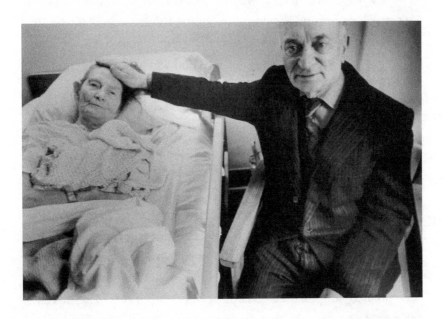

The last time I heard Raisa's voice was on November 24, 1989. I know the date because it was the day my mother married her second husband, a Moscow-born painter named Vitaly. A justice of the peace performed the ceremony at the Staten Island Borough Hall; it was less crowded than the one in Manhattan, and Vitaly and my mother wanted to take the morning ferry ride across the bay. Afterward, the three of us visited Raisa at a nursing home in Chinatown. The room was sparsely furnished and dark; I recall seeing the entrance to the Manhattan Bridge from the window. My mother leaned across the bed and told Raisa, loudly and slowly, that she was married— something my grandmother had long wanted. My mother held her hand, with the gold band on her finger, a few inches from her mother's face. Raisa made a few attempts to raise her head from the pillow and moved her lips soundlessly, as though rehearsing her line. Then she whispered, just loud enough to be heard, "Don't ever part."

Three springs later, shortly before the end of my senior year, my mother called early one morning to say that Raisa had died. I hitched a ride to New York with members of the Democratic Socialists of America who were on their way to a convention in Harlem. The service was held around the corner from the Ravenswood Houses, in a brick-faced synagogue on Crescent Street called Sons of Israel, where on Saturdays my grandfather said kaddish for his parents and his half brother, Roma.

After Raisa was gone, Semyon often looked lost. He'd kept himself busy with writing and mailing stacks of letters about various scientific topics to academics and congressmen, but now he didn't seem to know how to occupy his time. There were no more hospital visits to give shape to his days, and he rarely left the ground-floor one-bedroom apartment where he now lived alone. He seemed to spend entire days reading the *Times*, every section from beginning to end, writing comments and definitions in the margins in blue ballpoint script. He constantly misplaced keys, his bankbook, the wads of crumpled singles that he kept in various pockets. He looked at visitors quizzically, as though some question he'd asked long ago lingered, unanswered, in the air between them. His pallor turned grayer. When I visited, he kissed me wetly on the face, sat me down on the sofa, brought me a plate with a small ruddy apple and a thick slice of orange Department of Agriculture cheese, and set it on the table beside a glass of Ocean Spray cranberry drink. After Raisa died, a yellowish residue covered the plates, glasses and silverware; I began to think of it as the residue of old age.

Though he'd always been clean-shaven, Semyon let his facial hair grow out; he used a disposable plastic razor that sat in a soap dish on the sink, and after it got dull, he stopped shaving. This bothered me, and when I visited I brought a bag of orange-and-white razors. In the bathroom I stood beside my grandfather while he lathered up in the steamed-over mirror and absentmindedly dragged the razor across his cheeks. He particularly disliked the thick black hairs that grew out of his ears; he blamed them on an overzealous Vilnius barber from forty years earlier. While a Verdi opera blared on my old cassette boom box, I dabbed at his large ears with the razor, and he stood beside me quietly, satisfied, indifferent to the occasional nick.

Despite the befuddlement that never left him again, he retained an ironclad trust in science. The winter I was nineteen, I told my mother I was gay, precipitating five years of arguments about her squeamishness and disapproval, recriminations over my staying away from her, and months-long lulls between phone calls. Several years later, I decided to tell Semyon, too. On that morning I took the subway to Long Island City, watching the warehouses out the windows and wondering why I was determined to confuse and upset a widower in his seventies who said kaddish in shul for the souls of his long-gone family.

My confession came tumbling out moments after I walked into his apartment. We were still standing by the door. From behind his bifocals, my grandfather's magnified hazel eyes regarded me curiously while I told him that I'd gone on some dates with a boy from Joplin, Missouri. He scratched his head for a moment. "It's a perfectly normal abnormality," he declared finally. "It's well documented in the scientific literature that ten percent of all mammals and even birds engage in this sort of behavior." Then he began to talk about something else. I never felt more grateful to him—and to the natural sciences—than I did at that moment.

And so I knew something was wrong several years later, when he cautioned me on the phone about the cheap, roach-infested apartment I was sharing with my boyfriend in Brooklyn. "The big roaches," he whispered conspiratorially, "spread the HIV." He pronounced it "the heave." I called my mother. She said he'd been forgetting the day and the date lately, confusing her with me, and talking about Raisa as though she were still alive. Sometimes he became agitated or angry. Worse, he'd made certain "lewd" suggestions to his new home attendant, a gruff stocky woman from Port-au-Prince who reported him to her supervisor.

My mother asked a friend, a psychiatrist at Beth Israel, to evaluate him, and so Semyon spent several weeks on the hospital's psychiatric ward, a floor away from where he'd gone for years to see Raisa. One antipsychotic medication made him proposition the nurses; another made him too lethargic to leave bed.

When my boyfriend and I came to visit Semyon there, we found him in a holey pullover sweater, looking lost. He hugged each of us too strongly. The World Cup quarterfinals were being played that afternoon, and the three of us, on folding chairs, watched Germany play Croatia on the TV in the ward's common room. My grandfather kept asking about the score and the players and especially the German goalkeeper, whom he thought was Sepp Maier, a star player of the 1970s. At one point, he kissed my boyfriend on the cheek. His name—Doug—was too unfamiliar a name for Semyon to remember, so he called him Dagmar, a name that must've followed him from his years of speaking German. "My Dagmar!" Semyon said then, pleased with himself, and grinned. He looked happier than anytime since Raisa had been alive, and when I said we had to go, his eyes welled up and he kissed each of us on the face for too long before letting go.

The diagnosis was rapidly progressing dementia. The psychiatrist didn't think Semyon was safe living alone and required round-the-clock care. After a series of calls to specialists and social workers, my mother found him a vacant bed at the Bialystoker Home for the Aged, on East Broadway, in what had once been a Jewish section of the Lower East Side but had become the outer edge of Chinatown. When Semyon moved to the nursing home, my mother and I emptied out the old apartment in Ravenswood. After we gathered photo albums, war medals, a box of letters and documents, a few boxes of books and a good wool coat that fit me perfectly, Semyon's former neighbors dropped by and I told them to take what they wanted. Raul, a kind man in wire-rimmed glasses from Puerto Rico who lived several doors away, took the dusty stuffed waxbill perched on a section of branch on an inscribed wooden pedestal, a present from Semyon's zoology students in Vilnius. I took his students' other gift, a blue glass goblet inscribed in gold script with my grandfather's name and, in Latin, *"lectio ultima."*

On better days, Semyon played chess with the youngest resident on the floor, a former lawyer in his late forties who wore expensively tailored three-piece suits and suffered from early-onset Alzheimer's. Once a week, a rabbi helped him say kaddish. Semyon recognized my mother and me only intermittently, and I didn't visit as often as I should have. When I did, my grandfather and I sat beside each other on a bench in a fenced-off area outside, and sometimes he complained about whichever nurse was assigned to him; she was stealing, he said, though neither my mother nor I discovered any evidence of this. At other times he spoke about the war, about his mother and Roma, with an urgency and vividness that always surprised me. "Why didn't they come with me?" he asked me, almost pleading, as though I could've told him.

Three years after moving to the nursing home, he suffered a brain hemorrhage in his sleep; the doctors didn't think he would regain the ability to speak or eat on his own. While I stood by the side of his hospital bed, Semyon lay on his back, eyes shut tightly; his chest rose and fell heavily with each stertorous breath. When he opened his eyes, they looked as cloudy as ice. He'd told me, long ago, that he didn't want to linger after losing his ability to reason, and my mother signed a do-not-resuscitate form when he was checked back into Beth Israel. She and Vitaly had planned a trip to Italy, her first vacation in several years, and she couldn't decide whether she should go. I told her not to worry: I'd visit Semyon and keep in touch with his doctors; besides, his condition hadn't changed in months.

A few days after my mother left, Semyon suffered another stroke. The doctor phoned to say that he could no longer breathe on his own and would die within days, possibly hours, without a respirator. I called my mother at her hotel in Rome. Possibly out of fear or guilt, she reversed herself and wanted to agree to the respirator. What about Semyon's wishes? I asked. Judaism prescribed doing everything possible to save a life, she replied, and added that he was alive because God wanted him to live.

"Do you believe in God?" I asked.

"Yes," my mother said. "Do you?"

It was August 2001. A week later, after midnight on a Saturday, I was walking out of a Brooklyn bar with friends when I received a call from a Manhattan number. A nurse said that my grandfather had died and was on the seventh floor at Beth Israel, in case I wanted to see him.

That nurse, at her station, was the only person visible on the hospital's seventh floor when I showed up; it was silent except for the polyrhythmic beeping of the monitors. Semyon's room was lit with bright fluorescents. He lay on his back, zipped up to the sternum in a white plastic body bag, a sheet pulled over it in a kind of decorous afterthought. His skin looked waxy and dull. I'd never seen a dead person before. I had the acute apprehension that while this was my grandfather, it was also not: his body was there, but he wasn't in it. I stood beside him for some span of time before my mother and Vitaly, who'd returned from Rome a day earlier, walked in. My mother held Semyon's hand for a while and kissed him on the forehead, and then the nurse came in to ask whether it was okay to move him to the morgue.

Outside, I hailed a taxi. As it crossed the Brooklyn Bridge, I looked out at the downtown lights. Ever since I was a teenager returning from summer camp, their sight made me inexplicably happy, because it was the first sign of being home. The city teemed with life and motion: taxis rushed along the FDR, planes and helicopters blinked overhead, an illuminated tugboat puttered down the East River. I always preferred the view from the Brooklyn Bridge to any other in the city. Semyon once told me that New York was the happy ending to the twentieth century, and it never looked more so than on that night, with Manhattan's megawatt landscape set against a moonless sky. I took out my phone and called my boyfriend. "I'm coming home," I said.

CAMP SUCCESS

I LISTENED TO THE CLATTER OF WHEELS WHILE TRAIN 93 MOVED OVER THE bending track and felt my stomach settle. My father sat on the berth opposite mine and stared out the window, holding the silvered handle of a glass of tea. We hadn't seen each other in three years, not since I'd gone to meet his father, Vassily. But we were face-to-face again, riding to the country's interior in a luxury compartment—SV class—meaning two berths instead of four, and no soldiers snoring above us. My father's temples were grayer, and he'd changed his eyeglasses' prescription so that the lenses magnified his eyes, lending his face a slightly alarmed expression, but otherwise he looked as I remembered him. All afternoon he had been tying lures, delicate work that required the help of the bifocals that sat low on his nose; when he glanced up at me from time to time, his face looked comically abstracted.

The countryside outside was turning umber in the dusk, but I could still make out eerie white birches flashing under the electrical wire, the MMM of firs on the horizon, fences with missing slats like an endless bar code, and here and there clusters of bowlegged cabins that hugged the ground and petered out for no discernible reason. The beauty of the Russian countryside is mild and small of tooth. Except that it is endlessly vast, the landscape is composed of modest elements. Maybe that's why in Russia there has always been a tendency toward man-made gigantism—devising something to organize all the smallness, a flagpole planted on the steppe.

We were headed to the Volga, or more precisely to the confluence of two rivers—the Volga and the Akhtuba—to fish. The notion still sounded strange to me, because I am no angler; the pastime always struck me as cruel and possibly tedious. But my father made the trip to this stretch of muddy water about fifty kilometers north of the Caspian Sea every three or four months. The lower Volga happens to be one of the few places in the world where catfish grow immense— over a hundred kilos and more than three meters in length—and my father once won a national tournament when he reeled in an eighty-one-kilo specimen, though "reeled in" isn't exactly correct. The photo that accompanied the magazine article emailed to me by my half sister, Masha, showed my father and his fishing partner grinning in an inflatable craft. At their feet lay coiled a creature with an enormous bony head, a vestige of the Paleozoic. My father said it took him ninety minutes to tire out the fish; near the end, he stuck a rubber-gloved arm inside the creature's mouth and hauled it in by the jaw. Its eyes were purple-gray and opaque as graphite.

I hadn't picked up a fishing rod since catching a few crappies with balled-up pieces of Wonder Bread at a UJA-Federation summer camp in the Catskills more than twenty years earlier. My lack of experience didn't deter me. I'd been turning over the idea of joining my father on one of his trips to the Volga when I mentioned it to a magazine editor. He thought it would make a good travel story, about a place that "none of our readers would actually visit, but might like to read about." I called my father and outlined my plan: we'd travel together, I'd write about it and the magazine would cover the expenses. I half expected him to laugh it off. As the date of the flight to Moscow drew near, I also expected him to change his mind, as he did prior to the trip to Vinnytsia.

The trip would last nearly two weeks, the longest stretch my father and I been together since I was nine. We'd spend most of it in a cabin or a boat, surrounded by little besides tall grass and water, and this is what I was counting on. I wanted time with him in close quarters: I wanted to know why he hadn't left the country with my mother and me, why he didn't seem to want to be a father or a son, and why pleasure seemed to come to him most reliably in solitude. He told me once that when he visited the Volga, on some mornings he powered down the outboard and let the boat drift on the current for hours. "I get on the water at five, when it's still dark," he said, "and don't see another human being until I return to camp in the afternoon. Just birds."

I knew getting answers wasn't going to be easy. When my father met me at the airport in Moscow the previous morning, he gave me a brusque hug, and right away things fell into a familiar equipoise: he was happy to talk about anything as long as it wasn't us. He behaved as though we were old buddies picking up after years apart, and in the train compartment we talked about politics; books; jazz; his wife, Irina; my mother; and of course fishing. What he asked, without asking, was that I not revisit the past or muddy our time together by sorting out who'd done what and when to whom. Maybe he felt that it was too late to explain or rationalize his side of it. Maybe he simply found the prospect of talking about the past oppressive. "There is no more to be gained from sifting through the past than through cigarette ashes," he'd said to me once, years earlier, in Moscow.

I was going fishing, too, because I wanted to see what the country had become beyond the boulevards of Moscow and St. Petersburg, where the fantasy of a wealthy, orderly Russia was enacted for the benefit of government officials and foreign visitors. This mirage collapses minutes after one leaves the city centers, and by the time one crosses the city limits, the countryside seems to belong to a poor agrarian nation from half a century earlier. I suppose I wanted to know how most Russians saw their country and its leaders, and why democracy, invoked often during perestroika, hadn't taken root here. According to many people I'd spoken to, it never would.

It took twenty-seven hours to reach the village of Kharabali from Moscow, but I looked forward to our time aboard train 93, because trains may be the single finest thing about Russia. Like nothing else here, they are spotless and punctual, and long-distance train travel brings out a benevolence in Russians that's rarely on public display. Men take off their jackets and stand in black nylon socks in the corridors drinking tea and gazing at the passing countryside, looking as peaceful as large cattle. In-laws and grandparents sleep on the upper berths under coats or shawls. Passengers unpack vodka, sandwiches, cellophane bags of cucumbers and radishes; families play cards; time elongates. There is nowhere to go and nothing to be done about the rate of travel, and passengers grow courteous and content, as though the train were an elderly relative's name-day celebration.

In our darkening compartment, my father and I sat around the flip-up metal table. We picked at the sandwiches Irina had packed for us while he told fishing stories. Most of them concerned his friends— eight or nine men from Moscow of roughly the same age. Every year they spent several weeks together in a cluster of adjacent fishing lodges on a fan-shaped piece of land known prosaically as the Volga-Akhtuba floodplain. Like most of the others who fished there, these men were attorneys, midsize-business owners and high-ranking military and government staff, and they'd made serious money, at least by Russian standards. They arrived at the lodges in late-model German or Japanese SUVs stocked with cases of single-malt scotch, boxes of Cuban cigars, carbon-fiber rods and Gore-Tex waders. (My father, the least affluent among them, usually arrived by train.) Like many Russian stories, his dwelled on drunkenness and the absurd, and my father told them with expert comic timing and enough affection to make it clear that he thought of these men as family.

This is how the stories went. One night, one of the anglers, a colonel in the federal customs service, showed off his expensive new mobile phone and then, blind drunk, dropped it into the outhouse hole that he'd just replenished. Upon hearing of this, everyone back at the cabin fell over laughing. One of the men laughed so hard he vomited.

Here's another: After drinking for seventy-two hours straight with the anglers, the elderly father of a fishing-lodge night watchman attempted to ride his moped over a boggy field. Halfway across, the moped lost speed and toppled over. When spectators approached, they found the rider snoring on the spot where he'd hit the ground.

Then there's my father's friend who spent an afternoon in his tent with one of the local women—young and pretty enough, unsmiling, shabbily dressed, underemployed—who subject themselves to seasonal trysts with the visiting anglers. Mid-coitus, she looked up into the Muscovite's perspiring face and asked the amount of his annual salary.

On days when the wind and silence on the river got to them, the anglers drove to the surrounding villages in a caravan of luxury SUVs. Once, my father was riding in the passenger seat of a cream-leather-upholstered Range Rover when the driver pulled up beside a young woman walking by the side of the road. She was long-haired and slender, around twenty. The driver, a gas-company executive, rolled down the window and suggested, in a friendly but unambiguous way, that she come with them. Taking a sidelong glance at the vehicle's luminous paint job, the woman asked only, "Can I run home and get my toothbrush?"

"Don't think of us too harshly," my father said, catching what must've been a disapproving look on my face. "In Moscow, everyone is overworked and miserable; for a week on the river, we get to be a bunch of boys, and it's the most fun we have all year." I mustered a smile, not wanting to admit that his story—about a carful of men stopping to talk to a younger woman—had made me think of Vassily's.

It was late October. The compartment lights flickered on early. My father put away the lures and we sat watching the land flatten in the dusk. Trees grew farther apart until there was mostly tall grass. The cabins vanished. This was the farthest east in Russia I'd been, the closest to the Urals. I thought about the time I went to Yalta with Tamara and Mikhail Mikhailovich, the summer I was eight. I remembered spending hours looking out the window of their Zhiguli sedan and being astonished by the land's vastness, the way it went on and on with no end in sight. Years later, I was reminded of this when I discovered Chinese ink landscapes, where mountains and rivers overwhelmed the tiny figure of the hermit in his pavilion. On that night in 1978, I fell asleep somewhere among dark fields in Ukraine and woke in Crimea. It was morning, and overnight the firs and birches had turned into cypresses and palms; thinking we'd driven to another country, I nearly shouted with surprise. I wanted to tell my father about this memory, but when I looked up he was slumped back against the compartment wall, his glasses low on his nose, asleep.

KHARABALI APPEARED TO be sculpted out of mud. Several bulbs dangled from a wire, casting eerie aureoles on the packed dirt beside the train tracks. Two or three trees were visible on the periphery of the darkness. Beyond them, I could make out a row of single-story cinderblock bunkers, vestiges of a time when this place had been a heartland of Soviet collective farming.

We waited with a group of other passengers, bleary-eyed solidlooking men of vacationing age; they were zippered into high-end technical fabrics and carried fishing gear in purposeful dark cases. A column of Mitsubishis and Lexuses collected them, taking them to the nearby lodges. My father's ride turned out to be a mottled Brezhnev-era van. The driver, Andrei, a wild-haired teenager in a tracksuit, knew my father from previous visits, and for a while they made conversation about the weather and what was biting. I held on to the seat with both hands. The road was rutted with crenellations of dried mud so tall that it resembled the bottom of a prehistoric sea. Even at golf-cart speed, the van pitched so violently that a box of tackle went flying and burst open, covering the floor with wormy, feathery lures. We passed a van identical to our own, visible in the spillover from the headlights, lying on its side in a gully. "Tipped over this morning," Andrei reported cheerfully. "We're waiting on horses to haul it out." The Akhtuba, glowing the color of old silverware, finally swung into view at the bottom of an escarpment.

Andrei drove along the river at a precarious angle before pulling up in front of a guard booth and a lit plywood sign. We stood gratefully on solid ground and squinted into halogens under lettering that read, "Camp Success—the Greatest Fishing Lodge in the World!" The manager of the lodge, a boxy, businesslike man in a homemade sweater, trotted out of the darkness to welcome us. He shook our hands and asked where we were coming from. He did a double take when I told him. He said that a Czech, a Pole and even a Japanese had visited the local lodges, but I was the first American. He added with real satisfaction that I might be the last.

TWO HOURS AFTER we stepped off the train in Kharabali, my father and I sat bobbing in a boat he kept docked nearby, a shiny vessel of Finnish manufacture with the name *Silver Beaver* emblazoned in blue across the prow. We were on the Volga proper, a short ride from the Akhtuba along a marshy canal, and like the river in the famous Johnny Mercer song, it looked wider than a mile. We dropped anchor near a stand of old-growth trees known as the Oaks. It was about 6:30 a.m.—rush hour fishing-wise. The new day was beginning to suggest itself in the gloaming on the horizon, and the silence was the most silent I'd heard. We sat bobbing there until noon, and in that time we didn't see another human. The only break in the quiet was when a wild pig ran noisily out of the undergrowth to drink from the shallows.

After an afternoon on the water, my father and I had climbed out of the boat and were walking along the pier when the phone in my pocket buzzed. There was a spot, near the scale where anglers weighed their fish, where I could get one bar of reception. My mother was calling from New York, and for a few minutes we hollered at each over the dropouts. She was calling about Petya, my stepfather's son from his first marriage, who had gone with me to Vinnytsia to find Vassily. My mother was calling to say that Petya had died. Vitaly was in Moscow to organize his son's funeral and wake. She asked me to call him.

When I'd visited Petya a few days earlier, he didn't recognize me. He lay in a narrow bed tangled in sheets, his skin a dim shade of orange. His clouded eyes moved rapidly in their sockets, and when they paused on anyone's face, for an instant, they registered only fear and confusion. It was a humid day, and someone had opened all the windows at Botkin Hospital, Moscow's top infectious-disease center. Seven other men occupied the room, which was the size of an ordinary American hospital room but with the beds less than three feet apart and no curtains. One of them filled in Vitaly—Petya's father, my stepfather—about "the situation." Petya had rolled out of bed in the night, the man, a trombonist with the city's third-best orchestra, was saying. Because Petya was too heavy to lift, the man got out of bed and roamed the corridors to look for a nurse. The trombonist had a turban of gauze wound around his head and the dark eyes and aquiline nose of a Georgian. At the bed beside his, a woman fed soup to a frail old man who didn't once open his eyes.

Vitaly sat on the edge of Petya's bed and looked down blankly at his son. He and my mother had flown to Moscow several weeks earlier and were staying with Petya's mother, Vitaly's ex-wife, Irina, a tired-looking woman of indeterminate age who kept her dishwater hair tied back with a rubber band. She had gone to the pharmacy to buy adult diapers, because the hospital had run out of Petya's size. I didn't know that adult diapers came in sizes. I stood next to Petya's bed for a while and thought about putting my hand on Vitaly's shoulder. Instead, I walked to the bathroom. The hallway reeked because someone had propped the bathroom door open, and the toilets had clogged, and not recently. Inside, four patients stood smoking cigarettes and talking; one was tethered to an IV bag dangling from a metal pole.

Two years earlier, Petya had traveled to Grozny to photograph casualties of the war in Chechnya for a Moscow magazine: he said he had waded into ditches and took pictures of the dead, who lay everywhere. On the train home, he noticed that his skin had turned yellow. He got off at a station somewhere along the Volga—he didn't remember the name of the small city—and walked until someone gave him directions to a hospital. A doctor drew blood and diagnosed hepatitis B. When Petya asked how he might have contracted it, the doctor shrugged. Petya was given a bed, read magazines, swallowed a regimen of pills. After two weeks a doctor told him that he was better and ordered him to rest—don't go traipsing through any more war zones, he said—and signed a release.

A year and a half later, having turned yellow again and feeling worse than the first time, Petya checked himself into Botkin. A doctor there told him that treatment for hepatitis B required months of antibiotics, not weeks. After more tests, he told Petya that he had an eighty-year-old man's liver, and that it was failing. A second-opinion specialist confirmed that treatment would only slightly delay liver failure. He wasn't eligible for a transplant, the specialist told him, and was going to die within a year, maybe several months. Petya was thirty-seven.

I called him at the hospital when I heard. He sounded groggy but upbeat. He talked about us taking a train trip to Russia's far east—he called it "the sticks"—and working on a book together; he'd take the photos and I'd write the essay. I said it was a great idea and that I'd see him soon. In the meantime, toxins no longer eliminated by his liver began to infiltrate Petya's heart, kidneys and brain. Vitaly wanted to have him moved to a hospital in New York, but the doctor said he wouldn't survive the ten-hour flight.

By the time I saw him, Petya's muscular upper arms had swelled into yellowish cylinders; he no longer recognized his parents. Besides occasional visits by a tired-looking physician in a lab coat the color of car exhaust, no one at the hospital attended to him. When Vitaly told a nurse that Petya needed to be bathed, she said that for 150 rubles—about $5—she'd give him the key to the shower room. Standing behind him, Vitaly propped up Petya under both arms, walked him haltingly down the hallway, and undressed him. In his shirt, trousers and bare feet, Vitaly stood holding his son under the intermittently warm water. Vitaly's mother, Sofia, who'd raised Petya and was nearly ninety, was superstitious about hospitals and stayed away. She told Vitaly that if she came to see her grandson at the hospital, she was convinced he would die. Vitaly said he was going to die anyway.

I visited Petya on the day before taking the train to the Volga. I'd lingered too long in the lobby, putting on the green paper slippers that visitors were required to buy for thirty kopecks. Irina showed up with the adult diapers and sat staring at a wall, escaping to the bathroom every ten minutes to smoke with the invalids. This is hard on her, Vitaly said to no one in particular, as though it needed saying. My mother sat beside him. An unshaven man with bandaged legs in a nearby bed began telling me that when it got cold at night, he stuffed newspaper into the cracks around the windows. Also that, a few weeks earlier, an old man in the bed beside his died in the night, and no one came when he pressed the call button, which was probably broken, and it was morning before an orderly showed up to take the dead man to the morgue.

It was time to go, and I squeezed Petya's hand in mine, which made him convulse and scan the ceiling, startled. I spoke to him while his eyes roamed the walls. Some of the other patients watched. Out the window there was bright sunlight, and I could see workers in harnesses renovating an onion dome on the stately hospital chapel. With small rollers, methodically, they applied fresh sheets of gold.

I stood above the Akhtuba and the last reddish sliver of sun thinking about Petya. I was also rummaging for words. I couldn't speak to my stepfather in English—it would sound cold and strangely formal—but I didn't know what people said to one another in Russian when their children died. I told my father what had happened and asked him what to say, and he wrote several phrases on a sheet of notebook paper. *"Eto nasha obschaya tragedia"* (This is our collective tragedy) was the one I chose, and I practiced saying it a few times. Down near the fish scale, I dialed Moscow and repeated the phrase to Vitaly, telling him I was sorry. He thanked me, and we talked for a few minutes before hanging up. It was dark and the air was swollen with mosquitoes, and I climbed the hill to our cabin, because we had to be on the water by five thirty.

SERGEI GOLOVIN ONCE worked as an engineer at the Karl Marx Collective Farm. While we drove, he pointed out its chromed art deco sign on the side of a two-lane road. I liked Sergei right away. A night watchman at Camp Success, he was a nattily dressed man in his early fifties who exuded unfussy competence, a lack of sentimentality and

a wry sense of humor. On days when it rained, or I was too groggy to get up before dawn, Sergei drove me through the surrounding countryside, covering several hundred kilometers in his immaculate Soviet-era Zhiguli sedan, a Fiat clone with a neatly folded blanket across the backseat.

Once there were miles of potato fields here, Sergei said, and nearly everyone worked at the collective farms, where the famous Astrakhan watermelons grew alongside the equally famous tomatoes. The fields blew away in the early 1990s. The entire machinery of the U.S.S.R. had ground to a halt in a matter of weeks, and all that remained of the collective farms now were fallow dust lots, the arable land carried away by the winds that come off the river.

Like Kharabali, the local villages looked sculpted out of mud. One of the largest, Sasykoli, turned out to be a handful of perpendicular unpaved streets lined with plank or cinder-block houses and a sprinkling of antiquarian cars. Some houses were adorned with tires buried halfway in the ground—the lawn decoration of the poor the world over—or bald tractor-trailer tires piled up in twos and threes. Hay bales stood in loose pyramids. A skinny cow of unknown provenance wandered along a street chewing on bumps of browning grass and ignoring a pack of feral dogs that ran alongside it. Just after sunrise, the people outside were mostly the morning drunks with soiled shirtfronts staggering along the fences and blinking at the sun. A few were still in their teens, and it hurt to look at them.

In the afternoons, men sat on benches and logs in front of their houses; many were dressed in overalls and caps that had taken on the gray brown of the airborne dust. Some of the villagers worked at the canning plant in Kharabali. A handful of others commuted to jobs in Astrakhan or Volgograd. They were easy to pick out because of their better black-market forgeries, bought in the cities: leather boots with pointed toes, Guess jeans, chunky gold-framed sunglasses with the Gucci Gs at the temples.

Sergei drove from village to village, narrating the scenery. As much seemed to be happening outside the villages as in them. We had no destination, and there were few cars on the roads, so at times Sergei slowed down so we could take in the countryside at our leisure. We passed a man on the shoulder walking a bicycle laden with sacks of potatoes. We passed two men trying to fix a van; so many parts lay scattered in the grass that it looked as if they were trying to build an entirely different kind of machine from them. We passed a flock of crows winging noisily into the air, sounding like children complaining in a car's backseat. We passed women in loose floral-print tunics selling pink watery-looking tomatoes out of cardboard boxes. We passed a man in a denim cap sitting on a suitcase. Along a particularly unpeopled stretch of road, we passed some boisterous chestnut horses raising a plume of dust; we couldn't tell whether they belonged to anyone. At an intersection, Sergei pointed out a spot on the road where a sedan had flipped over. He said it had lain there, upside down, for more than a week.

In Bugor—the name means "hillock"—we stopped in front of a boxlike structure of brick and aluminum siding topped with five small bells, a cupola, two onion domes and Orthodox crosses. They were fashioned of sheet metal and looked homemade. After the Soviets came to Bugor, Sergei explained, they removed the church domes and turned the building into a gymnasium. Some seventy years later, the villagers made it into a church again and raised money for the domes to be put back, but just enough to make them out of sheet metal instead of gold. The domes glowed pewter gray in the sun, homely as kettles.

I asked Sergei what people here did for work after the collective farms closed. After the salaries dried up, he said, they continued to come to work and for a time were paid in barter. Sometimes they were paid in sugar, or rayon shirts, or ping-pong paddles, and a kind of ingenious swap meet rose up in the area: people drove hundreds of kilometers because someone five villages away was rumored to have a roll of insulation they might be willing to trade for some plastic tablecloths and a checkers set. The director of the Karl Marx Collective Farm knew the director of a porcelain factory somewhere farther north along the Volga, and for months Sergei received his wages in plates.

"In plates?" I repeated, not sure I'd heard him. He shrugged. Sergei's house in Sasykoli was an immaculate wood cabin. The spacious backyard had been turned into a vegetable garden where his wife grew cucumbers, tomatoes, lettuces, green onions and dill in pristine grids that took advantage of every last postage stamp of ground. Sergei led me to a shed in the back, opened a padlock, and swung open the doors. Inside, stacked nearly to the roof, were hundreds of unused white china dinner plates, some still in wrapping paper. "I thought someday I'd find a use for them," he said.

THE HORSES AND crows were the most mobile parts of the landscape. Everything else on the floodplain was low to the ground, still, brownish gray. The only place that could conceivably be called a destination was Selitrennoe. *Selitra* means "saltpeter," and for some reason my brain—stutter-stepping between Russian and English— indexed the village as Saltpetersburg. A short drive from Camp Success, it resembled the other villages except for the archaeological dig that had been maintained on its outskirts since the 1960s. As Sergei and I walked around Selitrennoe and he told me about its past, some of the windswept streets appeared nearly uninhabited. A black colt trotted by us and then turned onto a side street without pausing; he looked as if he had a destination in mind and was in a hurry. The horizon lay around us in every direction, a strange sensation for a city dweller. It was unsettling to think that some seven hundred years earlier, on the site of this inhospitable-looking village there stood a city more populous and important than Moscow.

The Mongol city was known as Sarai, or Sarai Batu, after the grandson of Genghis who, in the thirteenth century, conquered Russia and built his capital here, on the Caspian steppe, to take advantage of the river and the Silk Road's merchant caravans. Batu is said to have chosen the spot because it was far from trees. The Mongols were nomads who needed open grazing land for their horses and didn't bring with them any appreciation for colorful foliage.

The Mongols were as inevitable and unpredictable as weather. They passed through the countryside like a blizzard, entering the villages suddenly, at high gallop. Medieval church chronicles suggest how terrifying their arrivals must have been. When the unfamiliar horsemen first appeared on the steppe, many Russians assumed they were the people of Gog and Magog—mythical enemies of Alexander the Great—and signaled the coming apocalypse. About the last part they weren't altogether wrong.

The campaigns Batu waged against the people living on the territory of modern-day Russia inflicted killing and suffering on a scale unknown until the twentieth century. It had taken the Mongols sixty years to conquer China; they subjugated all of Russia in three. Instead of occupying its cities, Batu simply immolated them, after putting everyone inside their walls to death. Beginning in 1237, he razed Riazan, Kolomna, Kostroma, Yaroslavl, Uglich, Kashin, Ksnyatin, Galich, Gorodets, Kozelsk, Rostov, Suzdal, Volokolamsk, Chernigov, Smolensk, Pereslavl-Zalessky, Yuriev-Polsky, Dmitrov, Torzhok and Tver—among the larger cities, only Vladimir and Pskov were left standing. His army cut down some 270,000 people in Moscow alone. The Mongols put to death every man, woman and child in the city of Vladimir and nearly depopulated the Dnieper region.

In 1240, Batu reached Kiev. The most beautiful city in ancient Rus and its capital, Kiev was said to have exceeded western European cities in both size and splendor. It had been home to more than six hundred churches, and its noble families were related, by marriage or blood, to the monarchs of Byzantium, England and the Holy Roman Empire. After breaching Kiev's walls and killing nearly everyone inside, Batu's soldiers emptied the tombs as well, scattering the bones of the dead and smashing the skulls with their heels. Then they set fire to the city. The papal legate John of Plano Carpini, who passed through Kiev five years later, found fewer than two hundred houses standing and "an innumerable multitude of dead men's skulls and bones lying upon the earth."

When the Mongols approached a city, another chronicler recorded, the cries of their camels, the neighing of their horses and the din of their siege machinery drowned out conversations inside the city walls. They announced their arrival by lobbing burning projectiles over the walls, shot by Chinese catapults overseen personally by Genghis's youngest son, Tului. After sweeping through Russia, Poland, Silesia, Hungary, Serbia and Bulgaria with little difficulty, the Mongol army continued west. Other European countries would almost certainly have fallen, too, if the death of the Great Khan in 1241 hadn't convinced Batu that he should abandon the siege of Vienna and turn back to the Mongolian capital, Karakorum.

The Mongols—or Tatars, as the Russians called them—ruled Russia for more than 250 years with an officious and perplexing awfulness. They lived among the Persians and the Chinese after conquering them but kept their distance from the Russians, issuing orders from the steppe by proxy and eventually relying on local princes to collect tribute, enforce edicts and put down unrest in other principalities. The Tatars looted Russian villages seemingly for sport, burned crops and ran off cattle, conducted slave raids, took hostages. Their khans punished their subjects' political missteps and insubordination harshly and often. They sacked Moscow repeatedly. They razed Riazan so many times that eventually its residents gave up and rebuilt the city on another site. They enslaved the survivors of these campaigns, forced the young women into harems, and deported skilled laborers and artisans to the steppe to build Sarai and other Tatar cities. Only Orthodox monasteries were spared the random incursions and demands for tribute; the Tatars believed in the spiritual power of all religious men and left the bearded monks alone.

To be fair, the Russian princes were nearly as difficult to admire. They robbed their people with relish and warred with each other endlessly, sometimes enlisting the military aid of the Tatars in pursuing rivalries and vendettas. The khans seemed to enjoy pitting the Russians against one another: in 1327, Ivan Kalita of Moscow led a punitive Tatar-Russian army against the rebellious Aleksandr Mikhailovich of Tver (the younger brother of the memorably named Dmitri the Terrible Eyes). As a reward for victory, Ivan was given the title of grand prince and enthroned in Vladimir. Every prince was required to make weeks-long voyages to Sarai (and sometimes all the way to Karakorum) to pay tribute to and bribe Tatar officials and to settle disputes, pleading before the khan and, occasionally, one of the khan's powerful wives. Aleksandr Nevsky, the Russian war hero famous for victories over the Swedes and the Teutonic Knights, traveled repeatedly to Sarai to prostrate himself before Batu's son Sartaq. Nevsky—who was canonized by the Orthodox church—died while returning from one of these voyages.

The Tatars excelled at more than destruction. In the first half of the thirteenth century, on the site of Selitrennoe, they built a city as resplendent as any in the medieval world, a trading hub with mosques and palaces decorated with majolica inlays, carved alabaster and terra-cotta tiles. A network of underground pipes carried water from the Akhtuba, and there were quarters and marketplaces for many of the nationalities who traded there. Italian merchants alone operated two marketplaces in Sarai, one for the Genoese and another for the Venetians. At its zenith the city was home to nearly 600,000. For a great metropolis, however, Sarai proved remarkably short-lived. Tamerlane sacked it in 1395 and set fire to its libraries and archives. It remained standing for another century and a half, a time during which the Tatars grew divided and entropic, while the steppe gradually reverted to what it does best, which is emptiness.

The Tatars influenced Russian life in ways that are both mysterious and undeniable. The Russian vocabulary contains hundreds of remnants of the Tatar language, as conspicuous as the Russians' high cheekbones. The old way of bowing—by touching or beating the forehead on the ground—is a vestige of the Tatars, too. Ivan the Terrible once promised that "if the people of Novgorod beat their foreheads before me, I shall spare them." In tsarist times, peasants proudly showed off bumps on their foreheads that rose from bowing to their betters. But the Tatars' most indelible contribution to Russian culture is the despotism of the country's rulers and the people's acquiescence in it—even after the nation emancipated itself from the Tatars, its history amounted to a cyclical drama of victimization and submission played out by ordinary Russians, in a land that the nineteenth-century poet Mikhail Lermontov, in his famous poem, described as "a country of slaves, a country of masters." This cultural inheritance has been commented on practically since the Tatars left; the philosopher Pyotr Chaadaev stirred up a scandal in 1829 when he wrote that "our national rulers" inherited from the Tatars the spirit of "a cruel and humiliating foreign domination."

Some of the Russians' peculiarities that gall and mystify Westerners also date back centuries, sometimes all the way back to the Tatar occupation. After the Tatars left, the Russian suspicion of foreigners remained. In Selitrennoe, I wondered about the conviction, voiced so often in Russia, that foreigners and certain internal outsiders schemed to undermine the country and were to blame for its problems. At various times, these foreign and domestic antagonists included Swedes, Lithuanians, Turks, Japanese, Germans, Masons, Jews, Chechens, Americans, Protestants and, more recently, Chinese, Estonians, Georgians, Ukrainians and LGBT people. And from the Muslim culture of their conquerors, the Russians inherited the trope of "the decadent West," an imaginary place where wealthy, godless foreigners plotted against and heaped scorn on downtrodden, pious Russia.

Naturally, ever-present danger from both without and within the country demands a forceful, autocratic ruler. While this myth is perpetuated by the Kremlin and its official news outlets, in many Russians it resembles a gut feeling. Russians tend to anthropomorphize their country—always as a she, molested, beaten down, with infinite reserves of forbearance and a capacity to endure the unendurable. Of course they are describing themselves. The land had never belonged to them—it was the property of the perennial Landlord of All the Russias or a People's Commissar in St. Petersburg or Moscow—but Russia did. Perhaps only as an idea, but an irresistible, poetic one that formed a bedrock in the imagination. Yet Russians entrust the less poetic work of governing to the supreme leader in the capital, a strongman whom they've often simply called "Father," believing that it's necessary to give up the rights and protections of a lawful society to obtain stability and order.

Stalin was merely the most murderous in a long procession of "Fathers" (and several "Mothers"), and many of the seemingly novel features of Soviet totalitarianism long predated the Soviet state. NKVD agents like my grandfather resembled no one as much as Ivan the Terrible's *oprichniki*, who spied on, tortured and massacred all classes of Russians, employing terror as a form of mass control; like the NKVD, eventually the *oprichniki* themselves became the victims of their ruler's paranoia. And the Gulag, the Soviet penal archipelago, supplanted a centuries-old system of political exiles and ordinary prisoners who were made to march east along the world's longest roadway, the Great Siberian Tract, crossing the enormous country in manacled convoys, hungry, beaten by guards, freezing in winter and bitten by mosquitoes and horseflies in the sweltering summers. Stalin himself was one of these prisoners and escaped from his Siberian exile at least twice.

Russian authors who've dared to write frankly about their country often conceive of it as a problem in need of a solution: two well-known books about Russia, by Chernyshevsky and Lenin, are both titled *What Is to Be Done?*, while in 1995 Solzhenitsyn published *The Russian Question at the End of the Twentieth Century*. But many more Russians believe that to discuss the calamities of the past is to insult and demean their country, a conviction that also dates back to the Tatar conquest. During the time of the occupation, outcomes of military campaigns were reckoned to be divine verdicts on the righteousness of the Russian people and their one true church. "For our sins," a chronicler of Novgorod wrote of the Tatars, "unknown nations arrived." But how were the church scribes of the thirteenth and fourteenth centuries to explain Russia's complete defeat and lasting occupation? Though medieval chronicles are rife with accounts of the outlanders' pillaging and inhumanity, there's not a single allusion to the fact that the land as a whole was conquered and occupied by foreign infidels for more than two and a half centuries. It appears that the chroniclers chose simply not to acknowledge it. One historian named this the "ideology of silence."

Perhaps it was an attempt to save face before future generations, but in any case the penchant for rewriting and redacting history has lingered. A year before I visited Selitrennoe, a textbook was published with much fanfare in Moscow. *A Modern History of Russia, 1945–2006: A Manual for History Teachers* was said to be written under the direct supervision of the president, and upon its publication Putin himself addressed a teachers' convention. One of the stranger among the book's many novel theories suggests that Stalin's purges and the formation of the Gulag had been necessitated by American aggression. "In the circumstances of the Cold War," the textbook explains, "democratization was not an option for Stalin's government." Collectivization, famine and mass killings were the only possible response, its authors assure the reader, because the conditions of Russian society "demanded it."

Putin's desire to buff up the country's past like a Moscow boulevard also led his government, in 2014, to issue a classified order liquidating the personal records of the Gulag's prisoners—in many cases the last surviving documents of their existence. It was based on the fairy-tale notion that erasing historical records is the same as erasing the suffering they describe. "Russian history did contain some problematic pages," Putin told the history teachers gathered at the convention. "We have fewer of them than other countries. And they were less terrible than in some other countries. . . . We can't allow anyone to impose a sense of guilt on us."

As I wandered around Selitrennoe, it was difficult to believe that much about Russia—and about Russianness—was formed in this empty, haunted-looking place, the site of the nation's formative trauma. I've thought about Selitrennoe often, especially after learning about the Emory mouse study, and the other trauma transmission studies, some years later. What if Russia's peculiar cyclical history, I began to wonder, was guided by something more than precedent and tradition? What if we Russians were born to not only a set of cultural habits and assumptions, but into a reality that was genetically predetermined by a national catastrophe? If this was true, nearly eight centuries ago this Tatar settlement on the Akhtuba became the wellspring of an unstoppable chain reaction—an intergenerational transmission of fear, suspicion, grief, melancholy and rage that, over time, curdled into new historical calamities, new traumas to pass on to the young.

After all, what can be easier to empathize with than a trauma victim choosing safety over freedom? In his novel *Forever Flowing*, the novelist and journalist Vasily Grossman, sometimes called the Soviet Tolstoy, described the Russian soul as a "thousand-year-old slave." Surveying the country's brutal past, Chaadaev lamented that "we Russians, like illegitimate children, come to this world without patrimony." But the Russians' patrimony is all too easy to recognize in a nation of individuals fearful of foreigners, each other and the prospect of greater freedom, a people trembling seemingly without cause, like the lab mice at Emory.

The wind picked up. Sergei and I stood leaning on a fence and looked out at the steppe where Batu built his city. It was unlike the steppe farther west, where lush grass sometimes grows taller than a man; here, the yellowing grass was engaged in a squabble with patches of dusty earth, as though the land couldn't decide what it wanted. Sergei, usually even-tempered and wry, suddenly looked livid. Disgusted, he wiggled a loose plank in the fence. "People around here talk like everything is always changing," he said with unexpected feeling. "The Tatars, the Bolsheviks, the capitalists! Let me ask you—was life here ever different? The people here were slaves and farmers toiling in debt bondage under the princes, then became slaves under the Tatars, then serfs under the tsars. And what changed after the Reds came? More people learned to read, sure, more infants lived to adulthood. But they, too, spent their lives working on land they didn't own, and couldn't leave or travel, and knew nothing about the world out there." He pointed in the direction of the setting sun. "Maybe out there everything is always changing,

changing. But look—what's changed here?" He gestured at the village around us, with its hay bales, peeling paint and wooden homes snaking along a dirt road. Except for the sheet metal and the two or three rusted automobiles, it was easy to imagine that this is how the place looked two or even three hundred years earlier. "The Tatars never left," Sergei said darkly. "We *are* the Tatars." With this he spat, as though trying to get the flavor of the words out of his mouth, and walked to his car.

AT CAMP SUCCESS, when dawn lit the tops of the grass, my father and I shimmied down to the jetty and I untied the boat. He lowered the outboard into the cold water and gave it gas. The *Silver Beaver* took on speed and glided. Wind pulled at the surface of the river, and when we rode perpendicular to the current, the boat skidded like a stone, bouncing across the water with a metallic *chun-chun-chun*.

My father lowered two baited fishing hooks into the water behind us and crawled the boat along the good places. He was wrapped in a black Shimano jacket and a black hat with the Japanese company's logo; I think he enjoyed playing the sportsman. In those early hours the landscape was waking, minute by minute, and the small sounds and sensations unfolded in stark relief against the dark: the cackle of crows, the sputter of the outboard, the current tugging steadily on the line.

These were my favorite hours we spent together. My father and I sat in the boat stunned by wakefulness, surrounded by lavender on the horizon, and there wasn't much cause to talk. It was a way of being together that worked best. The busywork—tying lures, baiting hooks, fussing with the outboard—made our proximity enough. The silences felt abundant: we sat beside each other doing small, specific things, not speaking, the wide river and the sky and the stands of distant trees changing around us like a mobile stage set. For much of the mornings and early afternoons there were only the two of us there, sharing our primordial, biological bond. At these moments it was possible to believe that a lifetime of unspoken good intentions added up to a relationship, and that nothing was ever different, and that no one will leave and no one will die. When my father looked up at me I could tell he felt it, too. I think about these mornings often.

Our one-room cabin had a screened porch. On most nights, after a quick supper at the cafeteria we sat on the porch in plastic lawn chairs, propped our feet on the wooden railing and smoked my father's Winstons. We passed a flask of Moldovan five-star brandy, for sale at the cafeteria for nine U.S. dollars; its burn and sweet aftertaste agreed with the cigarettes. Inside, a nightstand and a small rug separated our beds, and before falling asleep we talked for a while, which allowed us to look at each other for stretches of time without awkwardness. At times I enjoyed this; at others I found myself becoming self-conscious at being studied by my father, becoming again his tentative, timid child, an almost physical sensation I couldn't bear for too long. Then one of us turned off the light, and then it was early morning and the alarm sounded, announcing it was time to head down to the jetty.

On several nights my father walked across the road to the adjacent fishing lodge, called Triangle, where he and his friends liked to stay. He told me he'd chosen Camp Success for us because I was an American accustomed to comfortable accommodations. To me this sounded like a reproach, though maybe I was being touchy. Camp Triangle was more communal, less upholstered, cheaper: instead of roomy cabins for two, visitors slept eight or ten to a room, in bunk beds. When my father went to visit his friends there, he didn't take me along. I wanted to meet them—I even suggested, somewhat disingenuously, that it would improve the article I was writing—but he waved this away and walked into the foggy trees alone. I read on the porch and waited. I wondered petulantly whether he was reluctant for me to meet his friends or for them to meet me. He returned late and in the mornings didn't say much about what he'd done, even when I asked.

A few days before we left the Volga, my father and I were trolling one of the reedy, shallow channels that connect the rivers. It was sunny and the sky was cloudless, decorated by a contrail left there by a single-engine plane that was round like a Japanese brushstroke. The boat was purring ahead when the rod in my hands jumped. I heard the reel unspooling and closed the bail, and the rod bent in an inverted U. "Hold on tight," my father yelled. There was a flash of silver in the water, and then the fish jumped, trying to dislodge the hook. I reeled it in slowly, the way my father showed me, and only after its head broke the water did I realize it was a pike perch, a broad silver-scaled fish with green-black eyes. "About six kilos," my father said after I hauled it in, nodding with approval. The pike perch lay between us, beating its flanks angrily on the boat's bottom.

We waited for it to stop moving, and then my father took out his camera, to photograph me with my first respectable trophy. I picked up the heavy fish and held it up with both hands while he focused the camera. Before he could trip the shutter, the pike perch convulsed in my hands and slipped loose. Unlike my father's purpose-made studded rubber gloves, mine were the ordinary leather ones I wore during New York winters, and after days of fishing they were covered with slime. I lunged after the pike perch, rocking the boat, but when I grabbed it my hands slid harmlessly down its sides. After a few more of my vaudevillian attempts to recapture the fish, it slipped over the side of the boat and bolted into the depths. My father looked on, his disbelief curdling into disgust. "You couldn't have planned *that* better," he grumbled finally, and stuck the camera back in the waterproof bag. "You'd never catch me doing something that stupid."

We didn't speak during the ride back to the lodge. I sat in the front of the boat and watched the low afternoon sun beat on the water. The contentment and affection we'd shared had come apart like a badly mended seam: my anger and shame came flooding back, and I huddled with my jaw clenched, refusing to look at my father. I felt the familiar helplessness, too, because I couldn't say to him the things I wanted to using the workmanlike, dull instrument of my Russian. Later that afternoon, on the porch, I tried anyway. "You made me feel ashamed," I said. "That's all you've ever done. I'd never do that to you." I spat the words out; I meant to sound hurt, but I was shaking with anger. My father looked up, considered saying something in response, then let out a long exasperated breath and walked into the cabin. He left me standing on the porch roiling with rage at him and at myself, and pity for him, and something that felt like grief. Suddenly it became painfully clear that he wouldn't, or couldn't, give me the answers I'd come for, and that there would be no accounting of the traumas he inherited, inflicted and suffered. Why was I seeing this only now? For as long as we'd known each other, my father had offered me the same answer: You'll have to do it yourself. All of it. My hurt at his absence—and hunger for his presence—were so intense that I never paused to consider that he was, in a certain way, right: I didn't need him to finish all the sentences he left incomplete. I could decide for myself.

We avoided each other until the evening, when he came out onto the porch, where I sat smoking his Winstons. We sat beside each other for a while, looking at the wash of darkening reds and yellows in the west. "Did you know that after you and your mother left, my father came to visit me?" he asked. I turned to look at him.

In 1985 or 1986—he didn't remember—he received a letter from Vassily. Fifteen years of silence was too long, Vassily wrote; it wasn't right for a father and a son to live as strangers. At the end of the letter, he added that in several weeks he'd be coming to Moscow and hoped to talk things over and apologize. "With love, your father," Vassily signed off. My father reread the letter several times but didn't write back.

By this time, he'd moved from the apartment where he had lived with me and my mother to a larger one in an adjacent building, something Vassily didn't know. (His letter was left on top of the mailboxes.) On the morning of his visit, a neighbor rang my father's doorbell. "There's an old man outside your old apartment, looking for you," she said. My father paused the story to light another Winston. "All I had to do was walk across a courtyard," he continued. "He was waiting less than a hundred meters away. I put my coat on and took it off several times, paced, smoked many cigarettes. In the end, I didn't see him. I couldn't. It was like an invisible hand held me in place. I heard later that Dad spent most of the day waiting there, in the hallway. I didn't hear from him after that."

It was the first time I'd heard my father refer to Vassily as "Dad"—*Papa*—and it sounded jarring, as if he were admitting for the first time that they were kin. I knew that the story was my father's offering to me—not the one I wanted, but nonetheless something real. We talked about other things for a while before he went to bed. I stayed outside and watched the smoke from my cigarette coil under the porch light, where it mingled with the frenzied moths. I thought about Vassily standing in the bare-concrete hallway I'd known as a child: the former KGB officer in his mid-seventies, waiting in a pressed suit for his estranged son. And I thought about my father, pacing with a cigarette in hand and deciding which urge to obey after years of separation. As it happened, I also knew about the "invisible hand." I thought about the countless times I'd wanted to ask or tell my father something, or simply hear his voice, when the hand—the residue of decades of hurt, disappointment and anger—stopped me from dialing his number. And when I considered what I would have done in my father's place on that morning in 1985 or 1986, I was surprised to realize that I didn't know.

That night, I had the dream again. I stand facing our summer-house in Stepanovskoye, holding on to the blue fence along the un-paved road where I fetched water from a well and first rode a bicycle, looking up at the lamplight behind the green shutters. I can smell the pine woods and the wood smoke from my great-grandmother's stove, and hear Lyudmila Andreevna from the adjacent yard singing over her berry bushes, and see the combine in the far-off wheat field. If I could only wake in this dream, I believe that I would be relieved to find myself in the village as it was then—the happiest place of my childhood. But I don't wake, not ever, and the barking of the bulldog behind the fence seizes my throat with fear. My mother, father, Tamara and Maria Nikolaevna are in the house, and I want badly to see them, and so like every time before, I throw open the gate and lunge for the door, and the bulldog lunges after me, snarling over my shoulder.

I woke with a yell in my throat. It was night, but to my surprise a lamp was on, and my father sat on the edge of my bed. "You were talking in your sleep," he said, "and then you yelled." I looked up at him. "I'm sorry," I replied, a little absurdly. My heartbeat still drummed in my ears. My father studied me with eyes magnified by reading glasses. "When I was a child and we lived in Moscow, your grandfather talked in his sleep, too," he said. "Sometimes he yelled or cried, and your grandmother woke him and talked to him until he fell asleep again." He thought for a moment. "I listened to them from behind a screen. And just now you sounded like him."

With his glasses on and his dentures out, my father looked older than I'd seen him. He patted the blanket over my legs, wished me good night and returned to his bed. I turned off the lamp. For a few moments after, I couldn't see or hear anything. The night on the Volga was lightless and the birds hadn't yet woken. Then I heard my father shifting and turning in his bed. We lay there for a long while, alone in our thoughts, before sleep overtook us.

ACKNOWLEDGMENTS

IN WRITING THIS BOOK, I'VE REQUIRED MORE ENCOURAGEMENT, ADVICE, FA-
vors, hand-holding, home-cooked meals, patience and time than
I'd like to admit. I've accrued quite a debt. This book would not
exist without John Jeremiah Sullivan, who first suggested that the
stories in it were worth writing, and generously introduced me to
people who helped make this happen. Joel Lovell and Jim Nelson
at *GQ* made the trip to meet Vassily possible. Nathan Lump at *T*
sent me fishing. Doug Dibbern helped shape the material, read
through many drafts, stoically suffered through its writing and
provided invaluable encouragement, advice and support. Thank
you, Doug.

The person who towed this book to shore is Andy Ward, my editor
at Random House. His masterful editing and tireless enthusiasm—as
well as his patience, generosity and talent for telling the truth—made
him a dream to work with. Any writer would be lucky to work with
Andy. At Random House I'd also like to thank Daniel Menaker, Jennifer Hershey, Chayenne Skeete, Craig Adams, London King, Ayelet
Gruenspecht, Jordan Pace and Anna Bauer.

My longtime agent and friend, Jin Auh, has been an editor, advo-
cate and protector. I adore her. At the Wylie Agency, I'd also like to

thank Tracy Bohan, Sarah Watling, Sarah Chalfant and Andrew Wylie. And thank you Bea Hemming and Dan Franklin at Jonathan Cape.

Heartfelt thanks to the brilliant and ebullient Andrew Chaikivsky, whose ability to detect errors, placeholders, assumptions and lazy logic is so formidable that it's slightly eerie. He made this a much better book.

I owe a massive debt to the McDowell Colony, Yaddo, Writers OMI at Ledig House, Summer Literary Seminars and the Brooklyn Writers Space for providing time, space and ego-boosting when I most needed them. In particular I'd like to thank Elaina Richardson, Candace Wait, Christy Williams, Michael Blake, David Macy, DW Gibson, Mikhail Iossel, Soren Stockman, Ann Ward, Scott Adkins, Erin Courtney and Jennifer Epstein.

The manuscript benefited from the attention of generous and attentive readers, including Alex Chasin, MT Connolly, Anne Fadiman, Boris Fishman, Elizabeth Kendall, Larry Krone, Michael Lowenthal, Lena Mandel, Maryse Meijer and Devika Rege. Olivia Laing, a beacon of encouragement and love, read through these pages at various stages, making me the beneficiary of her superb editorial eye and impeccable taste. Donald Antrim provided a wealth of much-needed advice, conversation and comfort during trying times. Simon Sebag Montefiore, Stephen Kotkin, Dovid Katz and the late Richard Pipes offered historical perspective and invaluable connections. Over the years, Boris Kerdimun provided personal recollections about Moscow in the 1940s as well as his unfailing friendship and love. And the late, sorely missed Pyotr Degtyarev shepherded me across Russia and Ukraine with good humor and unforgettable kindness.

Writing a book is, in the truest sense, a group effort, and I'd like to thank friends who cared for and encouraged me, in ways large and small, during a protracted and often difficult haul: Nick Abadzis, Hilton Als, Jim Andralis, Christian Barter, Cris Beam, Marcelle Beck, Jonathan Blessing, Ester Bloom, Paul Boyer, Colette Brooks, Alan

Burdick, Brooke Costello, Stanley Crouch, Kyle DeCamp, John De-
Vore, Lisa Dierbeck, Becky Doggett, Jeff Drouin, Laurel Farrin,
Aaron Foster, Ian Frazier, St. John Frizzell, Eric Gagne, Mary
Goldthwaite-Gagne, Donald Gray, Rahul Hamid, Trish Harnetiaux,
Maya Jasanoff, Alexander Kopelman, Jessica Lamb-Shapiro, Michael
Lashutka, Michael Lavorgna, Benjamin Lorr, Tamar Lusztig, Mitch
McCabe, Richard McCann, Kathleen McIntyre, John McManus,
Stephen Mejias, Hugh Merwin, Tzs Yan Ng, Garrett Oliver, Heidi
Parker, Michelle Radke, Tejal Rao, Yasmil Raymond, Herb Reichert,
Ragan Rhyne, Alex Rose, Karen Rush, Andrew Schulman, David
Seubert, Sumakshi Singh, Andrew Solomon, Wells Tower, Ellie
Tzortzi, Vint Virga, David Walker, Angela Watson, Anthony
Weigh, Dave Wondrich, John Wray and Wendy Xu.

Jonathan Allen weathered the writing of this book with endless
patience and care, read it carefully and provided crucial editorial advice. Over the years, my stepfather, Vitaly Komar, taught me much
about our former homeland. My half sister, Maria Cherkassova,
offered valuable insights into our family. Neither this book nor I
would exist without my mother, Anna Halberstadt, who brought
much of this material to life and was my partner in this project from
the beginning. I owe so much to her and to this book's other
protagonists—my late grandparents, Raisa and Semyon Galbershtad, Tamara Kamysheva and Vassily Chernopisky, and my father,
Viacheslav Chernopisky—that I will simply say спасибо.

PHOTO CREDITS

ABOUT THE AUTHOR

ALEX HALBERSTADT is the author of *Lonely Avenue: The Unlikely Life and Times of Doc Pomus*, which was named a *New York Times Book Review* Editors' Choice and a best book of the year by *The Times* of London. He has written for *The New Yorker*, *The New York Times Magazine*, *The New York Times Book Review*, *Travel + Leisure*, *GQ*, *Saveur* and *The Paris Review*. Nominated for two James Beard Awards, his journalism has been anthologized in *Best Food Writing 2014* and *The Best American Food Writing 2018*. He teaches at New York University and lives in Brooklyn, New York.

This book was set in Fournier, a typeface named for Pierre-Simon Fournier (1712–1768), the youngest son of a French printing family. He started out engraving woodblocks and large capitals, then moved on to fonts of type. In 1736 he began his own foundry and made several important contributions in the field of type design; he is said to have cut 147 alphabets of his own creation. Fournier is probably best remembered as the designer of St. Augustine Ordinaire, a face that served as the model for the Monotype Corporation's Fournier, which was released in 1925.